Date Due

EC477	³		
1LLO			
Sept 11/85			

The Best of Bob Edwards

EDITED BY
Hugh A. Dempsey

The Best of
Bob Edwards

EDITED BY
Hugh A. Dempsey

Hurtig Publishers
Edmonton

Hurtig Publishers
10560 105 Street
Edmonton, Alberta

ISBN 0-88830-096-4

Printed and bound in Canada

Contents

Introduction

Bob Edwards, the famous editor of the Calgary *Eye Opener,* is best remembered as a humorist who had an aphorism for every occasion. In addition, he had a vast treasury of jokes which were liberally sprinkled through his newspaper and dominated his pocket-sized *Summer Annuals.* Many of these jokes would be considered mildly ribald by today's standards, but in his period some were thought to be outright obscenities. As a result, the *Eye Opener* was banned from many God-fearing households while at the same time it enjoyed a mass circulation among the less devout all across Canada.

Yet Bob Edwards was more than a teller of off-color stories and the writer of one-line truisms. He was a man with a social conscience, an angry man lashing out at the inequities of Canadian society.

He was repelled by the hypocrisy of the established churches, the callousness of bureaucrats, the dishonesty of politicians, and the rapaciousness of corporate interests. All were fair game for his stinging comments, not just on an editorial page, but throughout the regular columns of his crusading journal. In truth, the *Eye Opener* was not a newspaper, but Bob Edwards's personal platform for social comment and humor.

The quiet, soft-spoken Scot was an unlikely crusader. Intelligent and well-educated, he had been a drifter and tramp journalist from the 1880s until he finally found a home in Calgary. Although interested in politics, he was no politician, and although he ran his own newspapers, he was no businessman.

And while he shrieked in fury and indignation through the columns of the *Eye Opener,* in public life he was the antithesis of a firebrand orator. A shy bachelor for most of his life, he enjoyed the companionship of a small circle of friends and followed a lonely path from hotel room, to hotel dining room, to hotel bar.

Robert Chambers Edwards was, according to his own account, born in Edinburgh on September 12, 1864, his middle name being handed down from his mother, a member of the famous Chambers publishing family in Scotland. The boy had an early start on a life of loneliness, for he was orphaned while still an infant. Taken in by a maiden aunt, he and his brother Jack were given a good education in Scottish grammar schools. From there, Bob went on to Glasgow University where he gained a solid training in classical literature, moral philosophy, logic and metaphysics—subjects which were important to the British in the Victorian era.

After graduation, young Edwards went to Europe where he followed his mother's family tradition by entering the newspaper business. His first effort was an English language paper, *The Traveller,* published on the Riviera for the benefit of wealthy tourists. It had a short life, but during that period Edwards travelled widely from Boulogne to Paris, Monte Carlo, and other watering places of the British elite. The experience was enough to convince him that the superficial life of the gentry was not for him.

Returning briefly to Scotland, Bob joined his brother Jack and in 1884 they left for the United States. Their original destination was to be Texas, but instead they went to Wyoming where, according to Edwards's own recollections, they raised livestock on Horse Shoe Creek. "As our horses ran on the range all winter and looked after themselves," he recalled, "we were able to spend the winters very comfortably down in Cheyenne. It was a wide-open city and there was lots of fun."[1]

After three years of the free and easy life in Wyoming, Bob drifted to Iowa where he found work on a farm. The agricultural life appealed to him, so he convinced his brother to join him there and together they bought a farm of their own. Edwards's own recollections are silent about the next decade but by early 1897 he had located in Wetaskiwin, about fifty miles south of Edmonton.

There, he worked at odd jobs for the first several months, and struck up a lifelong friendship with hotel operator Jerry Boyce. As before, Edwards found the new land to his liking, so he sent a letter off to brother Jack inviting him to join him. But this reunion was to be their last, for upon his arrival Jack went into a ranching partnership at Bittern Lake and died there a few weeks later.

Now Bob was truly alone. Cut off from his relatives in Scotland and lacking the support of his quieter and more successful brother, he looked around at the opportunities offered in Wetaskiwin. Recalling his earlier newspaper experience on the Riviera, he decided to launch a similar venture in the farming community. Financed by a dubious Jerry Boyce and other merchants, he made arrangements with the Calgary *Herald* to set his writings in type and to send the bundle of printed newspapers up to Wetaskiwin.

The weekly newspaper, named the Wetaskiwin *Free Lance*, came off the press on December 20, 1897, becoming the first paper to be published between Edmonton and Calgary. Described by the Macleod *Gazette* as "a bright newsy paper,"[2] it was an interesting combination of legitimate news and Edwards's satire. Unlike the later *Eye Opener*, where Edwards disdained the use of real news, his first ventures tried to fill both the roles of a small town weekly and a journal of social comment.

Edwards's literary talents were soon noticed by fellow journalists and others beyond Wetaskiwin's marketing area. The Calgary *Herald*, as his printers, suggested an arrangement whereby some of the type, after being used in the *Free Lance,* would also be carried in the pages of the *Daily Herald.* Under such titles as "This Week's Musings of the *Free Lance* Man,"[3] "Musings of the Wetaskiwin Sage,"[4] and "*Free Lance* Musings,"[5] Bob Edwards's writings soon became popular among a broad segment of the population. The reprinting of the articles in the *Herald* prompted demands for copies of the *Free Lance* as well, with the result that Edwards reported "quite a large circulation in the East."[6] These added subscriptions were a bonanza for at this time Wetaskiwin had a population of only 278, most of whom were caught up in a depression which had struck the West.

Bob Edwards was by now a lively and well-known figure who spent much of his time in Jerry Boyce's hotel bar. The extra money he received from his Ontario subscribers "kept half the town as full as a goat as long as the paper was running."[7] Spending the money on booze as quickly as he got it, Edwards carried on a carefree life which was reflected in the pages of his newspaper. "When the day of the week wore around for us to grind out copy to send down to the printers in Calgary," he recalled, "our office would be almost sure to be occupied by a hilarious bunch of drunks, singing songs, and shouting and yelling."[8]

One day, to escape the noise, Edwards went to the nearby Presbyterian church where, nipping from a flask, he finished his writing and shipped the copy off to the printers. However, in his rush he inadvertently left the empty flask behind the pulpit. Thus began the first of his several altercations with the established church. After the preacher took Edwards to task, the editor's star began to wane. A short time later, he could not resist injecting some biting humor into the news columns dealing with local merchants, with the result that they cancelled their much-needed advertising. In retaliation, Edwards published the names of "several patrons who have withdrawn their advertisements for some unexplained reason"[9] and in September 1898, he decided to move to Calgary.

By this time Edwards had made a number of friends in the southern city, in particular lawyer Paddy Nolan and publisher G. C. Porter. Although he continued to publish the Wetaskiwin *Free Lance*, it now became a newspaper dealing more with Calgary than the northern town, as Edwards catered to a readership beyond Wetaskiwin's subscribers. "Having temporarily abandoned Wetaskiwin," he told his readers, "we are in Calgary. Being in Calgary of course means being more or less in the soup, but being in Wetaskiwin means being on the hog."[10]

After a winter in Calgary, Bob Edwards abandoned the *Free Lance* and decided to seek his fortunes in Winnipeg; in April 1899, a number of admiring friends saw him off at the station. "Tears flowed copiously during the parting feature," observed the *Herald*.[11] Joining the staff of the Winnipeg *Free Press*, Edwards experienced an unhappy four months as a faceless writer for a large daily paper. Denied a by-line and lost in a city of strangers, he soon decided to return to small-town life. Learning that Jerry Boyce had opened a new hotel in Leduc, he travelled to that town and there published the first issue of the *Alberta Sun* late in September 1899.

"It didn't shine very long," commented Edwards. "It shone for about a year, if we remember rightly, which was not so bad, for it was a bum paper. Nor did the people like the way we handled local topics. They were scared to death of what we would say next."[12]

Within a matter of months, Edwards realized that the town could not support a newspaper, so he kept the name *Alberta Sun* but moved a few miles north to Strathcona, the sister city of Edmonton on the south side of the North Saskatchewan River. By this time, he had become something of a celebrity, as noted by the Macleod *Gazette* when he attended that town's fair. "Among the visitors was Robert Edwards, of Strathcona, the most famous editor of the Territories," it said. "His witty writings have made his name known all over western Canada."[13]

The *Alberta Sun* struggled along until the autumn of 1900 when, according to Edwards, his final issue went out in a blaze of glory. "We took devilish good care," he recalled, "to see that it was turned loose on the street by a friend only after the southbound train, with us on board, had pulled out."[14] Some of the items in that concluding issue related directly to merchants from whom Bob had been expected to curry favor. "Martin Doyle, our groceryman," stated one item, "is doing a poor business. His store is dirty and dusty and swarming with flies. How can he expect to do much?"[15] Then there was this one: "Rev. J. M. Broadhurst preached Sunday night on charity. This is a hell of a place to discourse on the subject of charity."

With those parting shots, Edwards went to the ranch of a friend near Wetaskiwin where he stayed for the winter. There, encouraged by his old companions, he decided to try another newspaper—his third in four years. Finding the economic climate much improved, he launched the Wetaskiwin *Breeze* in March 1901 and resumed his earlier arrangement with the Calgary *Herald* whereby they used his columns in exchange for printing services.

During these months, Bob Edwards was spending more time in Calgary than he was in the north. When he learned that Jerry Boyce was also moving south and would be opening a hotel in High River, he said farewell to the Wetaskiwin area for the last time. Setting up shop in High River, he produced the first issue of the *Eye Opener* on March 4, 1902. "The management has decided on the name 'Eye Opener,'" said Edwards, "because few people will resist taking it."[16]

Although it was the forerunner of the famous Calgary *Eye*

Opener, the paper was still a small-town weekly which carried its share of legitimate local news. In many ways, it was more like the old *Free Lance* than it was the *Eye Opener* of the future. Interestingly enough, when the first issue was due to appear, the Calgary *Herald* observed that "the financial end will belong to a New York syndicate,"[17] perhaps indicating that Edwards's reputation had indeed spread across the continent. Certainly, as early as 1898 he had papers in circulation all over Canada and in most of the northwestern states.

Initially, Edwards started the *Eye Opener* with a circulation of only 250, which was far less than the 600 copies he had been selling of his Wetaskiwin newspapers. But as soon as the word was out that Bob Edwards was back in business, subscriptions to the *Eye Opener* began rolling in.

Still a hard drinking, fun-loving man, Edwards confirmed the worst fears of the "respectable" element of High River. His frequent comments about booze in the town's only newspaper was the source of considerable embarrassment to them, even though the local cowboys, to use Edwards's own words, were "faithful readers of the *Eye Opener* who used to laugh uproariously whenever we got off a joke at their expense."[18]

During his two years at High River, Bob Edwards created some of the characters who became part of Alberta folklore. Most significant of these was Peter J. McGonigle, editor of the non-existent Midnapore *Gazette*. Setting them up at the bar of Nevermore House, McGonigle was a sage, a gentleman and a drunk—not unlike Edwards himself.

Eventually, the Midnapore *Gazette* became so famous that Edwards was obliged to "kill" its editor. This happened in 1910 when a young newspaperman named William De Graves began to bring out real issues of the *Gazette*. Over the years many avid readers of the *Eye Opener* had become convinced that there really was a Peter J. McGonigle and a Midnapore *Gazette*, so the issues were snapped up by souvenir hunters. Printed on bright pink paper, the newspaper sold by the hundreds to eager visitors who had come to the Calgary summer fair.

Emboldened by his initial success, De Graves and his backers continued to publish the *Gazette* during the fall of the year, constantly associating it with the *Eye Opener* and listing its editor as Peter J. McGonigle. After three issues of the newspaper had hit the Calgary streets, Edwards became concerned that it might prove to be a competitive threat to his own paper. Accordingly, in the next issue of the *Eye Opener*, Edwards carried a long story about the death of Peter McGonigle. To make the point perfectly clear, he summed up the tragedy by saying, "McGonigle now belongs to history and the *Gazette* is a thing of the past. Beware of spurious imitations."[19]

But the Midnapore *Gazette* did not die so easily. It continued to struggle along spasmodically until February 1911, when its editor and owner were charged with criminal libel and sued for $30,000 after the paper had attacked Calgary detective W. A. Grimsdall. As the case lingered before the courts, the *Gazette* finally came to an inglorious end.

Another character who first appeared during the High River days was Albert Buzzard-Cholomondeley, a British remittance man who, through the columns of the *Eye Opener*, wrote a series of letters home to his pater. In each case he found some ingenious method of extracting more funds from the family estate.

After less than a year at High River, Bob again ran afoul of the churches in two incidents which ultimately caused him to move to Calgary. The first occurred on a Saturday afternoon in January 1903, when a gramophone salesman came to town.

According to Edwards, the man "with scrubby whiskers, a very large satchel and an immense gramophone"[20] made his way to the local bar, where he enquired about the number of churches in High River. While sipping scotches and soda, he explained that his business was to sell recorded choir music to congregations that were having trouble keeping their own choirs. After playing a few sacred tunes for the admiring barflies, one of whom was suspected to be Bob Edwards himself, the salesman made arrangements for his demonstration at a church on the following day.

On Sunday evening the church was crowded and the salesman, at the appropriate moment, announced "Hark the Herald Angels Sing," by the Edison Quartette. As the sound of beautiful voices drifted over the admiring congregation, the preacher smiled and the salesman mentally calculated the size of his commission.

The next hymn announced was "Nearer My God to Thee" and the crowd leaned forward expectantly. A few moments passed before anyone realized what was happening; instead of a sacred hymn, the machine blared forth with the raucous strains of

"Just Because She Made Them Goo-Goo Eyes." When the flustered salesman put on another hymn, the congregation heard an instrumental solo by P. J. Cassidy, the Banjo King.

By the time Bob Edwards reported the incident in his next issue of the *Eye Opener*, everyone knew that some wag had switched records—probably in the bar. And although he never admitted it, the blame was placed squarely on Bob Edwards's shoulders by the church-going residents of High River.

This incident might have been forgotten if Edwards had not become involved in a heated argument with the Presbyterian minister a few months later. This man, newly-arrived from British Columbia, went to the *Eye Opener* office where he told Edwards bluntly that his paper "wasn't fit to be taken into a house where there were children."[21]

Bob was willing to let the remark pass, but a short time later he learned that the same minister had insulted his old friend Jerry Boyce. The minister had stopped Boyce on the street, demanded that he produce papers to show that he was a divorced man, and then told him he had no right to speak to the decent women of High River. The preacher concluded by telling the dumbfounded hotelkeeper that he was going to run him out of town.

Edwards was furious when he learned about the incident and devoted much of his next issue to the subject. Calling the minister a "misfit man of God,"[22] he likened him to the "tactless, offensive, conceited, self-sufficient, arrogant young parsons with no experience of men and things, uncultured by travel or reading, with absolutely no knowledge of the world, possessing a highly developed faculty for making themselves ridiculous and obnoxious, troubling the waters of a peaceful village, and sowing discord broadcast, having no rational argument in favor of their own existence."

The community was shocked by the outburst, which was closely followed by the Presbyterian minister arranging for an indignation meeting in his own defence. Even though this gathering proved, in Edwards's words, to be "a miserable fiasco,"[23] High River had become so divided that the *Eye Opener* was no longer assured of local support. So, after his second battle with the established churches, Bob Edwards decided to give up small-town life for the more impersonal atmosphere of Calgary.

Although Edwards continued to have trouble with the

churches, it never again reached the level that it achieved in 1903. In fact sixteen years later he was able to state that "we have lived in this neck of the woods for twenty-five years, and we do not know a single minister occupying a Calgary pulpit."[24] And there can be little doubt that Edwards preferred it that way.

Politically, Bob Edwards had always leaned towards the Conservatives, although he considered himself to be an independent. In Calgary, his *Eye Opener* more and more became a platform for political comment, and no public figure was immune to his stinging attacks. When the railway magnates Sir William Mackenzie and Sir Donald Mann (or simply "Bill and "Dan" in the *Eye Opener*) tried to sell their rights to the Winnipeg street railway system for $24 million, Edwards exposed their holdings as a pile of junk. When R. J. Stuart became a candidate for Calgary alderman, the *Eye Opener* used sarcasm, ridicule and direct attack to block his election. And even the prime minister of that period, Sir Wilfrid Laurier, was considered by Edwards to be the leader of a government which had become graft-ridden and corrupt.

Yet some Liberals received praise from the *Eye Opener*. Early in his career, Edwards had come to admire the Hon. Frank Oliver, member of parliament for Edmonton, and was his constant supporter. "He needs no boosting from this rag," he wrote in 1908. "We are quite aware that he regards the *Eye Opener* as a rag, and perhaps he is right."[25]

On the other hand, Conservatives who did not measure up to the *Eye Opener*'s standards were vigorously attacked and exposed. As the newspaper increased in popularity and influence, Edwards had no difficulty in finding disaffected party members or other informants who provided him with a hint of scandal. From there, Edwards made a diligent and usually successful effort to unearth the real facts before he printed the story.

Within two or three years, the *Eye Opener* had become a political force which could not be ignored. By 1908 it had a circulation of 18,500 copies, with 4,000 being sold in Toronto, 2,600 in Winnipeg, 1,000 in Vancouver, and 1,800 on the CPR trains. His articles also were being reprinted by leading daily newspapers in Canada and Great Britain. Much of this fame was based upon Edwards's biting satire and his ability to root out scandal and graft.

For example in 1908 he revealed that valuable contracts for

publishing Alberta textbooks were being fed through a Toronto agent to a non-union shop in New York. Similarly in 1907 he helped expose the Blairmore townsite scandal in which Malcolm McKenzie, a friend of the provincial government, was accused of receiving title to the townsite property under questionable circumstances.

One of the *Eye Opener's* bitterest opponents was Sir Clifford Sifton, whom Edwards in 1905 accused of having immoral relations with a married woman in Ottawa. This, he claimed was the real reason why Sifton had resigned from the Liberal cabinet, and not because of his publicly-announced opposition to the party's policy on the separate school question.

As the 1908 federal elections approached, Edwards heard a rumor that Sifton was supporting a Calgary newspaper, the *Daily News,* in an effort to counteract some of the bad publicity the Liberals were receiving in the *Eye Opener.* Yet Edwards was unprepared for the stinging personal attack which appeared in its columns on October 5, 1908. An article, signed "Nemesis" but actually written by owner Daniel McGillicuddy, was an obvious attempt to nullify Edwards's influence during the federal campaign.

While Edwards had frequently taken his opponents to task, he was careful to state his case in a form which was not libellous but rather to make his victims the butt of his sarcastic humor. McGillicuddy, on the other hand, waded into Edwards without regard for legal niceties. Calling him the "miserable wretch of a depraved existence that his is," he branded Edwards as a " 'four flusher,' a 'tin-horn' and a 'welcher' where poker debts are concerned." After mocking Edwards's slight speech impediment ("he has even captured Oscar Wilde's lisp"), he went on with the promise that "I intend to show that he is a libeller, a character thief, a coward, a liar, a drunkard, a dope-fiend and a degenerate." He also called Edwards "a physical coward of the meanest type and a ten-year-old boy, possessed of the courage of a jack-rabbit, could spit in his eye with impunity and Edwards would sprint in the opposite direction."[26]

Through his lawyer, Bob Edwards laid charges of criminal libel against his accuser. McGillicuddy in turn hired Vancouver lawyer E. P. Davis, and a short time later the case was heard by a jury in the courtroom of Judge N. D. Beck. In the end the jury found McGillicuddy guilty, but expressed dissatisfaction with some of the *Eye Opener* articles, which were in their view "obscene and suggestive" and asked the judge to caution the editor to use more discretion in the future or to have the paper suppressed.

In spite of the guilty verdict, McGillicuddy was fined only $100, half the maximum amount, thus convincing Edwards that the judge was playing politics. "Judge Beck was a Tory and he turned Grit to get his present job on the bench," said Edwards. "Judge Beck is first one thing and then another, but is always the same narrow, prejudiced, fanatical Beck."[27]

Bob Edwards was deeply hurt by the *Daily News* article and the inconclusive trial. He never forgave McGillicuddy—not even after the *Daily News* went broke. "Had it not been for the favoritism of the judge before whom he was convicted of libelling us," said Edwards, "he would have been wearing stripes in the penitentiary two years ago."[28]

Similarly he never forgave Judge Beck, whom he frequently roasted in his columns, or indeed E. P. Davis, the lawyer who had defended McGillicuddy. In fact it was his blind hatred for anyone connected with the McGillicuddy case which later led Edwards into his only conviction for libel as a result of his writings in the *Eye Opener*.

Shortly after the trial, Edwards had taken a mild swipe at E. P. Davis, telling of a humorous incident when he said the lawyer had drunkenly fallen into the Bow River at four o'clock in the morning. Four years later, his memory of the trial still with him, Edwards wrote another story, a tongue-in-cheek account of Davis being stranded on an island near Vancouver with a dozen bottles of scotch. When found E. P. Davis was "running about the island stark naked, with only his spectacles on, armed with a club and striking right and left at imaginary snakes."[29]

Although the piece was obviously fictional, Davis immediately charged Bob Edwards with libel. When the case was heard, the editor was found guilty and was instructed to publish an apology in the columns of the Calgary daily newspapers. Edwards had to comply but he tried to write off the incident by telling his readers that the "successful journal, like a successful man, has to be prepared for attacks from the incompetent ones who have failed."[30]

Yet it was a tribute to Bob Edwards's ability as a writer that the *Eye Opener* should lose only one case of libel in its twenty-year history. Skilfully couching his accusations in legally protective phrases, or using his humor with devastating effect, Edwards seldom saw the inside of a courtroom.

But there were exceptions. The first occurred in 1905 when J. S. Dennis of the CPR sued Edwards for criminal libel as a result of an article in the *Eye Opener* attacking the company's irrigation project. The future prime minister, R. B. Bennett, acted for the railway company, but in spite of his efforts the case was dismissed.

This incident launched Edwards on a vendetta against Bennett, Dennis, and the CPR. He accused the company of providing unsafe railway crossings within Calgary and used the columns of the *Eye Opener* to attack the railway and its hierarchy. His most stinging barbs, however, were saved for Bennett himself, who was railed and lampooned over the next six years. In the following year, for example, he said that "R. B. Bennett has been relieving his feelings by telling his friends that he will run the editor of the *Eye Opener* out of town."[31] And in 1910: "R. B. Bennett has been doing his utmost as solicitor for the CPR to throw obstacles in the way of the CNR coming into Calgary. It is all a question of money with Bennett. He only gets $1,000 as member, while he draws many thousands per annum from the CPR."[32]

By the time of the 1911 federal elections Edwards's anger had cooled sufficiently for him to recognize Bennett's positive qualities. Finally, in an abrupt turnabout, he announced to his readers that "in days gone by, the *Eye Opener* has ever and anon experienced hard feelings towards R.B., but time has healed all that."[33] A few weeks later the conversion was complete when he wrote, with prophet-like accuracy, "vote for R. B. Bennett, who may one day be prime minister of Canada."[34]

And while he was at it, Edwards gave up his fight with J. S. Dennis. "We have to take it all back," he said in 1911, "and fling a rose at the feet of John S. He has far more than made good and this humble little rag is only too delighted to be able to say so."[35]

Bob Edwards was known to have been involved in at least two other court cases. The first occurred in 1910 when the Lord's Day Alliance brought libel action against him in Winnipeg. In this case Edwards was acquitted. The other was in 1919 when Dr. P. C. Bruner tried to charge him with libel for exposing his dental office as a notorious dive. This time the case was brought to the supreme court where the Crown refused to proceed with the charge.

In addition there were three other lawsuits, or threatened lawsuits, because of articles in the *Eye Opener*. The most serious of these resulted from a long letter in the October 3, 1908 issue, in which Mrs. Maria Allison accused Conservative leader R. L. Borden of being the father of her daughter's illegitimate child. As a federal election was in the offing, Borden tried to prevent copies of the *Eye Opener* from being sold in his home constituency of Halifax. When the local distributor, Carruthers, ignored an order to halt the sale of the paper, he was hauled into court and charged with libel. The case dragged on for over a year but no charges were ever brought directly against Edwards or the *Eye Opener*.

The second case occurred in 1907 when a British magazine, *Nineteenth Century,* carried an article from the *Eye Opener* which attacked Borden. In spite of the fact that it was only a reprint and that no charges were being considered against Bob Edwards, the British magazine was obliged to print a retraction.

The third, and most ludicrous case, is almost legendary in the realm of Alberta folklore. On October 6, 1906 Bob Edwards carried a story about his mythical editor, Peter J. McGonigle, being released from jail after serving time on a horse-stealing charge. When McGonigle reached Calgary, a banquet was tendered for him by the board of trade and in the course of the evening the master of ceremonies read a letter, supposedly from Lord Strathcona. It said, in part: "The name of Peter McGonigle will ever stand high in the roll of eminent confiscators. Once, long ago, I myself came near achieving distinction in this direction when I performed some dexterous financing with the Bank of Montreal's funds. In consequence, however, of CPR stocks going up instead of down, I wound up in the House of Lords instead of Stony Mountain."[36]

According to the tale, Strathcona was infuriated when he learned of the article and instructed his solicitors to take legal action. However when their Calgary agents explained the nature of the *Eye Opener*, Strathcona was eventually persuaded to abandon the action.

Throughout Bob Edwards's career his avowed goal was justice for the common man. One of the ways he saw of achieving this was through honest government. Another method was the exposure of bunko artists and four-flushers who were victimizing small investors, and he enthusiastically attacked any elements of Canadian society which he felt were unfair to the working man.

Accordingly, he was sympathetic to the plight of prostitutes, lobbied for more relaxed divorce laws, spoke out against sweat shops and was opposed to Sunday "blue" laws. In specific instances he rose to the defence of members of the RNWMP who were being denied the rewards offered for the capture of train robber Jack Miner; he exposed real estate companies which were selling fraudulent townsite properties; he threatened to reveal the name of a Calgary dentist who was molesting young women; he exposed a well-known tailor who had fathered an illegitimate child; and he revealed that the second worst dive in Calgary was never raided because it was in a building owned by a local millionaire.

Ever since his French Riviera days, Bob Edwards had been impatient with the English upper class and the shallowness of society life. As a result, he invented his own "society notes" which became a hilarious and racy part of the *Eye Opener*. From there he branched out into medical advice and cooking recipes— all designed to ridicule the pretentiousness of society pages in the daily newspapers.

In one issue he even implied that he had engaged a local prostitute, "a creamy-complexioned lady" to do a society column for him every week. "She says she writes copy in a tea gown and slippers."[37] On another occasion he commented that "the society editress has begun to drink more than is good for her and has taken to laughing boisterously at pink teas."[38] Yet everyone knew the *Eye Opener* was strictly a one-man show.

The McGillicuddy case caused Bob Edwards to become disenchanted with his sojourn in Calgary. In particular, he resented the rebuke of the jury of local citizens and came to believe that he had lost his support in the prairie city.

For these reasons, in April 1909, he set out for Toronto where he hoped to relocate the *Eye Opener*. Finding conditions unfavorable there, he looked at Montreal before deciding to settle at Port Arthur. There, with the help of his faithful advertisers from Alberta, the *Eye Opener* resumed publication, and Edwards threw himself into the turmoil of Lakehead politics. However he soon discovered that Port Arthur was no better than Toronto, so at the end of the year he moved again to Winnipeg.

This city was no stranger to Edwards, for he had a number of friends on the daily newspapers there. It was also here that he realized he could publish the *Eye Opener* anywhere; his readers and advertisers simply followed him from place to place. Still being a westerner at heart, and mellowing in his attitudes about his treatment in Calgary, Edwards decided early in 1911 to return to the stampede city for good.

He was back home and well settled when the tenth anniversary of the *Eye Opener* was celebrated. "Starting with a circulation of 250," he recalled, "the rag embarked on a wild career, full of adventure by land and booze, plunging ahead regardless of the most appalling obstacles, and finally becoming an eight-page publication with a bona-fide circulation all over the Dominion of 35,000. In sending your congratulations, pray do not enclose a bottle, as we are strictly on the Water Wagon."[39]

Edwards's comments on booze were most appropriate, for although he was a success in the journalistic field, he never won his fight against the bottle. And the long battle was never easy. He would be sober for weeks at a time and then would suddenly disappear, only to surface several days or weeks later in Vancouver or perhaps in Dr. Brett's sanitarium at Banff. In the interim the *Eye Opener* failed to appear and everyone knew that Bob Edwards was drunk again.

Yet when the moral reformers launched a drive to introduce prohibition into Alberta, Edwards fully supported them. "The *Eye Opener* has no defence to offer for the booze traffic," he told his readers. "It is a bad business; none worse. We've been there. Nobody can tell us anything about it that we don't already know and our frank opinion is that the complete abolition of strong drink would solve the problem of the world's happiness."[40] With his active support the necessary legislation was passed and in 1916 Alberta became a dry province.

Then, just as he had supported the principle of prohibition, Edwards became an outspoken opponent of its actual implementation. He found that drinking was not halted; it simply moved from the bar into the home, and many women were now turning to booze. And even though he had been an alcoholic for years, he was appalled by the results of the new law. "God knows," he wrote, "we should be the last one to talk about other people drinking. Our own reputation as a booze artist used to be second to none, but such drinking as we did was always amongst men. In twenty years' residence in Calgary we have never had a drink in a private house, nor have we ever been to one of those drunken parties in the home that we hear so much about."[41]

During the 1910s the fiery Bob Edwards began to mellow. The pages of the *Eye Opener* were often devoted more to sports, theatrical news, humor and the broad aspects of social reform rather than to exposés of graft, corruption and moral laxity. "We cut out the rough stuff long ago," said Edwards in 1912, "and now the paper is welcomed in hundreds and hundreds of happy homes all over the land. Only last Sunday an article which appeared in the *Eye Opener* formed the basis of a sermon preached from a local pulpit."[42]

Now perhaps the *Eye Opener* wasn't all that innocent. Many young boys had to pay their nickels and read the off-color jokes out behind the woodshed, for the paper was still an anathema in countless Canadian homes. But its reputation as a crusader more than compensated for any loss of readership on moral grounds. And as Edwards grew older, he enjoyed the increasingly respectable role of the *Eye Opener*. On one occasion he even questioned the name of his paper. "It has often occurred to us," he said, "that the name of this paper is an unfortunate one. There is nothing dignified about the title 'Eye Opener.' "[43] He believed that public figures hesitated to quote him because the name lacked the respectability of the more common titles as the *Herald*, *Graphic* and *Times*.

Bob Edwards had remained a lonely bachelor during all his years in Alberta, so his readers were surprised in 1917 when, at the age of fifty-three, he married Kate Penman, a twenty-four-year-old Scottish girl. He had met her four years earlier, just after her arrival from the old country. Working in Bennett's law office and the land titles building, she had been a frequent visitor to the *Eye Opener* office in the months before the wedding. However, this union seems to have had little effect on Edwards and, except for a few random mentions in the *Eye Opener*, she was a closed part of his life.

Because of his well-established reputation as a humorist,

Bob Edwards was encouraged about this time to bring together some of his best writings in an anthology. Not satisfied with a purely editorial task, Edwards also added new stories and jokes, often embellishing the tales published a decade earlier. The result of this effort was the ninety-page *Bob Edwards Summer Annual,* a soft cover, pocket-sized book which was published in 1920. Selling for sixty cents a copy, it was snapped up by *Eye Opener* fans all across Canada, and enjoyed a particularly brisk trade among the news vendors on the CPR trains.

Heartened by the success of the venture, Edwards entered into an agreement with the Musson Book Company of Toronto to publish and distribute additional copies of the magazine. As a result, the *Summer Annual* appeared regularly each year for the rest of Edwards's life.

On many occasions, Bob Edwards had also been asked by political parties to join their ranks and to run for office. He had always resisted the temptation, preferring instead to take a neutral stand from which he could strike more effectively against the inequities of the political system. However in 1921 he finally succumbed, running as an independent and easily winning a seat in the Alberta legislature. Some measure of Edwards's popularity can be discerned from the fact that without advertising or public speaking tours, he polled the second largest vote in Calgary in a field of twenty candidates.

He sat for only one session of the legislature, commenting wonderingly, "Isn't it remarkable, here we are in the legislature and McGillicuddy is in hell?"[44] But even before he wrote those words, Edwards's health was failing to such a degree that he had been obliged to go to Vancouver for a complete rest. He made only one speech in the legislature, his maiden address, in which he condemned the devastating effects of the liquor traffic and prohibition. It was a subject which he knew all too well.

By the summer of 1922 he was a very sick man, publishing his last issue of the *Eye Opener* on July 29. Three and a half months later, on November 14, he died at the age of fifty-eight. Mourned across Canada, he was the subject of numerous tributes and editorials, all extolling his genius as one of the nation's leading humorists and social reformers.

A short time later his widow established the Bob Edwards Publishing Company and tried to carry on the *Eye Opener.* His eastern publishers also continued to glean stories from his back issues and they published posthumous editions of the *Summer Annual* in 1923 and 1924.

But everyone knew that Bob Edwards and the *Eye Opener* were one and the same. Gradually the effort to keep the newspaper and *Summer Annual* alive became something of a farce. At last the weekly newspaper ceased publication and all rights were sold to an eastern publishing house. There a cheap girlie magazine became the final and tragic beneficiary of a lifetime of Edwards's literary skills. As late as 1933 the Bob Edwards Publishing Co. of Montreal was still grinding out a pulp magazine of dirty jokes and cartoons under the title of *The Eye-Opener*. It was a far cry from the proud and defiant journal which had been a part of Canadian life for twenty years.

But the original *Eye Opener* survived the tawdriness of its shallow imitators and Edwards's reputation as a humorist and literary genius emerged unscathed. As editor of his "great moral journal," he had been a social conscience of the Canadian community. Far ahead of his time in matters of political and social reform, his writings have remained as a tribute to a lifetime of devotion to his fellow man. At the same time the pages of the *Eye Opener* reveal Bob Edwards's unique gift—the ability to make people laugh.

Hugh A. Dempsey

ONE

The Fair Sex

Nine-tenths of a woman's intuition is suspicion. [1]

*

Blessed are the pretty girls, for they shall inherit the men.[2]

*

A woman's idea of heaven is a place where she won't have to wash dishes. [3]

*

The secret of the success our western women have attained in public life is nothing else but the fact that they are such smooth speakers on the platform. They can talk a man blind and out-argue him at every turn, doing it in such a way that there is no come-back. Did you ever hear Nellie McClung when in good form? If not, you have missed the treat of your life. Woe betide the poor fish who interpolates a silly question. He gets his so quick that his head swims for about a week. We once went to hear this lady speak in the Grand Theatre, full of amused tolerance not unmixed with prejudice. After she got through, all we could gasp to the friend alongside was, "She wins." [4]

*

Prudes are women who are always looking for temptations to resist. [5]

*

To punish her little girl her mother put her in a closet. For fifteen long minutes the door was locked without a sound coming from behind it. Not a whimper nor a sniffle. At last the stern, but anxious parent unlocked the closet door and peered into the darkness. She could see nothing.

"What are you doing in there?" she cried.

Slowly and with emphasis a small voice made reply:

"I'm thpittin' on your new hat, and I'm thpittin' on your new dreth, and I'm thpittin' on your new thatin thlipperth, and—and—." There was a breathless pause.

"And what are you doing now?" anxiously cried the mother, who had been vainly trying to locate the hidden baby.

"Waitin' for thum more thpit!" said the voice of vengeance. [6]

*

This suffragette nonsense makes us very tired. There is only one way to head it off. Make the legal age for voting thirty-five instead of twenty-one. [7]

*

Apropos of the suffragettes, a friend was telling us rather a good yarn about them.

Premier Asquith, coming out of the House of Commons one day, was surrounded by a crowd of suffragettes. Lloyd George, who was standing by listening and looking on, remarked to a friend what a horribly ugly bunch of females they were. Half an hour later the women were arrested.

In the morning they were convicted and sentenced to thirty days each. Lloyd George, meeting Asquith on the street that afternoon, remarked that he had noticed that the suffragettes had been sent to jail.

"Yes," said Asquith, "that is the only opportunity they will have in their lives of being confined." [8]

*

Nothing succeeds like the efforts of a woman to be disagreeable. [9]

*

By George, we must get off some society stuff this issue or bust a gut. It is the height of the season and owing to several unfortunate jamborees at the time when the big functions were being pulled off we have not yet been able to get in our fine work. But better late than never.

Last Wednesday night a charming dance was given at the charming residence of the charming Mrs. W. Sloshcum-Kachorker. Old Sloshcum-Kachorker, who had inadvertently got drunk at the Mariaggi that afternoon, was unable to be present, but "a pleasant time was had" nevertheless. The rooms were tastefully decorated with flowers and ferns. Among those present were:

A beautiful gown of blue satin with net trimmings and sage and onion stuffing.

A charming gown of white crepe de Chine with apricot trimmings and apple dressing.

A cream brussels sprout net over silk, trimmed with old point lace.

A lovely gown of green satin, edged with point d'esprit and old rose silk, with touches of burlap.

There were many more beautiful gowns present and they appeared to be having a good time. It really does not matter who were inside the gowns. Towards the close of this most successful function old Sloshcum-Kachorker came lurching downstairs from an upper chamber looking for a drink and rather spoiled the general effect of the tout ensemble, but on the whole it was a most enjoyable affair and the charming hostess was warmly congratulated by her guests. [10]

*

It's awfully hard for a woman to pretend not to know the things she ought to know. [11]

*

Nothing pleases a girl more than to be mistaken for an actress. [12]

*

Now, here is something! Minister Sifton's statement that a Mrs. Livingston had gone to the old country and would bring out seventeen carloads of women servants, young girl nurses and governesses brings with it a gleam of hope to the weary bachelors of the North-West. The government will pay their

27

passage to Canada and the amount of the same will be refunded at the end of six months. The girls and women are to be turned loose in Canada to go to whichever province they choose.

But for fear they all get lost in the scramble those who need them most should apply in advance, giving a brief description of the sort of girl they want.

We have wired Sifton about the particular variety of femina divina we prefer. We want a freckled, pasty complexion, green-eyed blond, with a concave chest, height six feet, and able to dig post holes. We shall also insist on her wearing a wrapper and carpet slippers round the house, and she will also be expected to use hairpins. We cannot have our wife tying up her hair with binding twine. Neither must she be a hard drinker. If there is any drinking to be done, we will attend to it. She must have a trousseau that will last the rest of her natural life, as the *Free Lance* will not be in a position to blow itself for steel corsets and striped stockings for many a year to come. However, should she run out of carpet slippers we might strain a point and rustle her up a couple of old Peterboro' canoes in Edmonton.

As soon as we get her we will publish a cut of her in this paper. [13]

*

A girl of sixteen pretends to know a lot more than a woman of thirty will admit she knows. [14]

*

Society Note— Our genial friend, Mrs. Sophie MacHattie, known to many old-time Calgarians, who has been enjoying a prolonged visit at the Banff Dipsomaniac Retreat, returned home last Thursday. Her health is greatly improved, the purple streaks which lined her jocund countenance having almost entirely disappeared. Mrs. MacHattie has resumed her studies in Scotch whiskey. [15]

*

A despatch states that there is a split in the Alberta cabinet. She must be a suffragette. [16]

*

A Calgary waitress was room-hunting the other day and

called at a house that had the sign "Rooms to Rent" displayed in one of the windows. The lady of the house showed the young woman a nice comfortable room, which the latter decided to take. Suddenly the lady asked what employment she was engaged in and, when told "waiting table," stiffened up and said, "Oh, my dear young girl, you can't stay here. Why, there's a bank clerk on one side of the hall and a preacher on the other!"

The above incident is true. It has happened in Calgary in various forms many times before. In a Christian city like Calgary, where churches and Ladies' Aids and "movements" for the advancement of the women's cause are a predominating feature, it seems incredible that these hardworking young women should be turned down with a scornful curl of the lip by their own sex.

To be sure, there are some pretty fly and flip young ladies in the waitress line but, on the other hand, there are also some pretty fly and flip young ladies occupying superior stations in in life. It should be remembered that many highly respectable girls of respectable parents come to Calgary from neighbouring towns and districts to earn a living for themselves, which surely indicates a laudable spirit of independence. Every girl has not had the opportunity to attend business college and become a stenog. [17]

*

The more polite two women are when they meet the more they hate each other. [18]

*

The only period in a woman's life when she gives any thought to dress is between the cradle and the grave. [19]

*

Seasonable Recipes

Pea Soup: Take a lot of split peas and dump them into a pot of water. Let it boil a week. If the peas show no signs of softening, boil for another week. Time is no object with pea soup. Add an old boot to give it body. Also a pinch or two of salt. If not to your taste, chuck it out of the window.

Croutons: This goes with the pea soup. Take a loaf that is several days old and cut it into little cubes about the size of dice. Mark correct spots on cubes with India ink and put in oven till hard enough to crack the teeth. Guests can then extract them from the pea soup and agreeably while away the time shooting craps until the next course is served.

Hash à la Reine: See that the dog is a fairly fat one. Hit him over the head with an axe and allow him to boil three hours. Chop into mince meat and mix in a lot of potatoes, onions and sage. Serve hot. Cats take only twenty minutes.

Breaded Veal Cutlets: Select chops with nothing on them but bone and strips of gristly fat. Camouflage alleged chops by smearing them over with thick layer of bread crumbs, then stick in the oven until somebody orders "Breaded Veal Cutlets." Serve and then stand aside and watch the poor boob picking away at it. It is quite a study and is good for sixty cents. Or you can lay an old leaf of lettuce on the plate and charge six bits. [20]

*

A woman usually tells a joke the way she gets off a car. [21]

*

We got on to the following rather good morsel of gossip through the teacup route. It is said to be quite true.

A drayman was telephoned for to a certain house the other day to come and haul away a trunk. On driving up to the door the gentleman of the house came out and said he would help him carry down the trunk. While lugging it downstairs the husband grumblingly explained to the drayman, "I just got back from the coast an hour or two ago and find that my wife has packed up a lot of her old dresses and things to give to a friend who is not very well off. She must have put in a devil of a lot, for this old trunk weighs a ton."

After putting the trunk on the dray the gentleman paid the driver his fifty cents and returned indoors. As the rig was about to start the lady came tripping down the steps and, handing the driver a five-spot, said, "Don't take the trunk to the address my husband gave you. Take it to Room ——— in the ——— Block. When you get it there, open it and take out the parcel you will find inside. Here is the key."

As soon as the drayman got the trunk luggage up to the

room in the block, he unlocked it, opened the lid and out stepped a dishevelled young man with a rather scared express of counttenance.

"Now you keep mum about this. Do you understand? Here is a ten-spot."

"All right, sir," said the bewildered drayman. [22]

*

The laughter and tears of a woman are equally deceptive. [23]

*

Women are simply crazy to holler for suffrage. Few of them would vote intelligently anyhow. The maidens would all vote for the handsomest man with the cutest moustache, while the old hens would go for the candidates who wore spectacles and looked wise. Fathers, husbands and brothers could deliver the votes of their womenfolk to either side in a chunk. Were the female vote in doubt in any constituency all that the party in danger would have to do would be to put up a masher like Harold Jarvis or a matinee idol of the Dustin Farnum stamp and they would carry the seat a-flying. [24]

*

A woman is almost as sensitive about the size of her shoes as she is about her age. [25]

*

While we are on the subject of women, perhaps we might be permitted to express our wonder and astonishment over the question of where women get their information on which to base gossip? The curious part of it is that while their gossip may be tinkered a little to make their line of afternoon tea talk more spicy, their information is usually correct. Where do they get it?

We have finally arrived at the conclusion that wives hear all about what is going on downtown from their husbands, during the dead watches of the night before they fall asleep. The lady dishes it all out to her friends the following afternoon over the teacups, and there you are! [26]

*

A woman's best female friend will tell you more to her disadvantage in a minute than you can learn from her worst enemy in a month. [27]

*

If male preachers cannot fill their churches and attract the men who loaf around the street corners all day long on Sundays, why don't they give the women a chance?

Women have made a success of their homes; they are the props of the churches. Men have occupied the pulpits of the world for nineteen hundred and thirteen years, and a smaller percentage are going to church now than went when they first started in the business. If a woman with a bewitching smile asked a man to go to heaven with her he would take up his hat and go. If a man asks him the same question he promptly decides to take a chance on the other place.

Most of the men who are preaching today should be made janitors for a year or two, and women put in their places. If that would not fill the churches, let men preach to women and women to men, and then you would have a solution to the difficulty that made the Lord's Day Act people invoke the law. [28]

*

It is considered comme-il-faut for a woman to come down to breakfast in her nightgown and her hair done up in back numbers of the *Eye Opener*. It shows lack of good breeding. [29]

*

A woman begins to show her age only when she tries to hide it. [30]

*

Society Note— Miss Lena Bingham left on the eastbound last Thursday to visit friends in Winnipeg. Her many friends hope to see her back soon, also her front. [31]

*

There was a young woman of Natchez,
Who fell on some nettle weed patchez,
Now she sits in a room,
With a heart full of gloom,
And scratchez, and scratchez and scratchez. [32]

*

32

Society Note— Miss Mollie Poffkins, the amiable stenographer in a well-known law office in the city, desires us to state that she is not the Miss Poffkins who was arrested last week for stealing a crosscut saw and sledge hammer from Ashdown's Hardware. [33]

*

We actually need women in provincial politics. Women could never possibly participate in any graft system, owing to their inability to keep a secret. As publicity is the remedy for most political ills, women in politics should function admirably. [34]

*

Nothing pleases a pretty woman more than to be seen on the street with another woman who isn't pretty. [35]

*

A woman is always suspicious of another woman who dresses better than herself. [36]

*

Why is it that the prettiness of a pretty girl so often palls after you've got used to it? It surely must be because the flattery and attention she receives make her assume that her beauty is the only capital and stock-in-trade needful to enable her to pick and choose her own husband when the time comes, leading her to neglect cultivating other attractive qualities with which to bolster, support and fortify her good looks. These latter, it may be mentioned incidentally, seldom last into the home stretch.

Whenever a woman is pretty and knows it, then she isn't. Plain girls with winning ways can generally walk away from the pretty ones without winning ways. In any event, don't laugh at a girl with a pug nose. You never know what may turn up.

Something more than good features, disconcerting eyes and perfect lines are needed to build up a temple of human loveliness. Cultivation of mind, gentleness of heart, manners that are not of the Sawbath order, and a capacity for sinking the ego and making other mortals comfortable—all these are actual necessities. A brain that has developed through reading and study and a tongue that knows how to run right without slipping into gossip are great helps in social intercourse.

A pretty girl whose stock of conversation is confined to "well, I declare," "is that so?" and "well well!" is apt to become rather a bore after the glamor of her loveliness has worn off. The wise man does not marry dolls of this type, through a wholesome dread of being "well-I-declared" at breakfast, "is-that-soed" at dinner and "well-welled" at supper for the rest of his natural life. [37]

*

There are lots of funny things to be seen in this world, and among them is a fat woman sitting on a little piano stool. [38]

*

One thing we can never understand is why a woman looks straight into the mirror to adjust her belt at the back. [39]

*

Cooking Recipes

Bread Putting: Gather up all the chunks of bread that have been left over on the plates for the past week and dump them into a bucket of water. Let them soak overnight and in the morning pound into a pulp with the butt end of an empty beer bottle. Take a handful of plums and chuck into the mess. Stir with a big spoon and add a little sugar. Dump into a pan and stick it into the oven. As soon as it begins to look a trifle less disgusting, take it out and serve as plum pudding.

Stewed Chicken: Take the varicose veins of an aged chicken and wind them around the bones. Lay the flesh of the bird aside for private consumption the next day. Stick veins and bones in shallow pan and allow to simmer for a while, then serve in white sticky sauce. The latter can be procured in desired quantity from the Calgary Bill Posting Company Limited.

Pudding à la Reine: Take down flask from shelf and pour stiff horn down your throat. Whip five or six eggs into a fine lather and pour in a quart of milk. Add cupful of sugar. Have another drink. Add a little minced onion and the contents of a can of strawberries with pepper and salt to season. Flavor with vanilla and set away to cool. If the guests are not satisfied with this, tell them to go to hell and throw the pudding out of the window. Finish the flask.

34

Rabbit Stew: Take a good fat cat and give it a bat over the head in the cellar. Remove skin and dismember with sharp knife. Put in pan with a little water and allow to simmer slowly for a couple of hours. Season to taste.

Roast Turkey: Save up for months until you have price of good big bird. Then take money and send to Maple Creek for half a dozen bottles of Scotch. You won't want any turkey. [40]

*

Nature leaves a lot of work for the dressmaker to finish. [41]

*

Society Note— Last Wednesday night Mrs. Frederick Larkyn, whose grace and beauty the *Eye Opener* has frequently extolled, got out of her bed to take a snifter and came within an ace of swallowing a glass of water which stood on a table. Her many friends will be glad to learn that she has almost recovered from the shock. [42]

*

Women ought to make satisfactory angels because they are so fond of "harping."[43]

*

Some of the Women's Clubs in Alberta are agitating for a woman to be appointed to the Canadian Senate. This is a new departure in politics and is creating some stir. Might we suggest "Blondie" Jorkin as a suitable candidate? She could hold her own admirably in Ottawa, as an accomplished booze artist. Blondie is amply bibulous for the job. [44]

*

Women will never make good on juries until they get to be as ignorant as men. [45]

*

It is pleasant to note that the girls in this neck of the woods no longer—or, at least, very seldom—chew gum in public. This was indeed a most vulgar and unsightly habit. A woman, no matter how pretty or how attractively she is dressed, has absolutely no attraction when her jaws are working like a steam engine. They have been rather long finding this out, but better late than never. [46]

*

Society Note— Mrs. J. B. Scluff, of Fourteenth Ave. W., entertained some of her neighbors informally last Monday afternoon. That is to say, she and her cook had a quarrel on the front porch. [47]

*

Mrs. John M. Snufflebuster denies the rumor that an interesting event is expected in her family in the fall. She says it is a canard, or words to that effect. [48]

*

Girls with the most cheek do the least blushing. [49]

*

Events in the legislature suggest the well-known toast, "Here is to woman, once our superior, now our equal." [50]

*

Society Note— Miss Annie Jugglebuster has left for her home in Hamilton, Ont. What is Hamilton's loss is our gain. [51]

Politics

Probably the saddest thing about Ottawa is the number of fourth-rate intellects applied to first-rate problems. [1]

*

Yes, the plug was pulled out. That curious soughing noise you hear is doubtless the late Grit government going down the pipe. [2]

*

They are getting very toney up in Edmonton, with their fair and inauguration festivities in sight. Many of the smart young ladies have taken to wearing open-work shoes to display pretty hosiery, a charming idea. It is now in order for the men of Edmonton to start wearing open-work hats for the purpose of displaying the wheels revolving in their heads. [3]

*

We understand—ha ha!—that—haw haw!—R. J. Stuart—ah-yaw-haw—ha ha ha!—is going to run oh oh ha ha—for alderman—ha ha ha ha ha ha!—Ha ha ha ha ha ha—ha ha ha ha ha ha ha ha ha! [4]

*

"It's funny," said R. B. Bennett one day, "but nobody ever seems to be glad to see me."

"And haven't you ever found out the cause of your unpopularity?" inquired his candid friend, who, being from New Brunswick also was permitted to take liberties.

"No, I can't discover it."

"Well, well, it's right under your very nose." [5]

*

What is this we hear about W. C. Armstrong going to run for alderman in the third ward? This, if true, is the most consummate a piece of gall we ever heard tell of, even in this town. Which is saying a good deal. Armstrong, it will be remembered, was a prominent member of the syndicate which so nearly did up the citizens of Calgary on the notorious city lot deal. For this man even to allow his name to be breathed in connection with a seat in the city council is an insult to the community. [6]

*

One watched pot that does boil is the political pot. [7]

*

The *Eye Opener* wants to know why the Grits are so anxious for another term of power. There is nothing left to steal. Everything is cleaned up. What, then, can be their object? [8]

*

The devil knew what he was doing when he invented politics, all right. [9]

*

There is neither rhyme nor reason in trying to make a heroic figure out of Laurier in his hour of defeat. Laurier may be a picturesque enough figure, but hanged if we can see anything heroic about a politician who has been turned down by the voters of the country. The situation is quite commonplace. It is occurring all the time all over the world where there is popular franchise. One bunch of politicians who have got gay by too long tenure of power get chucked out and another bunch get chucked in. The latter last long enough to get fat and gay and then they get chucked out too and the other bunch get chucked back again. That is all there is to it.

Political parties, like many individuals we know, cannot stand prosperity. After a party has been in power for a number of years it becomes stodgy and self-complacent and its members in office by a continuous absorption of flattery from fawning lightweights at home, get to imagine that they are devilish important, devilish important. Drunken with a sense of power and immunity, the more unscrupulous ones become careless and corrupt. The canker of graft takes hold and spreads, immorality is added to corruption, scandals creep forth, an alert opposition press gets busy and the electors do the rest.

In the recent election the Liberal government got canned because the people of Canada had a very shrewd suspicion that their own premier was trying to sell them out. They were willing to stand for a lot from Sir Wilfrid, but they couldn't stand for that!

That a proper amount of B.S. will raise a man above his fellows by causing them to think him wondrous wise, might be illustrated by the following yarn:

There were three pigs in a poke. The overcrowding was scandalous. Each accounted for the evil in a different manner.

The first pig said, "This overcrowding is terrible; it is because we are in a poke."

The second pig said, "This overcrowding is disastrous; it is because we are pigs."

The third pig spoke as follows, "The overcrowding is undoubtedly appalling, but you are both mistaken as to the conditions that have caused it. It is not due to our being in a poke; neither is it due to our being pigs. The evil is the direct and inevitable outcome of certain spasmodic variations in the Law of Economic Utility."

The other two pigs were much impressed, and without more ado elected the third pig leader among them. Still the overcrowding remained as bad as ever. [10]

*

Some fellow made the remark the other day that there was small difference between the Liberal and the Conservative parties. There is all the difference in the world. One is in and the other is out. [11]

*

Most of any government's troubles come from trying to uphold the blunders it makes. [12]

*

The Hon. W. R. Motherwell, minister of something or other in the former Saskatchewan government, on August 13 got the following off his chest:

"The Regina *Standard* quotes me as saying, 'I do not take much notice of the *Standard*.' That is true. I do not. But I would rather depend on the *Standard* than on the Calgary *Eye Opener*."

That's all right old cockie, but we helped put you where you belong anyway—on the scrap pile. [13]

*

Many an aspirant occupies the political grave he dug for the other fellow. [14]

*

We were once a very active Conservative ourself. The reason we are not so any longer is because there is no Conservative party to belong to. It is dead as a mackerel. As a party to be reckoned with it is non-existent. A few of the old brigade will hang on from habit or from congenital inability to keep up with the bandwagon of progress. Fresh ideas are elbowing out the old ones; labor is coming into its own; the farmer has already compelled long-deferred recognition; social problems are being handled from a new angle and nothing is allowed to go stagnant any more. Even the church has caught the alert spirit of the times and is in the throes of a great Forward Movement. Things look good all round.

The very name, "Conservative," sounds out of place these days. It has a standing still and even a retrogressive tinkle. They will never get anywhere with a name like that. Suggestions, emanating from some boobies in the East, have been made recently to the effect that a new party called the "National Party" should be organized, but they can't fool us out here with raw camouflage of that sort. It would just be the old hidebound, high-protectionist, Manufacturers' Association party over again, operating under a deliberately misleading name. [15]

*

Politics has not ceased to make strange bedfellows, or, at least, the politicians of both parties continue to share the same bunk. You know the kind of bunk we mean. [16]

*

40

The Sifton government and the McBride government are both doomed to defeat next time they venture to go to the country. Sifton and McBride have each turned some queer tricks which have smothered them in a cloud of suspicion. People are getting sick and tired of graft suspects in high places and are becoming especially intolerant of those of whom they have good grounds for suspicion, yet who are too foxy to be caught. [17]

*

Except for politics, Satan would lose his grip on some men. [18]

*

What can be said of Lougheed, the leader of the Conservatives in the Senate? Not only is he an offensively aggressive promoter of corporation interests to the detriment of the people, but he is the only public man we know of in Canada who has openly shown himself to be the direct enemy of the laboring classes. There can be but little doubt that Lougheed intrigued for this appointment in the Senate in order to be in line for cabinet office in the sweet bye and bye, but so long as men like him are allowed to retain positions of this kind in the party the chances of the Conservatives ever regaining power are too slim to be worth considering. [19]

*

All that the country has to do to improve the government at Ottawa is to change it. [20]

*

Politics is a good game, but a mighty poor business. [21]

*

The history of the Conservative party in western Canada for the past ten years has been one long, continuous blunder. They have done every d——d thing they ought not to have done, and haven't done a single thing any sane man might be expected to do. [22]

*

A father, wishing to satisfy himself as to the future prospects of his son, decided to make the following test. "Now," he said, "I will put here, where he will see them the first thing when he comes in, a Bible, some money, and a bottle of whiskey. If he takes the Bible he will be a preacher, if he takes the money he will be a business man, and if he takes the whiskey he will be no good."

Having thus decided on the plan, he arranged the articles and concealed himself to await the son and watch results. Presently in came the boy, saw the money and put it in his pocket, took up the bottle of whiskey and drank it, put the Bible under his arm and walked out whistling.

"My gracious!" exclaimed the father, "He will be a member of parliament!" [23]

*

This is indeed the land of opportunity. There is no other country on the face of the earth so available as Canada where a man has such glorious opportunities to make a fool of himself in politics. [24]

*

Sample debate in the Canadian House of Commons:

Mr. John Herron (Alberta) moved the following resolution: That the circumstances attendant upon the murder of his mother-in-law by John T. Peterkins, inspector of swamp lands in Ungava, and subsequent disgraceful distribution of her body amongst the wolves of that country, and the continued retention of said official in office without investigation, reflects discredit upon the government and should receive the disapproval of this House.

Mr. Bourassa asked if the government intended to take any steps to remove from office John T. Peterkins, inspector of swamp lands in Ungava, who had recently become notorious through strangling his mother-in-law in her shack, cutting up her body into small chunks, filling them with assafoetida and strychnine, and setting them out as bait for wolves, on which there was a bounty of $1 a head. By these shocking means Peterkins had collected $145 from the government.

Hon. Frank Oliver: The honorable member has been misinformed as usual. It seems a pity that honorable members do not obtain more exact information on which to base their

42

charges against the government. The number of pelts paid for by the government in this district was only 85, of which number Peterkins had a claim against 53. This money has not yet been paid over to the claimants, but the government sees no reason why Peterkins' claim should not be settled along with the rest. The territory of Ungava has for years been terrorized by large and ferocious bands of wolves, and the department considers that Mr. Peterkins has done the state no small service in ridding his district of the number of wild animals indicated.

Mr. Bourassa: Will the right honorable the minister of the interior inform the House whether or not the government proposes to retain Peterkins in the public service with this awful charge hanging over his head.

Hon. Frank Oliver: I cannot see whereof consists the "awful charge." No complaint has reached the department that Mr. Peterkins neglected the swamp lands of Ungava while sporadically engaged in trapping wolves. If it can be shown that the swamp lands were in any way neglected or allowed to fall into decay through lack of inspection, then the department may take steps to make further investigation into the matter. (Cheers.)

W. F. Maclean: That is not the point. The charge has been made that this government official, Peterkins, strangled his mother-in-law and fed her to the wolves. Surely such a monstrous piece of business should be looked into.

Sir Wilfrid Laurier: I must protest against the time of the House being frittered away in this manner. Mr. Peterkins' record as a swamp inspector is unrivalled in the annals of swamp lore. The Ungava swamps have thriven as they never throve before, under his inspection, and it does credit to his nobility of disposition that he devoted his leisure moments to the eradication of wild animals which had become a menace to the country. (Loud cheers.)

Mr. Bourassa: The right honorable the premier begs the question. It has been proven beyond the shadow of a doubt that this man murdered his mother-in-law and threw her in sections to the wolves. What is the government going to do about it? Surely I am entitled to an answer to my question.

Hon. Frank Oliver: The department lays down no hard and fast rules as to what kind of bait shall be used in the case of wild animals on whose pelts a bounty is paid by the government. Ordinary meat is liable to be in a frozen condition at this time of the year, and poison administered through the medium of frozen meat takes longer to work on the vitals of a wolf. Even frozen hard it takes quite a while to melt after being swallowed, and the animal may stray for miles before the strychnine gets in its fine work, thus rendering impotent the work of the man who is out for the pelt. Fresh meat, when obtainable, is the most efficacious form of bait. Old trappers of the Hudson's Bay are unanimous in this opinion. Mr. Peterkins is one of the most zealous servants in the employ of the government and I certainly see no reason for his removal, as suggested by my honorable friend. I might mention that Ungava is a great lone land, and it is sometimes hard to find a competent man to remain there for any lengthy period in the government service. However, I am happy to be in a position to inform the House that Mr. Peterkins is about to take himself another wife and will shortly marry into a prominent Esquimaux family.

M. S. McCarthy: Out of bait again?

W. F. Maclean: Wants some more fresh meat probably.

The Speaker: Order, order.

In concluding the debate, the premier asked the government members to vote down this frivolous resolution, as it involved an attack upon the government.

Upon a division being taken, Mr. Herron's resolution was defeated by a vote of ninety to forty-one.

The House then went into Committee of Ways and Means. [25]

*

"I beg pardon," said a man to Clifford Sifton one day last session, "but am I rightly informed that it costs you $50,000 a year to live?"

"You are."

"Then why do you do it?" [26]

*

As the dominion parliament always contains such a plethora of cerebral miscarriages in the shape of human beings it doubtless can get along very well without the society of Simmons. [27]

*

There is intense enthusiasm at Edmonton over their chances

44

for becoming the permanent capital. Even the women are in a frenzy, with an eye to future balls and society functions at the capital. Of course the babies are crying for it also. The Edmontonian tells you calmly that they have the C. & E., the CNR, the Grand Trunk and—Frank Oliver, and that Calgary has no more chance of becoming the capital than Sifton has of entering the kingdom of heaven. They are a hard lot of citizens up there, for a fact. [28]

*

Politically, man is but a flash in the pan. Who can remember today and call off without a mistake all the men who have chortled and slobbered round Sir Wilfrid's cabinet table since '96? There has been an awful bunch of them. [29]

*

[The following "news" story was written by Bob Edwards about five months before Alberta became a province and before Hon. G. H. V. Bulyea was chosen as the province's first lieutenant-governor.]

Dr. Lafferty yesterday became the first lieutenant-governor of the new province of Alberta. Edmonton was en fête. It was her first gala day since the hanging of King at the fort.

Lafferty was in great form. Every eye was bent on that weird figure as he was driven amid wild huzzahs to the scene of his inauguration, escorted by a body guard of influential real estate sharks. The tepees and shacks on either side of Main Street were tastefully decorated with bunting and streamers, appropriate mottoes—"God bless Lafferty," "How would you like to be the Iceman," and so forth—catching the eye on every hand, while the goats on the roofs of the Irish quarter shook their shaggy beards in sympathy with the occasion.

The new lieutenant-governor ever and anon stood up in his carriage and raised his hat, smiling fatuously and wagging his head, at which hundreds and hundreds of partially Seagramized citizens raised their voices in enthusiastic acclaim. Nellie Brown and Lil Whatshername, of the old-timers' committee, strewed roses in front of the carriage, performing the while a complicated variation of the once-famous koutchee-koutchee dance, to the intense delight of the populace. The scene was oriental. Behind the gubernatorial equipage came the town band, discoursing martial music for all it was worth. The sound of cannons issued from every billiard hall, and the screams from the neighboring asylum gave the scene a characteristic local tone.

At the Grand Central Hotel a stop was made for a drink, the occupants of all the carriages descending and lining up in front of an affable young man who wore a spotless white vest and an interrogative smile. The lieutenant-governor did the honors and made a rather witty speech from the top of the bar, whither he had been hoisted, announcing that the treat was on him. By common impulse, as if some electric communication had passed through the crowd, the whole mass moved forward. It was fully fifteen minutes before the procession was ready to proceed.

A similar stop was made at every hotel on Jasper Avenue, and by the time the lieutenant-governor and his suite arrived at the fair grounds, where he was to be sworn in, the crowd was feeling all right, thank you. When his honor mounted the judges' stand, which had been transformed into a throne, a roar of applause rent the air. The grandstand, as well as the race track from the turn into the home stretch, was one seething mass of humanity. The spectacle was one of exceeding splendor. From beginning to end the ceremonies that followed were as dignified, impressive and picturesque as such ceremonies could possibly be.

The enthusiasm may, in a measure, be explained. His honor having duly set 'em up at eight different hotels en route to the grounds, it was felt that the affairs of a great, free and enlightened people were in just the proper hands, especially if he kept up the good work.

As the sublime Dr. Lafferty, gorgeously attired in his new Windsor uniform and with a four-point Hudson's Bay blanket carelessly thrown over his shoulders to keep out any drafts that might be drawn on him, reached the throne he bowed graciously right and left. With bared head he repeated after the chief justice the simple and impressive oath of office, after which he solemnly stroked his whiskers and kissed the open pages of the Bible held out before him.

A wave of emotion passed over the surging mass of human beings and press reporters. Women sobbed with uncontrollable emotion, while strong men wept. The half-breed quartette relieved the strain by striking up "Alouette, gentille Alouette," in the chorus of which the people joined, those on the grounds

46

catching up the refrain and making the welkin ring with this most convivial of ditties.

At this juncture Bishop Legal, representing the pope, stepped forward to place the cocked hat on Lafferty's head and crown him lord of all, but the new ruler of this glorious province seized the cocked hat and with his own hands placed it on his massive koko, thus following in the footsteps of his great prototype, Napoleon. This episode will no doubt become equally historic, especially if John A. McDougall gets out another book.

The new lieutenant-governor had risen to the occasion. It was universally remarked, in Edmonton colloquialism, that there were no flies on him. He was self-possession itself. Lighting a cigar of Edmonton manufacture, he calmly eyed the cheering multitude with impassive face. Patiently he waited until the crowd settled itself and perfect order obtained, and, having smoked down to the cabbage in his cigar, he dropped it on the head of a spectator and proceeded to deliver the speech from the throne.

"Ladies and gentlemen, as personal representative of the British monarch, I have the honor to inform you that it affords King Edward and myself unalloyed pleasure to greet you on this the red letter day of the new province of Alberta. My appointment meets with our joint approval. I know of no act of the Liberal party which has given His Majesty and myself such sincere gratification. (Cheers.) A cablegram reached me this morning from Buckingham Palace, which I am sure you would all like to hear: 'Buckingham Palace, Old Kent Road, London. His Majesty desires me to state that he is all tickled up the back. Ponsonby, secretary.' (Prolonged cheering and cries of 'Wot's the matter with Lafferty? Lafferty's all right!')

"I am sorry my old friend, James Reilly, is not here today to participate in your acclamations. Doubtless, like many of my appendicitis patients, he feels considerably cut up, but there is still room for him in the Senate as a retired sage should he care to hire a slab in our national mausoleum. ('Good boy, Lafferty!' 'Stay with it!') Those who feel moved to write panegyrics about myself are requested to send copies to my friend Reilly, to alleviate his pain. ('You bet!' 'Keep a-goin!' 'Soop her up!')

"It grieves me, however, to inform you, ladies and gentlemen— but it is my duty to do so—that there is but little probability of

Edmonton becoming the permanent capital. ('Wow, wow, wow!' 'Wot's that?') As a Calgarian of many years standing, ('Lynch him!' 'Eat 'em up!' 'Tear down the throne!') I must say that we have your northern burg faded. ('Soak him!' 'Duck him in the river!') No, gentlemen, you won't duck me in the river. In an official sense I am Edward the Seventh, King of Great Britain and Ireland. If you duck me in the river you will be ducking the king, and that will be lese majestie. ('Knock off his cocked hat!') Do you know what lese majestie means? ('Go to hell!') No, it does not mean that either. It means that you will all be jugged. ('Oh, come off the perch!' 'Soak your head!' 'Chuck a brace!') Gentlemen, if you carry on in this style, what am I to say in reply to His Gracious Majesty's message from across the sea? Am I to tell His Majesty that you are all bughouse? ('Certainly! Tell him the truth!' 'Go on!' 'Shut up!') Gentlemen, I almost wish my friend Reilly had received this appointment. ('Yawp!') Indeed I do. Were it not that Mr. Reilly has just joined a sect which is waiting for the world to come to an end, I should be tempted to turn over my cocked hat to him. I would, so help me, Johnnie Rodgers. But I fear I bore you. ('You do!' 'Dry up!' 'Not at all!' 'Shut up!') As Lady Godiva said when returning from her ride, 'I am now drawing near my clothes.' (Roars of laughter.) By way of propitiating the furies, I beg to invite you all to accompany me up town and we shall again visit all the hotels at my expense. (Wild burst of applause and frantic shouts of 'Lafferty's all right!' 'Good boy, Lafferty!' 'Long live Lafferty!' 'Three cheers for Lafferty!' 'Laf-laf-laf-ferty-ferty-ferty! Lafferty—hoopla!') Pray, gentlemen, contain yourselves while the chaplain pronounces a benediction on these impressive exercises. ('All right, hurry up!' 'Get a move on!' 'Cut it short!' 'Shut up!')"

The procession was quickly reformed and the lieutenant-governor returned to the city with the whole male population trailing along close behind his carriage. The much-heralded inauguration ball in the evening turned out a fizzle. Only ladies were present and there was consequently no dancing. The men were all busily engaged with His Honor, doing up the town. Their yells were distinctly heard in the ballroom, and many of the ladies returned home early in disgust. It seems a pity that our citizens cannot comport themselves decently on an occasion of this kind.

It is needless to say that Dr. Lafferty has endeared himself to the residents of this burg. A leading bartender was heard to remark that he was "quite a sport," while another gave it out officially as his opinion that the worthy doctor would need three or four Collinses tomorrow morning before he could get on his cocked hat. This stamps him as an acclimated Edmontonian and the *Bulletin* extends a hearty welcome. We bespeak for the genial doctor a reign of unexampled popularity. [30]

*

R. L. Borden does not let a little thing like a rainstorm interfere with his campaign speechifying. That is the advantage of having two suits of clothes. [31]

*

In a national sense Canada is at present rushing down a steep hill into the sea. Its economies are those of a spendthrift who is blind to the financial obligations of the morrow. Our politicians seem to be actuated with the same spirit as that shown by the ordinary real estate wild cat operator. They appear to be either blind or indifferent to the requirements of the country. Their object seems to be to feather their own nests and then to clear out to spend an honorable old age in affluence, either in the French Riviera, or California. [32]

*

Politicians resemble shoes in one respect—the higher grade is not machine made. [33]

*

Earl Grey's reception in Calgary last week registered thirty-eight degrees below. The city council had invited His Excellency to a reception at the drill hall and only two of them showed up. Out of our boasted population of 20,000 more or less, only seven gentlemen put in an appearance to greet the governor general at the reception to which he had been invited by the city.

The noble earl was justly angry. In fact, he was as mad as a hatter. When His Excellency looked around the large bare hall with its half-dozen uncomfortable-looking citizens, not to mention the gaping faces of the irrepressible rubbernecks peering in from sundry apertures, and noticed the icicles forming in the surrounding frost, he beckoned to the major, to Mr. McCarthy,

M.P., and to Senator Lougheed and told them plainly what he thought of the whole shooting match.

His exact words, as near as we can learn, were these: "You are aware, gentlemen, that I am the representative of the king in Canada and was invited as such to a reception in your city. I consider this reception an insult to His Majesty. Please ask the band to play 'God Save the King' and have my carriage called at once."

"Have my carriage called at once" was productive of still further confusion. When His Excellency walked forth in a state of suppressed indignation to enter his carriage, there was no carriage there. Nothing in sight, not even a delivery wagon. After waiting around awhile and seeing that efforts to procure a rig of some kind were unavailing, the vice-regal party started off on foot and walked all the way back to their car at the depot. Lord Howick, who had left his coat and hat in the carriage which fetched the party to the drill hall, expecting to return in the same vehicle, had to walk back without a hat with a cold sharp wind blowing a gale. Fortunately His Lordship does not wear whiskers.

This rings the death knell of the present city council. The earl was their guest, asked by special invitation to participate in a public reception in his honor. Having sent this invitation to the king's representative they did not have manners enough to be present as his hosts. They have made Calgary the laughing stock of Canada, and it is up to the citizens to sweep them out of office holus-bolus next election. Let no bum alderman escape. The council, and the council alone, is to blame for this ridiculous and humiliating fiasco.

The mayor especially is to blame. We always knew that he was unfit for his office, but never imagined he was quite so rotten a mayor as he proved himself to be on this disastrous occasion. The reception was not advertised, nor were the citizens notified as to what was expected of them. The correct thing to have done was to send out invitations to as many presentable citizens as possible, requesting them to be present with their wives and daughters at the civic reception to the governor general. This would have ensured a pretty fair attendance anyhow, and saved the situation.

The council appropriated $50 for the governor general's entertainment. What we want to know, and what the ratepayers

should insist on knowing, is what has become of the balance of
$45 left over? It is up to the council to issue a detailed state-
ment of how the five dollars was expended. There was no bunting, no banquet, no nothing. Is John S. Hall to be permitted to
get hold of this $45 to loan out at six percent? Whither are we
drifting?

Our readers will note that we are concentrating the blame
on the dunderheads who compose our council for their pitiful
exhibition of ignorance of the most primitive rule of social life, to
wit—when you ask a man to your house, be there to receive him.
Lord Grey has no call to feel bitter against or to say unkind
things about the citizens of Calgary. They had nothing to do with
this mess. [34]

*

When a man quits turning around to look at a pretty girl he
is old enough, almost, for the Senate. [35]

*

Why is it that all the rogues manage to get into the other
political party? [36]

*

The appointment of Mackenzie King as Liberal leader has
effectually squelched any chances that party may have had at
the next general election. Though a young man, single and
physically sound, he took no part in the war. This puts the everlasting kibosh on the Liberal party for some time to come.

Mackenzie King dwelt snugly and comfortably over in the
States while the war was in progress, having gone over the
border two months after the war started. He took a safe trip to
England after the armistice was signed and returned to Canada
only a week or so before the convention. He has not figured even
in a casual capacity in connection with the Red Cross or other
patriotic war work. Obviously it was the Quebec bunch who
elected him leader, his war activities being of the kind to meet
with the warm approval of the Peasoupsters. [37]

*

After nine years' steady hammering the *Eye Opener* has at
last the satisfaction of seeing the Liberal government broken
into fragments.

51

A pitiful spectacle indeed!
Our heart goes out to the bunch. It does for a fact.
Wiped out.
Annihilated.
Bartender! Bartender! Come hither! [38]

*

The eyes of all Canada are on Saskatchewan, and will remain focussed thereon until the people of that province say by their votes on August 14 whether they desire to have a clean, independent, popular government that is autonomous within its own boundaries, or whether they prefer to continue piking along a foul path as the creatures of a groggy Ottawa hierarchy that is fighting for its worthless life.

It is up to the men of Saskatchewan. [39]

*

As reported, Sir Wilfrid Laurier's last speech was very short, because all the bunk was cut out. [40]

*

The attention of Providence having been called to the infamous condition of Canadian politics, it was some time ago decided to send Moses down to take a hand in the game and, if possible, introduce a little purity by way of a novel experiment.

Moses, it will be remembered, was at one time leader of the Opposition in his own country, and, like that other lawgiver of glorious, pious and immortal memory, R. B. Bennett, succeeded in having only two of his candidates, Messrs. Joshua and Caleb, representing his party in the House.

The local House in Egypt was even then strongly Conservative, the Israelite party being in an almost hopeless minority—Joshua and Caleb, like Hiebert and Robertson, vying for the leadership. Moses, however, had an excellent record as a legislator, having brought down no less than ten measures which are still on the statute book.

On his arrival at Ottawa, where he brought letters of introduction to Sir Frederick Borden, Charles Hyman and Clifford Sifton, Moses registered at the Russell House and was at once taken up by the more prominent members of the Liberal party. Sir Wilfrid assured him that he would speedily find him a constituency. He was fortunate, also, in being endorsed by Emerson, who invited him to spend a weekend at St. Lawrence Hall, and, altogether, "a pleasant time was had."

The electoral district of Midnapore, Alberta, happening to be open owing to the retirement of the sitting member, Peter J. McGonigle, who had been ordered by his physicians to take a post-alcoholic course at the Calgary Boozorium, Moses was declared elected to that constituency by acclamation.

In introducing the new member to his constituency, Mr. McGonigle, the retiring member who, we understand, is slated for a position in the excise department as inspector of bonded warehouses, in a voice broken with emotion and booze, took occasion to refer to his own record as representative of the growing and thriving district of Midnapore. During his regime a new wing had been added to Ed Johnson's hotel and a new set of bar fixtures installed. It was now the finest bar west of the Great Lakes. He might refer to several other local improvements, but would not weary his hearers with matters of lesser importance. The Midnapore *Gazette* would soon be on a paying basis, and the new member might always rely on its loyal support. Some of his hearers had, no doubt, already heard of Moses, who was a contemporary of Sir Richard Cartwright and the Hon. R. W. Scott. Although not a native of Canada, Moses' record would stand inspection. He was of good birth, being connected with a very good old Egyptian family, the Pharoahs of Bullrush Park. Should he fall in line with the existing conditions which have made the Liberal party what it is today, he predicted for him a bright future.

The party then adjourned to Mr. Johnson's hostelry, where a sumptuous banquet, consisting of pig's cheek and cabbage and unlimited lush, was partaken of with hearty relish.

Moses, M.P., left at midnight on the Okotoks Flyer for Ottawa, taking his seat with him and arriving at the capital in time to take part in the debate on the timber limits.

Having listened attentively to Mr. Ames for about three days the member for Midnapore began to see things in a somewhat different light. He learned from private and authentic sources that most of the members had bought their way into parliament with money and subsequently reimbursed themselves by huge steals of public property. He found that the whole system was permeated with graft from the heads of departments down to

53

the meanest little stinker with a government job, each with his mitt out in proportion to the size of his position.

So incensed did the member for Midnapore become over these enormities that, to the amazement of his leader, who had already arranged as to who should catch the Speaker's eye, he arose in his place on the fourth day and delivered an address such as had not hitherto been heard within the legislative halls of Canada. In trumpet tones he inveighed against the criminal enormities which had been perpetrated by their rulers against the people of Canada. He raked his own party fore and aft. He went after the Siftons and the Burrows, and denounced Turriff in most scathing language, saying, amid loud applause from the Opposition, that he was a Turriff for revenue only. He expressed unfeigned astonishment at the indecency which permitted the spoliation of the public domain without remonstrance from the men who could prevent it. There were lots more respectable people in certain districts of hell than were to be found in the parliaments of Canada.

At this point ex-Honorable J. A. Calder of Saskatchewan, who was an interested listener in the Distinguished Strangers' Gallery, abruptly left the chamber.

The speech of Moses, M.P., caused the greatest possible excitement in every quarter of the House, which shortly afterwards adjourned.

A heated discussion took place in the corridor among the premier, Clifford Sifton, and the member for Midnapore, Sir Wilfrid expostulating with Moses on his unheard of impudence. The member for Midnapore was heard to reply:

"I meant every word I said. You are surrounded by a lot of cold-blooded grafters and if you don't know it, you ought to know it. It's your business to know. You go around with a sunny smile while your lieutenants are rifling the pockets of the people."

"But you must not forget," said Sir Wilfrid, somewhat staggered at being spoken to thus frankly, "that Canada now occupies a foremost position amongst the daughters of the Empire."

"Empire be damned!" cried the infuriated member. "This kind of twaddle makes me sick. Canada is known throughout the civilized world today as the crookedest, most immoral, psalm-singing, hypocritical, grafting country on the face of the globe. You are the man to blame for this condition of affairs. If you, Sir Wilfrid, were half as honest as you pretend to be, you could

54

put a stop to this business in ten minutes and you would have the people of Canada at your back in doing so."

"But what would I get in that event?" put in Clifford Sifton.

"You would get it in the neck," said Moses, "if this gentleman here was attending to the business of the people who put him there. But he is what he always was, an easy mark for every plausible Grit grafter that knew his way about. You grafters have grafters under you, and these grafters in turn have grafters under them, and so on away down the line until the whole system is one grand honeycomb of graft from start to finish."

"Tut, tut," ejaculated Sir Wilfrid, "I don't know of any such thing."

"That's the hell of it," retorted Moses. "You're not supposed to see anything. Your role is to hold the attention of the audience and keep them in good humor while the other fellows are going through their pockets."

"You can't prove anything of that kind against us," said Clifford, rather red in the face.

"I know enough about you," said Moses, looking Sifton squarely in the face, "to know that you are pretty clever at covering up your tracks, but your own record convicts you. You know how you were fixed when you left Winnipeg in '96 and today you own mansions in Ottawa, summer palaces at Brockville, steam yachts, newspapers, timber lands, coal lands, mineral lands, as well as a wad of the long green that a greyhound couldn't jump over. You live in the style of a Russian grand duke and you scatter money abroad to minister to your own pleasure. Your only available source of income has been your salary as minister of the interior and private member. What I should like to know is, *where did you get it?*"

"I don't know that Mr. Sifton is as rich as you think he is," said Sir Wilfrid mildly.

"Oh, there's a heap of things you don't know," responded Moses, "and that is where you are going to get left some day. You are the only man in Canada who doesn't seem to know anything about Sir Frederick Borden, Emmerson, Hyman and several other scallywags whom I might mention, but you'll find out all about it some day to your cost."

"I don't know that that's any of your business anyhow," said Sifton warmly.

"Touched a raw spot there, eh?" replied Moses, giving Sifton a grim smile. "It may not be my business, but it's the people's business, and the day will come when you'll find out that the people of this country decline to accept as their rulers men who are a disgrace to the country which supports them. For my part, I'm going back home. You can work out your own destruction. If hell is any worse than this place, it must be a daisy."

Moses, M.P., before leaving Ottawa, placed his resignation in the hands of the Speaker and left for heaven on the westbound express. [41]

*

Society Note— It is unlikely that T. B. Mulligan will run for the council, as announced in the press. Mr. Mulligan does not get out of jail until December 20, too late to file his nomination papers. [42]

*

Can anyone inform us what our provincial legislators do between times for the good of their country? They gather at Edmonton for one lugubrious four-weeks' session, and then what becomes of them? Pray tell us, what do they do towards helping out the development and expansion of the province during the other eleven months of the year?

(Not a damned thing—Ed.)

That is absolutely true. They don't do a damned thing. They hie up to Edmonton for their stupid little session, ratify what has already been done by the government, throw a few shots of booze into themselves, make a ridiculous attempt to look like statesmen, wind up with a mutual admiration banquet or two, and then return home to resume their various occupations. [43]

*

Premier Sifton continues to take himself seriously, which shows how useless it is for anybody to try to teach him anything. [44]

*

Does anybody remember what reasons Alberta voters had for electing this silly Grit government at Edmonton? No? Then what in h—l did you do it for? [45]

*

The Socialist party of Calgary are early in the field. Already they are figuring on putting up a candidate at the ensuing federal election. At this stage of the world's progress Socialism should have made better headway, and in view of the fact that many of their tenets are undeniably sound, we are forced to the conclusion that their failure to advance as a political body is due to the drastic and all-too-sudden character of their reforms and to the crude rambunctiousness of their leaders. Socialism in its milder form is what we are all working for. But not, Brabantio, in its strenuous form. Not on your life. [46]

*

Puerile and pusillanimous, our government is a strange compound of picayunishness and prodigality. Picayunish where they should be prodigal, and prodigal where they should be at least economical! They are perfectly willing to pay Captain O'Brien $500 for census work that should occupy a few weeks, but are only willing to pay $280 for a year's mail contract, involving five post offices, in a country difficult to negotiate. [47]

*

One of the consoling things about public life is that no matter what kind of a spectacular ass a man may make of himself in public matters, he will always receive a stack of letters commending his course. [48]

*

In these trying times, no matter how one tries to think of other things, one's mind involuntarily wanders back to politics. [49]

*

A certain lawyer who was a candidate for a municipal office went out canvassing one day and knocked at a cottage door. The door was opened by a woman.

"Is your husband in, Mrs. ———?" inquired the lawyer.

"No, sir," was the reply, "but I know what you want. My husband is sure to vote for you because you got him off for stealing that ham last week."

"No, no—alleged stealing of the ham," corrected the lawyer.

57

"Alleged be blowed!" was the woman's reply. "We've got a bit of it left yet. Come in and have a ham sandwich." [50]

*

Maybe it would be a good idea to have less politics in politics. [51]

*

At an election meeting, one of the speakers was tormented by an interrupter who was constantly jumping up and hurling insinuations. Finally the speaker turned on him.

"You, sir," he shouted, pointing a bony finger, "remind me of an aeolian harp that has just been struck by lightning. I will tell you why. An aeolian harp is a lyre. And a lyre that has been struck by lightning is a blasted lyre. And that's what you are!" [52]

*

Dear me! It is all of three weeks now since we had a speech from Sir Wilfrid Laurier on the subject of the ties of blood which bind the colonies to the mother country. He must be sick. [53]

*

As for our own success at the polls—well, now, what the devil are we going to say about that? That we deeply and gratefully appreciate the kindness shown on every side, goes without saying. (Business of placing hand on heart and making low bow.) No speeches were made on our behalf; no meetings held. The only appeal to the electorate was the silent one of a clean sheet covering twenty years. To this might be added the kindly feeling of personal friendship towards ourself on the part of the citizens generally, who had us doped out as "a good old scout." It was a combination impossible to beat.

Up in Edmonton, when the time arrives to go there, we shall reciprocate by exercising diligence in performing the duties of an accredited representative. Perhaps an independent member may not be able to cut much swath, but if he knows enough to take his duties seriously and not be content with the role of innocent bystander, he can at least exercise some influence by participating intelligently in the proceedings of the House and keeping his eye on the indicator.

In order to try and find out what kind of speeches my constituents expect me to make in the House, I sent out some questionnaires the other day to a lot of people in different walks of life. Quite a number of sample speeches have come pouring in, samples of what they claim to be looking for. It will be very difficult to please 'em all, since no two of the specimen addresses are in any way alike. For instance, a gentleman living over in Hillhurst writes to say that he will be greatly disappointed if our first speech does not run something like this:

"Mr. Speaker, in speaking to the resolution placed in my name with the clerk of the House praying for a generous, liberal and elaborate recrudescence of lager beer in the Province of Alberta, I take this opportunity of introducing an amendment to the Weights and Measures Act which will authorize three pints to the quart. (Cheers.) Allaying the unrest of the people is as nothing compared to allaying their thirst (Loud cheers.) and I think, Mr. Speaker, that God in his mercy would not be averse to seeing a spirited beer policy carried out by the government (Hear, hear!) at their earliest possible convenience. I might remind the House that in Great Britain. . . ."

But why continue? He goes on like this for ten pages. Must be bughouse.

We can only say that the variety of samples sent in are rather bewildering. One gentleman's oration is one long eloquent suggestion that the sessions of the House be held in the Macdonald Hotel to save car fare. He cites several reasons, with which the availability of booze is not unconnected. This speech is not such a bad one, but hopelessly impracticable and could not be delivered in the House without causing a disturbance. Guess we had better invent our own speeches. [54]

THREE

Religion

Lord, let me keep a straight way in the path of honor—and a straight face in the presence of solemn asses. Let me not truckle to the high, nor bulldoze the low; let me frolic with the jack and the joker and win the game. Lead me unto Truth and Beauty—and tell me her name. Keep me sane, but not too sane. Let me not take the world or myself too seriously, and grant more people to laugh with and fewer to laugh at. Let me condemn no man because of his grammar and no woman on account of her morals, neither being responsible for either. Preserve my sense of humor and of values and proportions. Let me be healthy while I live, but not live too long. Which is about all for today, Lord. Amen. [1]

*

How many people do you know—including yourself—who can repeat the ten commandments? [2]

*

If you must play golf on Sunday, play good golf. [3]

*

The Ford is my jitney;
I shall not want for whiskey;
It maketh me to lie down in wet waters;
It soileth my clothes;
It leadeth me into deep waters;

It leadeth me into paths of ridicule for its namesake;
It prepareth a breakdown for me in the presence of mine
enemies;
Yes, though I run through the valleys, I am towed up the
hills.
I fear great evil when it is with me;
Its rods and its engines discomfort me.
It anointeth my face with oil,
Its tank runneth over.
Surely to goodness, if this thing follows me all the days of
my life I shall dwell in the house of Ponoka forever. [4]

*

The pope rises at 5:30 every morning. This should give him
time for at least three eye-openers before breakfast. [5]

*

Remember that Jonah said to the whale, "you can't keep a
good man down." [6]

*

Etiquette— Entering into a heated altercation with your
pastor with regard to the relative merits of rye and Scotch is
considered bad form. If he prefers rye that is none of your
business. [7]

*

How many men do you know who let their religion interfere
with their business? [8]

*

Which is the worse from a moral standpoint: a man drinking a glass of beer or a preacher stuffing a kid's head full of a
lot of supernatural nonsense? [9]

*

The Rev. Mr. Slensby came up from the south and preached
at Midnapore last Sunday. Not feeling very well, the reverend
gentleman remained overnight at the home of Mr. and Mrs.
Kachorker.

"I am so sorry you are not feeling well, Mr. Slensby," said
Mrs. Kachorker after the evening service.

"That reminds me, Mrs. Kachorker," said the preacher gravely. "You should avoid altogether the appearance of evil."

"Why, Mr. Slensby, what have I been doing now?"

"I observe that on your sideboard you have several cut-glass decanters and that each of them is half-filled with what appears to be ardent spirits."

"Well, now, it isn't anything of the kind. The bottles look so pretty on the sideboard that I just filled them half way up with some floor stain and furniture polish, just for appearance."

"That's why I'm cautioning you, Mrs. Kachorker. Before going over to the church I took a great big jolt out of the big bottle in the middle. I came very near throwing up my guts during the second hymn. Have you none of the real stuff handy?" [10]

*

Some people are too good to be interesting. [11]

*

Mustapha Sweeney Bey, the prophet of Hootch, Alta., sends in the following weird stuff:

Take heed that you be not deceived, for many shall come in the name of Democracy and say the time of Liberty draweth near.

Go ye not therefore after them.

Faction shall rise against faction, and province against province, and great riots shall be in the land, and famines and floods.

Food shall be stored by the men in high places, and doled out to the hungry at huge profits.

Pestilence shall follow in the wake of famine; but be ye content, for your peers of yesterday are today robed in purple and fine linen.

But before all these things they shall lay hands on you and persecute you.

They shall protect the wealthy and him that is of high degree that he may increase, and shall take from him that hath little, even all that he hath.

Railways shall be granted permission to augment their tolls beyond equity, and delay cars without reason, but the poor must treble his tax for demurrage.

Be not disturbed, for when all this is away from you taken, the grafters shall cease from their robbing.

You shall be taken before kings and judges, and if your offence be trivial, your punishment shall be the greater, but rulers and knights shall be exempted, and those who have seized your resources shall by the sovereign be honored.

And ye shall be betrayed, both by parents and brethren, and kinsfolk and friends, and they shall turn thy land to traitors on promise of spoils to be shared.

Ye shall be hated of all men for your independence, but there shall not an hair of your head perish.

In your patience possess ye your souls.

And when ye shall see Ottawa, compassed with looters, then know that the desolation thereof is nigh.

Then let them that are in Canada not flee to the mountains, and let them which are in the midst of it not depart out.

For these be the days of vengeance, and all wrongs shall be righted.

But woe unto them that are sick in these days, for there shall be great distress in the land, for profiteers shall rise in all quarters, and extort to the uttermost farthing.

There shall be signs in the sun, and upon the earth, distress of nations, with perplexity. Men's hearts failing for fear and for looking after those things which are coming on the earth.

Then shall they see Liberty, coming with power and great glory.

But be ye steadfast for your country, spare not to drive the enemy from your gates, knowing well that when he shall be destroyed, ye shall have time to put your house in order.

And when these things begin to come to pass, then look up, and lift up your heads, for your redemption draweth nigh. [12]

*

A Scottish minister was asked to pray for rain. He did so and the rain came down in floods and destroyed the crops. "This comes o' intrustin' sic a request to a meenister who isna acquent wi' agriculture," growled one elder to another. [13]

*

A good many people do not believe in the efficacy of prayer

because the Lord gives them what they deserve instead of what they ask for. [14]

*

Endue our ministers with righteousness, O Lord, and make thy chosen people less bughouse. [15]

*

We thought we had roasted everything in sight, but it seems we forgot the bishops. How we came to overlook these grave and reverend signors with their buckled shoes, shovel hats and cute little knickerbockers, is hard to understand, as we have always had a sneaking regard for bishops. It would perhaps be stretching the truth to aver in these columns that they have any special partiality for us, but even bishops do not always know a good thing when they see it. The unctuous wordiness and monumental humbug of some bishops is well-illustrated in the following incidents in which a couple of northwestern bishops figure. It is worth reading.

When Johnny Burke and Fletcher Breden, whom we all know as popular old-timers, were up on the Mackenzie River last March buying fur and trading for an Edmonton firm, they had occasion to build a boat; and in order to house themselves during this work and while waiting for the river to break up, they asked for the use of a vacant kitchen belonging to the Church Missionary Society. They applied to the Right Reverend Bishop Reeve, now of Fort Simpson (then of Fort Wrigley), and received a reply refusing permission to occupy the vacant kitchen because—to literally quote the letter—"we have to be very careful not to help the opponents of the company." This allusion was to the Hudson's Bay Co'y, and the letter is in existence to substantiate this pitiful example of serfdom. This gentleman has accepted money from Canada for his missions, and when Canadians go up into his country, might at least "reciprocate." The thing at stake was only a kitchen with a fireplace in it. Not much, was it? The missionary in charge was agreeable that they should have it, but, to make sure that he might not be making a bad break by doing an act of humanity at the expense of the H.B.C., he saw the bishop who at once refused to allow Burke and Breden to occupy the shack. This was not in Cuba.

In the spring of '95 it was decided by the settlers at Buffalo

Lake to build a church. They all jumped in and helped to build it. When it was completed Bishop Pinkham was to have come up to open it but not having openers, he deputed Dr. Cooper to come up and do the business. The church was formally opened on the 28th of June that year. Dr. Cooper apologized for the absence of the bishop, and said he was sorry that he could not consecrate the church on account of it being a log building.

They had a few services about this time, but altogether since then, from the opening till the present date, there have not been more than twenty services, and for the last twelve months none at all. As they were having no services at all, several clergymen of other denominations offered to come out and hold regular services provided they could get the use of the church, and they all agreed that it would be a very good thing and should be pushed along. It reached the bishop's ears that such a thing was on the tapis, and he didn't do a thing but come right up and consecrate the church, thus barring out the other preachers.

A bishop declining to consecrate a church built of logs is a good deal like Sullivan refusing to meet Peter Jackson on account of his color, and quite as unreasonable. [16]

*

Bishop Legal, coadjutor of St. Albert, was in town last Tuesday, having come up from Hobbema. He leaves shortly for France with Father Belleviere, of Duhamel. This is the second bishop who has visited Wetaskiwin within the last two weeks without dropping in to see us. The next bishop that comes along and don't drop in at the *Free Lance* office and leave a six months' subscription we fear we will have to roast in these columns. Even Ole Oleson and Ivan Snorkavorivitch pay us a visit once in a while. As a matter of fact, a bishop ought to be good for a whole year's subscription. [17]

*

Men are sick to death of religion in so far as it is only a statement of creed and collection of nickels. Preachers who incommode themselves to lift the fallen from the dust and the beggar from the dunghill are as scarce as hen's teeth. Clever sermons will not alone win men to Christ. [18]

*

65

You may break all the commandments in the code. Provided that you do it à la mode. [19]

*

The Lord freezes the water, but we are expected to cut our own ice. [20]

*

The Roman Catholic religion was severely criticized at the Methodist Ministerial Association meeting held at the Wesley College in Winnipeg last week. This surely was in very bad taste. The Methodists ought to "cut it out" and not bother with other people's particular brand of religion, especially when the latter is apt to be just as sound in its way as their own.

The Methodists have nothing to brag about anyhow. The biggest rascals and hypocrites we ever knew were Methodists. Old McGillicuddy, of Calgary, for example, is a Methodist. So is W. H. Cushing. And there you are. The only low-down mean tricks ever played on us have been the work of Methodists. We don't know how it is in Canada, but when we lived in the States the Methodist camp meetings and picnics invariably resulted in a generous contribution to the world's population. The lofty morals of the rank and file were nothing to cable home to auntie about. We would in all seriousness advise the Methodist Ministerial Association to leave other sects alone and gang their ane gait. [21]

*

The Lord will provide—that is, he will provide us with the ability to provide for ourselves. The manna-from-heaven stunt has never responded to an encore. [22]

*

It may seem rather a crude thing to say, but, if the truth were told, very few people believe in the immortality of the soul or in the hereafter. What makes us think so is this, that you never hear anybody talking about it in conversation. Do you suppose for a moment, if men really believed in a future life—as almost all profess to do—that every man over fifty years of age wouldn't be making due preparation and at least occasionally referring to it in the course of chats with his friends?

66

But no! You never hear a word about it outside of the pulpit of a Sunday. The elderly man planning to visit Europe next year prattles about it all the time and bores his friends to death telling them of how he is going to look over the battle-scarred fields of Flanders, and makes tremendous preparations for his trip; but the same elderly man, with the prospect of the longest journey of all a few short years ahead of him, and the added prospect of an entirely new existence that is to last to all eternity, does not seemingly bother his head about it. He doesn't take it seriously and makes absolutely no preparation.

And about the Bible. The Christian world concedes that it is the greatest book in existence, a wondrous piece of sacred literature. And yet you never catch anybody reading it. Did you ever see a man in the rotunda of a hotel sitting comfortably smoking and perusing the Bible? You never did. How often have you visited a private home in Calgary and discovered a member of the family reading the Bible? Never. The only people who seem to indulge in honest perusal of the Bible are men about to be hanged. And even then, should a reprieve arrive, they will switch off to the Bob Edwards *Summer Annual* as quickly as possible. [23]

*

The best brand of religion is the kind a man uses in his business. [24]

*

A Protestant evangelist minister entered the train and found the seats all occupied except one near a Roman Catholic bishop. After some hesitation he sat down beside the bishop, who was reading.

"Good day, sir," he said.

"Good day," replied the bishop, continuing his reading.

Half an hour elapsed and the evangelist, who had been getting very uneasy, said, "My dear sir—"

"Well, sir?"

"Do you know, I don't believe in purgatory."

"Then you can go to hell," rejoined the bishop absent-mindedly, as he turned over a leaf and went on reading. [25]

*

Religion is, after all, a very personal and intimate affair. How many regular churchgoers go down on their knees in the quiet of their chamber and hold communion with their God? Precious few, we take it. The church can have its eloquent preachers, swell choirs, accomplished organists and ultra-respectable vestries, but if the Sunday devotions are not merged in the daily lives of those who profess Christianity by attendance at church, then the ultimate effect is nil.

Still, one must not get into the habit of decrying the church or belittling the efforts of those engaged in church work. The latter is uphill work indeed. Perhaps if the preachers could get a little closer to the people by participating more in their amusements, recreations and so on, it might help some. Unfortunately, the job of a preacher is something like that of a Supreme Court judge; it automatically keeps the ubiquitous hoi polloi at arms' length, Which is unfortunate, but true.

Take our own case. We have lived in this neck of the woods for twenty-five years, exactly a quarter of a century, and we do not know a single minister occupying a Calgary pulpit. Not only do we not know any of them personally, but we don't even know one of them by sight, always excepting Bishop Pinkham. This is a literal fact. How do you account for it? We know almost everybody else.

There must be something wrong. From what we hear from others, our Calgary ministers must be very likeable men. But where do they keep themselves? On Sundays a fairy waves a wand and lo! there they are standing in front of you in church as large as life, telling you all about the children of Israel. At the close of the evening service the fairy once more waves her wand, and the preacher disappears. [26]

*

About the only people who won't quarrel over religion are the people who haven't got any. [27]

*

The Okotoks Methodist Ladies' Aid will give a bean supper from 6 to 8 P.M., to be followed by a musical program. [28]

*

Rev. Kerby disapproves of Sunday golf, eh? Well, what of it? Who cares? We don't. [29]

*

Oh, for a prophet to appear and teach us how to have a riproaring time decently! How to raise merry hell without hurting anybody, including ourselves! We know all the rules for being good. Will someone please rise and explain how we may be good, though full of physical electricity? [30]

Sticky Fingers

Much that is labelled "financial success" is plain graft. [1]

*

One of the chief reasons why graft is so prevalent these days is because the people evince not the slightest indignation over the tricks turned at their expense by the grafters. If the public, who are directly affected, don't care, why should the grafters lose any sleep? In parliament, political grafters are protected by their party even to the length of jeopardizing the safety of that party. In business establishments, an employee who is suspected of crooked work is fired, simply out of consideration for the interests of the shareholders in the business. Not so with an Ottawa government. Business lines do not prevail there. [2]

*

The way some of those political grafters quietly heel themselves against a rainy day reminds one of the custom prevalent amongst dogs of burying bones in the backyard. [3]

*

There is another lot scandal in full blast in Calgary. For the information of readers elsewhere we shall briefly summarize it.

The Hon. W. H. Cushing summoned the members of the school board to a meeting last Saturday afternoon to decide upon the purchase of a site for the normal school, which is to be a magnificent $85,000 structure, and thus of great enhancing value to the property adjacent. The members of the school board considered the matter, hesitated and asked for time for consideration. This would be about three o'clock in the afternoon. At seven o'clock they were to give Mr. Cushing their decision. (In order to follow subsequent events, you must keep these hours in mind.)

At about a quarter to six o'clock on Saturday afternoon, Mr. Bennett, the real estate man, came rushing, literally out of breath, into the *Herald* office and shouted for McAra, foreman of the job department. Mr. McAra owned six lots right alongside of where the site of the normal school had been secretly decided upon, an hour or so before, by the school board. Mr. McAra knew nothing about this and was in no particular hurry to sell, so he told Bennett to come around and talk the matter over on Monday.

"Oh, there's no time for that!" cried the breathless Bennett. "My customer is leaving on the 6:45 train."

McAra, succumbing to the old familiar rush act, then and there sold his lots.

On Monday morning Mr. McAra discovered the cause of Bennett's unseemly haste in getting the lots. It may be said right here that Mr. McAra was perfectly satisfied with the price he got for the lots, though he admits that he could have got considerably more had he known what Bennett knew. However, that has no bearing on the yarn.

Being asked about the mysterious customer who was going away on the 6:45 train, Bennett laughed and turned it off with a josh. He then told Mr. McAra that he had bought the lots for Comer and Waines.

Mr. Comer is a member of the school board; Mr. Waines is the secretary.

And there you are.

Comment is superfluous. Here were men, elected as representatives of the people, taking advantage of information obtained at a secret meeting of the school board, of which they were officials, to feather their own nests, to the direct financial loss of the people they caught. It is a scandalous abuse of trust.

We are surprised at Charlie Comer's name being mixed up in this and hope that he can successfully explain matters.

The last city lot scandal was engineered by some local Masons, and it would make the secret societies of Calgary somewhat ridiculous if this affair was shown to have been pushed through by a boss Odd Fellow.

No one can be surprised, however, at anything Mr. Waines may do. He was trained in Lougheed & Bennett's office. [4]

*

Perhaps a shorter definition of graft and one that would fit in the vocabulary of politicians is: "A good thing that you are not in on." [5]

*

Many an honest man might be otherwise but lacks the opportunity. That is so. But opportunity was not lacking last summer during the oil excitement—and since. Our oil boom in Calgary showed up some prominent men in a decidedly queer light and put the kibosh on them as local leaders for evermore. [6]

*

For the fourth time within five years the "Who's Who" stunt has been pulled off with financial éclat in our midst. *The History of Alberta* is the latest. We don't know who got this thing up, but whoever it was must have made a pot of money. The work is in two volumes and has hundreds of biographies of the Great Men of Alberta, such as Terry McGraw and Mike McCoole, with steel engravings and all the rest of it. Getting one's pikcher in the book along with a high-sounding biography cost $250, with a copy of the book thrown in. Great stuff, eh? We counted 582 biographies. Of course it didn't cost so much without the pikcher.

Only those who consented to cough up to those brigands got a mention in this *History*, or *Who's Who*, or whatever it is. The three Calgarians who are most widely known throughout the Dominion of Canada, to wit, P. J. Nolan, M. S. McCarthy and R. B. Bennett, are not mentioned at all. The promoters of this soft thing were wise enough to enlist the services of a prominent man of good repute to write the actual history of the province, in order to give the thing tone and a touch of authority. They got Dr. A. O. MacRae, Ph.D., to write it and he made an excellent job of it. Indeed, this part is the only redeeming feature and is too valuable a piece of work to be thrust into a mass of wriggling biographies of eminent bounders.

We venture a quote from a few of these $250 biographies. Let us take the biography of John P. Cleghorn, for instance:

"Among the most popular and progressive cleaners and pressers of clothes in the city of Calgary must be mentioned John P. Cleghorn. Mr. Cleghorn has been prominently and successfully identified for many years with the pants of many of Calgary's leading citizens and is an earnest church worker. Born at an early age in St. Thomas, Ont., Mr. Cleghorn received a liberal education and came west, where he quickly showed a great avidity for booze. Having by persistence and courage and a sublime faith in his own destiny succeeded in weathering a number of exceptionally severe attacks of delirium tremens, Mr. Cleghorn pushed ahead, overcame every obstacle, and now is justly regarded throughout the length and breadth of the City of the Foothills as one of the most successful, enterprising, prominent, distinguished, phenomenal, collateral, respected, honored and public spirited exponents of the clothes-pressing art in the civilized world today."

(This costs Johnnie two hundred and fifty bucks.)

Then we pick out the biography of Robert T. Renwick:

"Probably no man living today in the civilized world is held in higher esteem by the leading and prominent citizens of Calgary than Robert T. Renwick, the talented liveryman. Mr. Renwick was born south of the line, being the son of the late Peter Renwick, who was hanged at Shelby Junction in 1893 for stealing horses from the Fleury ranch. The subject of our sketch moved to Alberta in the fall of '93 with the horses which his father was hanged for stealing and has since conducted a thriving business as a conscientious horse trader, winning not only affluence, but also the kindly regard of all people with whom he has never done any business. His specialty is filing the teeth of aged horses, showing his tenderness of heart in thus alleviating the antiquity and preserving the youth of man's greatest friend. Mr. Renwick is a member of several churches and belongs to the Eagles. He is a bird. The greatest regret of his life is that he never learned to play golf. He is yet on the threshold of life, and if his future success is at all commensurate with his gall, Mr. Renwick should become one of the wealthiest men in the province as he is now one of the most enterprising. We predict a bright future for Robert."

(Another 250 bucks.)

73

But why proceed with any more? The biographies are all couched in the same strain. Each and every man written up is the most successful, the most pop'lar and the most prom'nent cit'zen that ever came over the pike. We wonder how the man that got up this book knew that we didn't have 250 bucks. Somebody must have told him. Poverty hath its recompense. What? [7]

*

It seems as if the world is divided into two sets of people—one set are engaged in making money by productive labor and the other set are simultaneously engaged in taking it away from them. [8]

*

Graft is that portion of the money taken by a public official to which his constituents tumble. It becomes graft only when discovered. Otherwise the fattening of the bank account is merely the result of good business investments. [9]

*

No explanation yet from the Alberta government in regard to the American Publishing Company of New York being given the job of printing and publishing for ten long years the school books of this province.

Not a word. Quiet as a mouse. Silent as the grave. As a matter of fact they are feeling not a little ashamed of themselves for having allowed Calder and Morang to pull the wool over their eyes. This is, after all, the only serious blunder they have made since taking office, but it is a bad one, a very bad one.

By maintaining a discreet silence and ignoring the statements made in this paper, the Alberta government fondly hopes (no doubt) that public interest in this matter will die out and that the incident will close of its own accord.

Fatuous hope!

If the provincial cabinet thinks for a moment that we are going to sit quietly by and see our school books printed and published for the next *ten years*—till 1918—in New York City, they have not got us sized up right. They may ignore the *Eye Opener* all they have a mind to, but they cannot very well afford to ignore the trades unions—at least, not in Calgary and Edmonton. At election time the school book contract will cut tons and tons of ice.

The case at present stands like this: Alberta publishing houses were passed up altogether when it came to getting out new school books for the province and a ten-year contract was given to a man called Morang in Toronto. Morang, having no plant, has the books printed and published in New York City by a firm of which he is the Canadian agent—the American Book Company—a shady, unscrupulous outfit operating throughout the States under various names. To make matters worse from the labor standpoint, the American Book Company is a non-union firm, employs cheap labor and makes its employees work longer hours than printing plants operating under "fair" conditions.

If Premier Rutherford ever consults the political barometer he had better take a good searching look at it right now before it is too late, and either cancel that ten-year contract or cut it down to two years. All this comes of the government having twenty-three members to the right of the Speaker's chair as against two to the left. The result in such cases is invariably the same. The government feels safe, confident and secure in its bulging strength and feels that it can do whatever it d——d well pleases without suffering ill consequences. They are a short-sighted bunch. We won't say that they are drunk with power, but they certainly have acted as if half-shot.

Even now the taxpayers of Alberta and Saskatchewan are paying thousands upon thousands of dollars to this New York firm. Three or four years hence, as the West gets filled up, they will be sending hundreds of thousands of dollars annually over to the other side for work that should be done in Canada. And the taxpayers will have to stand this for ten years! If there is any doubt in the minds of our readers as to the methods of this organization, perhaps the following Associated Press despatch will help dispel them:

"Austin, Tex., June 20— The attorney general filed suits in court here today against the American Book Company for penalties aggregating $3,080,000 and demanded the company's ouster from the state for violations of the anti-trust law covering a period of nearly two years.

"One suit is against the New York corporation and another against the New Jersey corporation, both having the same name and being composed of the same persons."

This is what Morang says about it in an interview:

"Mr. Morang, when seen by a representative of *The Bookseller and Stationer* in regard to the attack made upon him by the Calgary *Eye Opener*, stated that he did not deem it worthwhile to take cognizance of such libelous statements from an irresponsible and sensational sheet like the *Eye Opener*. He intimated that if any reputable newspaper would repeat the charges or publish the allegations contained therein he would at once institute action for criminal libel. Mr. Morang did not care to discuss specifically the points of attack, but, in the course of an informal conversation, vigorously denied that the American Book Company of New York had any connection whatever with the contract. The Morang Company submitted the plates, proofs and bindings to the minister of Education at Edmonton and was awarded the contract solely on the merit of their goods and the low figure at which they tendered. The American Book Company had nothing to do directly or indirectly with the tender, and the firm in Toronto has no relations with that company beyond acting as agents or representatives in Canada for certain copyright books which they place on the Canadian market.

"Mr. Morang says that so long as the government has no complaint to make he should not take notice of these misleading statements. That the work was done in New York he freely admits, but says there was nothing in his contract which stipulated where the printing, press work and binding should be executed. The governments of Alberta and Saskatchewan did not care where operations were carried out, whether in Zululand or Hong Kong, so long as the books, which were required at the shortest possible notice, were up to the standard in all respects. Considering that it was the 20th of January before the contract was signed, so that the Morang Company could proceed with the work and that they had to deliver to the governments of Saskatchewan and Alberta by the middle of June no less than 160,000 of the Alexandra readers, it was a matter of the utmost importance that the work should be carried out as expeditiously as possible. There was no bookbinding establishment in the West which could do the binding of the character of these readers, which made the volumes practically indestructible; so far as the printing and press work were concerned, the low figure at which the job was secured made it imperative, along with the demand of the government for haste, that these things be done where it was possible to secure the cheapest and speediest work.

"Mr. Morang stated that the Alexandra set of readers would compare favorably in the binding, printing, press and color work with any American set of readers, and that, in many respects, they were superior. Some of the plates were made in Toronto and some in New York. So long as the Alberta government secured the output, which it desired in the time stipulated, it did not care where the work was done so long as it was satisfactory in character and equal to the specimens submitted. The American Book Company had nothing to do directly or indirectly with the contract for the Alexandra readers, which was awarded solely and exclusively to Morang & Company."

Morang, it will be observed, prattles about "the low price at which the job was secured." He must think we are all batty out here. It was proved in the Regina House that the Canada Publishing Company's *retail* price was lower than Morang's *wholesale* price. And there you are.

Morang must not run away with the idea that his quibbling explanation will either fool the western public or cause our pen to falter for an instant. He may have experienced little or no difficulty in working the Alberta government, but both he and the Alberta government are up against *the people* this time, which is another proposition entirely. So far as threats of criminal libel go, every shyster we ever exposed in these columns has threatened the same thing. It does not scare this chicken a little bit. We know when we are right and when we are wrong.

Morang's denial that the American Book Company had any connection with the contract is rather amazing to an outsider in the light of his own admission that he is this notorious firm's agent in Canada, that the plates were made by this American firm, and that all the printing, binding and mechanical work is done by them in New York City. It is a wonder some of the Toronto roosters didn't crow thrice when Morang made his denial.

It is, to say the least, ungenerous of Morang to try and lay the onus on the provincial government by saying that "the government of Alberta did not care where operations were carried out, whether in Zululand or Hong Kong," because such a statement, if true, places the life of Premier Rutherford's government in jeopardy. Still, we are charitable enough to believe that Premier Rutherford had no idea when he gave the ten-year contract to these people that the printing and publishing of the Alberta school books was to be turned over to an American concern.

Morang, it will be observed, admits the truth of all the *Eye Opener's* allegations, except the one to the effect that the American Book Company had any connection with the contract.

Well, the American Book Co. have *got* the work the contract calls for, haven't they? And Morang is their Canadian agent, isn't he? What is he trying to lie out of it for? He must take us folk for a lot of come-ons. [10]

*

Some agent is at work in the East selling lots in a subdivision called Belfast, which is away off to hell and gone in a northeasterly direction. You know where the sporting houses on Nose Creek are, of course? Well, Belfast is one mile due north of that, beyond the Morris subdivision. Some Johnny in Ottawa writes to say that he has bought fifty feet, or two lots, in Belfast for $600 and wants to know if it is any good. We have not the heart to answer this man's letter. [11]

*

The process in all graft, where a member of the government is concerned, is the same. He gets away with the graft first and salts the good thing away. Long afterwards, when the inevitable investigation and disclosures occur, his party protects and whitewashes him for obvious political reasons and that is all there is to it. He still has the goods. Which is the main thing. [12]

*

The *Albertan* very properly administers a stinging rebuke to the city council for the complacency with which they regard Alderman Pitman's recent petty little piece of graft, which consisted of the illegal selling of a bill of goods from his store to the city. Because the graft was not of ample enough dimensions, they let it slide, ignoring the principle of the thing altogether. Every year there is some alderman who is guilty of an indiscretion.

Another alderman who has been guilty of what might be construed into a grave indiscretion is Alderman Stuart. This gentleman is chairman of the police committee and, incidentally, is in the insurance business. Now, what do you suppose he has been up to, this immaculate stickler for the higher morality? He has been working the policemen for insurance in his company and has already written up policies for five or six of them. Amongst those of the force whom he has written up are the three new policemen who were taken on the other day. How could these men refuse the chairman of the police committee to whom they owed their jobs?

This proceeding on the part of Alderman Stuart does not, of course, come under the head of graft, for there are no strings on him so far as his business is concerned, but it is certainly imprudence of the most glaring kind to lay himself open to the charge of using the weight of his official position as chairman of the police committee to induce the policemen to buy insurance from him. There may be nothing wrong about it technically, but it looks rotten. [13]

*

Without the periodical scandals at Ottawa lots of decent people in the West would never hear of the place. [14]

*

Watch out and don't let 'em get you on Tofield subdivisions. Tofield itself may be all right, but beware of its subdivisions. That is unless you have already made arrangements with the Almighty to let you live until you are 200 years old. [15]

*

In Okotoks, where no village official has ever yet been accused of graft, the inhabitants are wondering whether they are better than other people or only duller. [16]

*

A certain real estate man in Calgary who is known to his associates far and wide as "Honest John," on account of his favorite text in the Bible, "Suffer the suckers to come at me," has been guilty of the most serious crime known to modern society, that of getting found out. "Honest John" originated a syndicate of himself and four leading citizens of Calgary to buy a certain corner and was entrusted by the syndicate to do the buying. This he did for $80,000, receiving from the vendors the usual five percent for making the sale. He then put it in to the syndicate, his own syndicate, for $100,000, thus skinning off for himself some $20,000 from his partners' pockets. This smooth piece of work soon leaked out in real estate circles. We are surprised at John, Honest John. We are, for a fact. He reminds us of the famous poem:

"John, John, the piper's son,
Stole a pig and away he run." [17]

*

A man can claim to have "arrived" when his private affairs begin to interest the public. [18]

*

There are three things in the West that need either readjusting or busting. These are the lumber combine, the beef combine and the grain combine.

Under the lumber combine it costs the settler the value of two acres of $6 land to purchase 1,000 feet of rough boards.

Under the beef combine no small rancher, or group of small ranchers, can ship east on their own account, for the reason that on reaching Winnipeg they find themselves at the mercy of Gordon & Ironsides, whose favorite method on the arrival of independent shipments is to protest that they are "full up," "have more than they can handle," etc., knowing that they have the shipper faded and far from home. The lesson thus inculcated in the small ranchman's mind is that it will be better for him in future to sell to the monopoly that exercises exclusive control over his home district, and take what he can get.

As for the grain combine, its finish, thanks to the probing of the royal grain commission and the red-hot agitation of the Winnipeg *Tribune* (the only friend the farmer and rancher seem to have these days), seems to be in sight. [19]

*

The irresponsible freaks, highball guzzlers and unabashed grafters who have been ruling the roost in Ontario for so long are at last within measurable distance of their finish. The soup vats are ready. [20]

*

In both Vancouver and Victoria there are swell ground-floor Edson real estate offices. We were told that the Vancouver firm was selling lots in Edson on the south side of the railway track, where the town isn't. If this is so, their conscience needs fixing. Once more we warn people about investing in Edson lots. If there is a river running through your town, chuck your money into it instead. It will save a whole lot of trouble making out papers, paying instalments and so forth. [21]

*

That the Canadian bench is corrupt there is not the shadow of a doubt. It is not venal, it does not sell its decisions for actual money. But venality is only one form of corruption. A man who is free from cancer may suffer from blood poisoning. Wherever any question of politics enters into legal proceedings the bench is thoroughly corrupt. It even goes further than that. Persons who are political enemies of the judges' party are not always safe in their courts, and persons with whom they are politically allied are often favored.

This is a much more difficult question to get to the bottom of than might be thought. There are two ideas about the doing of justice. The one is that it resides in the people, who are the final court of appeal, the other that it comes through a polished legal lense in the person of a judge as nearly impersonal as may be.

The wholly impersonal legal lense is an impossibility in this imperfect world. Every judge is a human being and must have his prejudices and prepossessions, surrounding him like an atmosphere and refracting the judicial light he sheds. If this aura happens to embody the highest thought, best aspiration and absolute impartiality of mind, it is all right. If it does not, it is all wrong.

Canadian judges are appointed in exactly the same way as British judges. They are taken from the legal ranks of the political party in power and preferment is often bestowed as a reward for political service. The trouble is that their mental environment and atmosphere are different. It is limited by partisan prejudices and prepossessions. In many Canadian courts the litigant is not in a Canadian court at all, but in a Liberal court or a Conservative court, and we find a disgusting jockeying for position on grounds which have nothing to do with the cause in action.

Of course, there are perfectly tangible excuses for this condition of the Canadian bench. The root cause is the avenue to judicial preferment. The surest way to become a judge in Canada is to have balked a parliamentary inquiry by legal chicanery or legal hectoring, to have covered up some scandal, administered and smothered the tracks of electoral corruption, concealed some dirty work by clever special pleading, or shown diplomatic skill in adjusting the sawoffs which balance the crimes of both sides. We draw our judges from infected sources. The legal ethics renders members of the legal profession liable to infection. A lawyer is the only man who may be thoroughly unmoral in his whole mental attitude (it is not said that all of them are) and yet enjoy the external reputation of probity.

Another very potent cause of corruption is that a man's career has not reached its summit with a judicial appointment. Even if he does not hop off into public life again as some do, there are always fat royal commissions, investigations and inquiries regarding probably a certain careful avoidance of the grass, and flexibility in reports anticipated and demanded. A Canadian judge is often still a backstairs climber with muddy feet from the outside staircase before he hits the carpeted interior.

So just as we find the highest judicial probity in the Supreme Court, because there is no higher to go, so we have a more supple morality lower down because there is, and the occupants of the bench are habituated to, a certain method of climbing.

The remedy is simple but uncommonly difficult to put in practice. But a bold public opinion which will pursue some of our judges with openly expressed contempt holds out the best prospect of improvement. Judges who are not respectable should not be respected because they are judges, and open contempt is the sorest discipline for men in high office. [22]

*

Society Note— Mr. George J. Jinks, the popular Calgary real

estate agent, is on his way home from England. At least this is the information received by Chief Cuddy from Scotland Yard. He is said to be accompanied by a rather nifty piece of goods. [23]

*

There is a bunch of Spokane land sharks in town that will bear watching. They are smooth as they make 'em and are preparing for a raid on the public's money in the spring. We hereby serve notice on this bunch of advertising sharks that whenever they attempt to put on any of their sky blue additions this spring, we will investigate and expose every one of them. [24]

*

Ho hum! It's a dull world. Can't somebody start a scandal or something? [25]

Peter J. McGonigle

Peter Jonah McGonigle, B.A., the brilliant editor of the Midnapore *Gazette,* was born in the county of Huron, Ontario. His parents were very Irish. He was educated at Toronto University, where, under the careful eye of Professor McConkey, he achieved brilliant results and finally took his degree of B.A. (Boozological Artist). Mr. McGonigle decided to come west and finally settled down in Winnipeg where he was shown much attention in police circles. From Winnipeg he moved to Stoney Mountain, where he resided continuously for seven years, after which he came further west to engage in journalism. Midnapore looked good to McGonigle and here he established the famous Midnapore *Gazette.* This publication is a weekly and enjoys a large circulation. [1]

*

Mr. Peter J. McGonigle is being groomed down at Midnapore for his big campaign at the forthcoming dominion elections. He has made arrangements with Mr. J. Young Byers, of Calgary, to run the *Gazette* during his speaking tour through the riding. Mr. McGonigle has cut out the booze and is getting down to business. His friends think he will make a strong run.

In view of the prominence which Mr. McGonigle has suddenly attained through his determination to run as an independent Conservative in the Calgary district, it may interest the public to read some extracts from last week's issue of his stirring weekly, the Midnapore *Gazette.*

"Mr. John Googlund, our wide awake real estate man, while driving a prospective settler over the country east of town Tuesday, fell out of the rig and was brought back to the city unconscious. The stranger whom he was driving is authority for the statement that Mr. Googlund was very drunk. The many friends of Mr. Googlund will be distressed to learn of this untoward incident, but hope he will soon be up and around.

"Our talented young friend, Al Hopkins, has accepted a position tending bar in Calgary. The *Gazette* predicts a bright future for Al.

"Mrs. Jeraboam Q. Slopmagulcher, the acknowledged leader of Midnapore's haut ton, gave a pink tea Thursday afternoon. It was a delightful affair, Old Slopmagulcher, however, who had been playing freeze-out for the drinks over at the hotel all day, rolled home a couple of hours too early and lurched right into the recherche parlor, kicking over the tea table and throwing bric-a-brac at the guests. He was put to bed with difficulty and Mrs. Slop laughingly apologized to her guests, who told her not to mention it as it was of no consequence." [2]

*

A girl seldom falls in love with a man unless there is some reason that she shouldn't.—McGonigle. [3]

*

P. J. McGonigle, the Midnapore journalist, is the most unfortunate of men. It appears that during the despondent stage following hard upon his last drunk Mr. McGonigle got religion and joined the church. Having a voice far louder and more raucous than any of Mr. Brodeur's St. Lawrence River foghorns, they put him into the choir and he distinguished himself the very first Sunday by nearly shattering the "Rock of Ages" into a thousand fragments. The trustees asked him to draw it mild, but as he has since been fired out of the church altogether, this makes no material difference.

There happened to be a rather pretty widow who sang contralto in the choir and Peter warmed up to her in great shape. They sang out of the same hymn book and all that sort of thing. The other fellows naturally grew a bit jealous, though they did not seriously think that an ornery-looking slob like McGonigle would have much chance with the merry widow. However, the

85

hot running made by the celebrated editor made them not a little uneasy.

Now it must be explained that on Mondays, Tuesdays and Wednesdays, when he didn't have to write stuff for the *Gazette,* Mr. McGonigle turned an honest penny by selling sewing machines. He bethought him one evening that to try and sell a sewing machine to the widow would be an excellent excuse for calling. So between eight and nine o'clock, accompanied by his faithful dog, he knocked at the front door of the lady's residence, and, on being admitted, ordered the little dog to lie down on the porch outside and wait for him.

While he was inside doing the polite, the dog sprang down from the porch to run after a passing rig, and during the five minutes that the dog was absent Mr. McGonigle rose to say goodbye. He meandered down to the hotel to get a drink before the bar closed and then went home to bed, wondering lazily what had become of the dog.

It seems that the dog, after chasing the rig for quite a distance down the road, returned to the porch of the widow's cottage and lay down to wait for his master. He was a very faithful animal. Between five and six o'clock the next morning some Midnaporeites who had to get up early to do their chores espied McGonigle's dog lying asleep at the widow's front door and drew their own conclusions.

Before ten o'clock it was the scandal of the town. In vain did McGonigle try to explain. In vain did the poor widow try to make the womenfolk believe in her innocence. The minister called at the *Gazette* office and cancelled the editor's membership in his church. McGonigle threatened to write the whole lot of them up, but inadvertently got drunk instead. In point of fact, there was no issue last week and it is not likely there will be another for a month, as this drunk looks as if it was going to be a prolonged one. The widow has "gone east to visit friends," and the confounded little dog may be seen at any hour of the day lying outside the bar-room door of the Nevermore Hotel waiting for his master. Mr. McGonigle threatens to move his plant to Okotoks. [4]

*

All things conspire to the glory of Alberta. The Hon. Peter J. McGonigle of Midnapore has consented to act as judge of the baby show at the dominion fair. If Mr. McGonigle proves as excellent a judge of babies as he is of whiskey, the mothers of this great land will have no kick coming. [5]

*

We are indebted to the pen of our dear old college chum and journalistic confrere, Peter J. McGonigle of the Midnapore *Gazette,* for the following account of the grand opening of the boozorium:

My Dear Bob—
You often told me I would wind up in the bughouse if I kept on drinking Midnapore whiskey, and I guess you're right. I was kidnapped last Saturday night after a high old time with the boys, and carted over the hills and far away until I reached this place, which, from what I can gather, is the kind of place you used to talk about, except that they call it a boozorium. The morning after the day I arrived the formal opening of the institution took place, and it certainly was a daisy. In honor of the occasion all restrictions were removed and booze was flowing far more copiously than water does through the CPR ditch. We had Scotch, rye, brandy, Tom gin, square gin, beer and lots of other stuff, and although I sampled them all I found nothing to compare with the good old Midnapore Killmequick, with its benzine and fishhooks.

The opening was a grand affair. Lieutenant-Governor Bulyea came down from Edmonton to preside over the function. He drank comparatively little for a man in his position. The speech he delivered was the same speech that he opened the bull show with last spring, but none of the patients seemed to mind it. He was shown around the boozorium and seemed highly pleased with what he saw. The museum occupied most of his attention, His Honor being particularly struck with snakery. One of the patients who accompanied him invited him into the room where he said he had several other varieties on view, but although the governor went with him he said he could not see them. This is the first day since I came here that I have been able to use a pen, but am tapering off nicely, being down to forty whiskies a day, with a little lager beer for a chaser. Tomorrow I hope to be put into the bromide class and if I have any kind of luck I ought to be promoted into the calomel department early next week.

Several of the patients have endeavored to get leave to go downtown for the mail, as they expect some important letters, but they have been refused permission. Another patient received a telegram, which he unfortunately lost, saying that his mother was dead in Ontario and he had to go east at once. He, too, was turned down, on the ground that the old lady had just telephoned up from town to know how he was getting on. Another patient was most anxious to consult a firm of lawyers downtown about a big land deal he was swinging, but was informed that this same firm had left instructions that he was on no account to be set at large before October 1. All the other fellows are doing nicely and we are all perfectly contented and well satisfied. Yours as ever,

PETER J. McGONIGLE

P.S. If by any chance you could manage to fetch me up a couple of bottles of Scotch without letting these people here get on to it, you would be doing a service which I shall never forget. Come as soon as you can. Don't delay. I need it. [6]

*

Sport: You lose, P. J. McGonigle's father died peacefully in his bed. He had been suffering from tumors in his stomach, the complaint being aggravated by his inordinate love of Burke's beer, the rosin of which helped along the disease. The old gentleman passed away full of years and tumors in '98, leaving a large family, of which Peter J. is the eldest, to mourn his loss. His further family history may be found in Burke's Beerage. It was probably the grandfather you were thinking of. He was hanged at Fort Walsh in '85. [7]

*

As banquets and luncheons seem to be the order of the day in Calgary, we offer no apology for presenting an absolutely correct report of a pleasant function which was pulled off last week.

The banquet tendered by the Calgary board of trade to Mr. Peter McGonigle on the occasion of his release from the Edmonton penitentiary, where he had spent some time trying to live down a conviction of horse stealing, proved a great success. Quite a number of prominent citizens were present, and, with Mayor Emerson in the chair, the songs, toasts and speeches passed off with all the éclat available at such short notice.

Letters of regret were read from Lord Strathcona, Earl Grey, Premier Rutherford, Charles Wagner, Joseph Seagram, Josh Calloway, W. Callahan, Col. G. C. Porter, W. F. Maclean, Joseph Fahy, Rev. John A. McDougall, Con. Leary and others.

Lord Strathcona's letter reads as follows:

John Emerson, Esq., Mayor, Calgary.

Dear Jack,—You don't mind me calling you Jack, do you, old cock? I regret exceedingly that I shall be unable to attend the McGonigle banquet at Calgary, but, believe me, my sympathies go out to your honored guest. The name of Peter McGonigle will ever stand high in the roll of eminent confiscators. Once, long ago, I myself came near achieving distinction in this direction when I performed some dexterous financing with the Bank of Montreal's funds. In consequence, however, of CPR stocks going up instead of down, I wound up in the House of Lords instead of Stoney Mountain.

Believe me, dear Jack,

Yours very truly,
STRATHCONA

Joseph Seagram, M.P., wrote:

Dear Mr. Mayor,—Though unable to be with you in the flesh, my spirit is no doubt with you in sufficient quantities. Wishing Mr. McGonigle all luck in his next venture.

Yours truly,
JOSEPH SEAGRAM

The sumptuous repast, of which we give the menu, was provided by Messrs. Wing and Kidney, the well-known caterers.

Soup
Bouillon Macaulaise
Skilly à la Matt

Fish
Suckers à la Hanson
Henglish Erring à la Hemerson

Entrees
Calf's head without brains, Commission style
Muttonhead Cutlets à la city council
Commission Croquettes cut on the bias

Boiled
Owls, aldermanic variety

Roasts
Herald
Albertan
Eye Opener

Dessert
Assorted Fruit
Receptions glacees à la Grey
Kitheth à la Gillith
Cafe Chantant, with or without
Tea Deum

As the walnuts and the prunes and the wine came on, cigars were lit and the mayor rose to propose the toast of the king. His Honor expressed his entire satisfaction with His Majesty's reign. Indeed, he expressed a very high opinion of His Majesty and thought that he was as good a king as they could possibly get for the money. (Hear, hear.) He did not think the time yet ripe for the British Empire to be ruled by a commission. They had tried it in Calgary and it was found to be a failure. He was quite agreeable that the king should remain on the throne till the end of his term. (Loud cheers.)

The toast of the Army, Navy and Reserve Forces was ably responded to by Major Charles Fisher, speaker of the Alberta House. In graphic language he sketched the careers of great soldiers from Julius Caesar down to Major Walker, outlined the strategy of Napoleon and pointed out his tactical blunders, criticised in caustic language Nelson's clumsy handling of his ships at the battle of Trafalgar, showed up to the merciless light of day the deficiencies in the military training of Von Moltke, and wound up with a glowing eulogy of the Alberta Light Horse and a fervid appeal for an open canteen. The major resumed his seat amidst thunderous applause.

Mr. R. J. Hutchings, in replying to the toast of the Great West, said: "Mr. Chairman, I presume this toast has special reference to the firm with which I have been connected more or less along these lines for the past number of years. I must say, Mr. Chairman, that we have endeavored to the best of our capacity to show what is in us and we hope to keep our-our-our shoulder to the wheel along those lines. (Hear, hear.) The country around us is developing fast. I might almost say that it is developing at a great rate. (Loud applause.) The government at Edmonton is constructing long distance telephone lines throughout the province and we hope—we trust—nay, we propose, to develop our business along those lines. (Cheers.) I am proud to say that the guest of the evening is a most remarkable man and endowed with a marvellous sense of discrimination. Even in the moment of abstraction, when he took the horse, he selected one of our magnificent sets of single harness from the owner's stable and, having secured the lines, removed the animal along those lines. (Cheers.) I earnestly trust that Mr. McGonigle, whose pallid countenance and general appearance show the effects of his residence in Edmonton, will soon fatten up and be able to resume his chosen avocation along those lines. (Hear, hear.) Before sitting down, Mr. Chairman, I might perhaps be permitted to say that if, as has been suggested, a company is to be formed to harness Kananaskis Falls, —er— might I suggest that they look in on our firm before going elsewhere?" (Loud and prolonged cheering.)

Mr. C. W. Bowley, in response to loud cries, obliged with his great song, "Ye Banks and Brays," and was loudly applauded.

The chairman, Mayor Emerson, on rising to propose the toast of Our Guest, was greeted with vociferous applause.

"Gentlemen, I am 'eartily pleased to be with you this evening to endeavor, if possible, to liven things up a bit. ('Ear, 'ear! and cries of 'Put him out!') My duties as mayor of this great city are sometimes difficult. As is my custom, I 'ad intended to read a little address to our guest, but Gillies refused to write one for me. 'Owever, 'ere goes for a few extempore remarks. ('Stay with it!' 'Put him out!' 'Shut up!') Although not as a rule a believer in a third term, yet, since learning that I am to be succeeded by either Mr. Clifford Jones or Mr. R. J. Stuart, my views on the subject have very materially changed.

"I have frequently, in the dear old mother country which we all love so well (loud and prolonged cheers), as well as in the North-West, shaken 'ands with royalty, but, gentlemen, I 'ave never forgotten the kindly words of friendliness which was spoken to me by 'Is Royal 'Ighness, Prince Harthur of Connaught, when he grasped my 'and at the station and said, 'John, you are the limit.' (Cheers.) Only the hother day at the magnificent reception which me and Gillies got up for Earl Grey, although I tried to look as mild as possible, I overheard 'Is Excellency remark to 'is missus that I was pretty fierce. (Roars of laughter.) It is simple marks of condescension such as these that endear us common folk to royalty. ('Have another prune, John!' 'Shut up!' 'Give him a show!' 'Rats!')

"As you are all aware, our guest has for some time past been most hospitably entertained by His Majesty at his Edmonton shooting box, where he had the honor of meeting our talented and popular fellow-townsman, Mr. Callahan, who is sought after everywhere, and young Mr. Wilson, the Macleod chicken fancier. This district is splendidly adapted for gentlemen of Mr. McGonigle's pursuits, and owing to the persistent reduction of the police force he can conduct his business without serious molestation. As the poet says:

I knew by the smoke that so gracefully curled,
From out the green coulee that a rustler was near,
And I said, if there's peace to be found in this world,
The 'eart that is 'umble may 'ope for it 'ere."

(Tremendous cheers.)

Mr. McGonigle's rising was the signal for a loud and vociferous outburst of applause. It was fully ten minutes before the guest of the evening, who was visibly affected by the warmth of his reception, was allowed to proceed. On quiet being restored, Mr. McGonigle proceeded to thank those present for their cordial greeting, and said that owing to the many kindnesses which had been shown him that afternoon he felt entirely too full to express his appreciation of the honor done him. ("Good boy!" "Stay with it!") He was willing to let the dead past bury its dead. The horse in question had died shortly after he was parted from it. As a matter of fact, he had been working for a dead horse for a number of years. (Applause.) Had it not been for the ignorance of his lawyer he might have been acquitted, for the horse he stole was not a horse at all, but a mare. This point was entirely overlooked at the trial. It was a horse on him, anyhow.

The speaker paid a high tribute to the hospitality of his Edmonton host, Mr. McCauley, whom he was proud to see there that evening, though he lamented that in spite of the number of bars on his premises there was nothing of an enlivening nature to drink. They were sorry to lose Mr. Callahan from their pleasant little house party. His suite of rooms, however, were being prepared for the long-expected visit of Mr. Philipp Wagner, the distinguished Galician financier.

Mr. McGonigle could not close without making a pathetic reference to the gross partiality of the trial judge, who absolutely ignored his proposition to return the horse and say no more about it. He would ask the company to charge their glasses and drink a silent toast to the memory of the dead horse. (Prolonged cheering.)

Mr. Matt McCauley of Edmonton, being called upon for a song, obliged the company with "Abide with Me," which he rendered with deep feeling in a rich staccato voice, which would be none the worse of a little sandpapering. Mr. Frank Wrigley played the accompaniment.

Mr. C. W. Rowley, manager of the Canadian Bank of Commerce and president of the board of trade, in replying to the toast of Frenzied Finance said: "Mr. Chairman and gentlemen, in my capacity as manager of the Canadian Bank of Commerce and president of the board of trade I have developed great faith in the future of this particular district. Yet, Mr. Chairman and gentlemen, I must admit that had Mr. H. Byron Walker, my chief in the Canadian Bank of Commerce, seen fit to send me to conduct a branch of the Canadian Bank of Commerce at Jackfish Bay on the bleak north shore, I should naturally have shown the same faith in the agricultural possibilities of that as yet undeveloped district. (Loud cheers.) I have also great faith in the Canadian Bank of Commerce and its manager, and I would caution the public against doing business anywhere else than with us.

"As president of the board of trade I devote a large portion of my time to drawing the attention of the eastern provinces and the northern states to the CPR irrigation ditch, thus creating the healthy impression that nothing can grow here except on land irrigated from this ditch. (Hear, hear.) It is eminently desirable that people from abroad should be made to believe that this country is as dry as a bone, because so many newcomers dislike a damp climate and the sale of the CPR lands adjacent to the ditch is of paramount importance to the company. (Loud cheers.) Every visitor to Calgary is driven out to the ditch. No visitor has escaped yet. The board of trade has made a specialty of showing off this ditch to every bunch of eastern and American newspaper men that come along, in order that the main feature of their published descriptions of the Calgary district may be set forth in large type as "The Arid Lands of Alberta Saved by a Benevolent CPR Irrigation System." (Vociferous cheering.) Our rate of interest in the Canadian Bank of Commerce will compare favorably with that of any other financial institution in the city and the clearing house returns furnish ample evidence of our increasing popularity. To our great president, the illustrious philanthropist George A. Cox, as well as myself, may be attributed the astonishing success of the Canadian Bank of Commerce.

"As regards the guest of the evening, whom we are assembled 'to have the pleasure to meet' tonight, I can only say that I shall have him driven out to have a look at the ditch in the morning." (Prolonged cheering.)

The chairman here called upon Messrs. Hiebert and Robertson, the sweet warblers, for a song. They cheerfully complied with the well-known duet, "Oh, That We Two Were Haying," after which Mr. Robertson in response to the encore, sang "Okotoks, The Gem of the Ocean."

Alderman Stuart, in replying to the toast of the City Police, said that he had become a prominent citizen mainly through the efforts of Lougheed and Bennett in securing his election to the city council. It had been said that honesty was the best policy, but he believed that the twenty-year payment policy issued by his company was by far and away the best. As chairman of the police committee he had deemed it his duty to convince the members of the police force of the necessity of insuring with him, and he had already succeeded in frightening several of the newer and greener members into taking out policies. (Cheers.) He had also scared the life out of the two young lady typewriters at the city hall who were afraid of losing their $40 jobs by incurring his aldermanic displeasure, and had bulldozed them into taking out policies in his company. (Hear, hear, and laughter.) He flattered himself that he had succeeded in insuring all who could not afford to quarrel with him.

This city hall graft was invaluable to a man in his line, and he was going to have himself elected to another term in order to help along his insurance business. Indeed, he hoped to be their next mayor. (Roars of laughter.) He thought that office would give him a wider field for butting in.

In conclusion, Alderman Stuart stated that he had much

pleasure in announcing that the guest of the evening had decided to take out an accident policy in his company in case at any future time he might again be placed horse de combat. (Applause.)

A song, "If I Were Only Long Enough, A Sodjer I Would Be," by Joseph Hicks of Macleod, elicited great enthusiasm and he was forced to give his great Shakespearian recitation, "Anthony's address to a Macleod jury."

The proceedings were thereafter brought to a close with "God Save the King" and three cheers for Peter McGonigle, the guest of the evening. [8]

*

Peter J. McGonigle, editor of the popular Midnapore *Gazette*, has not had an issue of his paper out for several weeks. He has been down to High River on a business trip. As is well known, a business trip to High River involves considerable drinking, and it will be distressing to many of Mr. McGonigle's friends to learn that he forgot his pledge and, as the local preacher put it, went the whole hog. He was so near the willies that they shut down on giving him any more booze, and he became a perfect nuisance round the St. George Hotel, where he was stopping. Finally he approached Phil Weinard, the presiding genius of the gurgling bottle, and made a fervid appeal for just one jolt.

"Not on your life, Pete," said Phil, wiping off the bar with great deliberation.

"Then," cried McGonigle in an excess of despair, "I'll be desperate. I'll get a rope and hang myself to the telephone pole in front of the hotel."

"How many times have I got to tell you that I don't want you hanging around here?" shouted Phil.

But Phil, realizing that he had got off something good, relented and passed up the bottle. A valuable life was thus saved and much credit is due Mr. Weinard for his noble magnanimity on this occasion. Jack Binns could have done no more. The next number of the Midnapore *Gazette* will appear shortly if not sooner. [9]

*

The father of the Calgary girl whom Peter J. McGonigle, of the Midnapore *Gazette*, contemplates marrying in the spring, seems to have soured on his future son-in-law. At least, he ordered him peremptorily from the house the other night. It appears that Peter was slightly under the influence of bugjuice. Not much, but just enough to be cheeky. The old man was on the prod, and said: "There's no use talking, McGonigle, my daughter can never be yours."

"Of course she can't be my daughter," replied Peter, with offensive gaiety. "Who said she could be my daughter? But she's going to be my wife, and the sooner you get the idea out of your head that she isn't, the sooner you'll have room under your lid for another idea. How's that, old cockie?"

Then the old gentleman rose from his seat. [10]

*

There has been so much interest displayed by the reading public in the McGonigle family that we have decided to present the portraits of the late Mr. J. McGonigle Sr. and his son Mr. Peter J. McGonigle, editor of the Midnapore *Gazette*. The elder Mr. McGonigle died very suddenly a number of year ago, in Choteau county, Montana, between Choteau and Ponderay. His grave may still be seen, though it is off the beaten track. There being no flowers in this desolate cow country, his friends have kept his grave green with that which he loved so well in life, kegs and bottles. This is how he himself would have wished to have it. The band of mares, which was the immediate cause of his taking off, were duly returned to their rightful owners.

Peter J. McGonigle is the editor and sole proprietor of the Midnapore *Gazette*, one of the most popular family journals in western Canada. Its circulation within the past few years has bounded up from 375 to over 600, and is still on the rise. The *Gazette* is independent in politics, the editor favoring the side that "comes through." Owing to the close proximity of the Nevermore Hotel there are occasions when the paper fails to appear, but Mr. McGonigle invariably manages to pacify his infuriated subscribers by getting out an extra good number the next time he prints. Mr. McGonigle is well known in Calgary, and is a great favorite with the sisters of the Holy Cross Hospital, which he never fails to visit when in town, usually with the D.T.s. He is a bachelor, but expects shortly to marry a charming lady in Calgary.

96

The social life of Midnapore fluctuates considerably. It is only nine miles from Calgary, and frequently, when there is a musical comedy playing at one of the theatres, the local sports will give the chorus girls a flying trip down to the little burg in automobiles. On these occasions Mr. McGonigle is routed out of bed, and he and Jimmy see that the visitors have a good time. They can kick up all the row they like, for the cattle on the range don't mind and the coyotes rather seem to enjoy it. We predict a great future for Midnapore. [11]

*

"What are your views on currency," asked a stranger of McGonigle, the sage of Midnapore.

"Mostly sad and reminiscent," was the reply, "but if it's a drink you're after, I've got a shillin'." [12]

*

The engagement of Miss Phoebe Delaney of Calgary to Mr. Peter J. McGonigle of Midnapore is at last announced. The wedding has been set for March 17, to be followed by an extended honeymoon to Macleod via Okotoks, High River, Nanton, Staveley and Granum. The happy couple will thereafter take up residence in Midnapore, where Mr. McGonigle has extensive business interests. Midnapore society is all agog over this delightful society event and many balls, routs, dinner parties, pink teas and receptions will be gotten up in their honor.

Mr. McGonigle gave a charming pink whiskey to his male friends last Monday afternoon in the spacious parlors of the Nevermore Hotel, when he formally announced his approaching marriage. A pleasant time was had. The function, which was quite a recherche affair, is still in progress, according to a despatch received at this office before going to press. The guests are engaged in a delightful game of progressive poker, the prizes being round and flat objects d'art of various hues, white, red, blue and yellow. A little bird has whispered that Mr. John M. Delaney will settle $500 on his daughter, which should enable Mr. McGonigle to get in a new Gordon press for job printing, the old one having been smashed in a fracas last election. In the meantime a ward is being held in readiness for Mr. McGonigle at the Holy Cross Hospital in Calgary, where he will recuperate from his very successful pink whiskey under the care of the family physician and a trained snake charmer. There will be no issue of the *Gazette* next week. [13]

*

A pretty anecdote is related in connection with the recent McGonigle nuptials at Midnapore. At the wedding breakfast it appears that Mr. McGonigle, in the exuberance of the moment, seized a bottle of whiskey and applied it to his mouth, drinking with great long gulps.

"My dear sir," interposed the minister, "be careful, be careful! I once knew a man who drank from a bottle with such haste and avidity that he dropped dead before he finished it."

"You don't say!" said the happy bridegroom, pausing with a look of unfeigned interest. "And what did they do with the rest of the bottle?" [14]

*

The wedding of Mr. Peter J. McGonigle of Midnapore and Miss Phoebe Delaney of Calgary was duly solemnized on March 17. The happy couple left immediately after the ceremony for Edmonton, where they travelled by stage into the north country. Mr. McGonigle proposes to study the habits of the Indians up there, and with this purpose in view both he and Mrs. McGonigle have taken up their abode in their midst, adopting their dress and so forth. During Mr. McGonigle's absence the Midnapore *Gazette* is being conducted by the Hon. Thomas Mewburn of Calgary. [15]

*

Mr. and Mrs. Peter J. McGonigle returned a couple of weeks ago from their honeymoon and have taken up residence in the charming flat above the printing office. Two new chairs and a family Bible have been installed, also a clock. Mrs. McGonigle will receive for the first time next Wednesday afternoon. Mr. McGonigle has only had one mild toot since his wedding, and that was at Edmonton on the trip down from the far north. He would appear to have met the Hon. Joseph Adair. Mr. McGonigle has so far nobly kept his promise to his bride to never again enter the Nevermore Hotel. Jimmy, the faithful bartender, has to slip over every once in a while with a bottle while the happy couple are billing and cooing along the violet-strewn banks of Fish Creek and cache it away in the hell box.

The first tiff of the happy couple came from the family Bible aforesaid, for which Mrs. McGonigle had paid $1.60 in Calgary. On looking over the good book and idly turning over the pages she discovered that her Peter had been using the leaves for cigarette papers, probably because they were so thin. On close scrutiny she found that her husband, whom she thought so noble, so high-minded, so god-like, had smoked up all the gospels and about half of Ezekiel. There was also a suspicious gap in the Psalms. However, Peter J., who is pretty smooth, fixed it up somehow and the goose is now hanging at frightful altitude.

Mr. McGonigle was highly pleased at the manner in which Mr. Thomas Mewburn conducted the *Gazette* during his absence and, by way of remuneration, waved his hand airily and said he "would make it all right with him." McGonigle has a great heart. [16]

*

Mr. McGonigle of Midnapore had to tear himself away from his bride last week and run up to Calgary on some business connected with the *Gazette*. Of course he had to drop in to have a chat with Fred Adams at the Victoria, and then he had to call around and congratulate Jack Moseley on getting hold of the Imperial, and then he had to see if the same old barkeeps were on deck at the Yale, and then he had to investigate Bart's Beautiful Budge at the Grand Central, and then—he got spifflicated, this making his second fall from grace since his marriage. He was extremely dubious about returning home on the evening train.

Passing Terrill's florist emporium he was struck with a brilliant idea of taking home a floral peace offering to Mrs. McGonigle. He pointed out some flowers that he thought would do the trick, and the florist made up a dozen for him. As he was leaving he turned to inquire the name of the flowers.

"Wash you call these flowrsh?"

The florist told him they were chrysanthemums, whereupon Mr. McGonigle shook his head sadly.

"Mush have shumthing easier than that," he said, "lemme have shumthing I can say—gimme a dozen pinks." [17]

*

The Pan-Boozological Congress of Demented Bartenders was held in Winnipeg this year and met in session last week at the Royal Alexandra. Delegates from all the provinces, with the exception of Quebec, were present. The Quebec delegates had been detained by the Eucharistic Congress in Montreal and could not get here for the opening session. However, a pleasant time was had as the *Free Press* would say.

Mr. Peter J. McGonigle, the distinguished journalist of Midnapore, who was on his way home after taking the jag cure at Port Arthur, was invited to be present and address the delegates. This he kindly consented to do, and in the course of the morning prepared a thoughtful address on "The Horrors of Square Gin." Being unused to public speaking, Mr. McGonigle nerved himself for the ordeal by slipping round to the bar before the proceedings commenced and throwing three or four stiff old hookers into himself. He argued that one little flurry of rye would not materially affect the good results of his recent cure.

The Chairman, Mr. J. Collins, in introducing the distinguished guest, said that it was indeed an honor to the Pan-Boozological Congress to have Mr. McGonigle with them on this auspicious occasion. Mr. McGonigle was a man who had probably done more for the cause of booze than any other living man. (Cheers.) He had long been an honor to the bar. It was understood that his onerous labors on behalf of the alcoholic industries of this country had constrained his physicians to order a complete rest, but it was to be hoped that in a few months, if not weeks, he would be sufficiently restored to resume active operations in the field where he had attained such lofty pre-eminence. (Loud applause.)

"I take pleasure," concluded the chairman, "in introducing Mr. Peter McGonigle, the champeen heavyweight booze-fighter of the West."

Mr. McGonigle, on rising, was received with tumultuous applause, the delegates rising to their feet and singing "We Won't Go Home Till Morning" with fine effect. Mr. McGonigle's speech, in part, was as follows:

"Mr. Chairman and gentlemen, I am profoundly touched by the warmth of your reception. There are many faces here of which I have a very distinct recollection, while there are others of which I have only an indistinct recollection, but I am glad to be with you all today. The remarkable reception which you have accorded me will ever live in my memory and will be handed down as a family legend to my children, if I ever have any, and to my children's children, if they ever have any. (Loud and prolonged applause.) Mr. Chairman, I had intended addressing your congress this afternoon on the horrors of square gin, but I think it would be more in accordance with the proprieties of the occasion if I simply offered a few remarks on the complex subject of boozology as a general proposition. (Hear, hear!)

"There may be some here who prefer Square Face to Old Tom and it is far from my intention, I assure you, to wound the susceptibilities of any one by lauding one kind of gin to the detriment of another. When a booze artist of average intelligence regards his past life he has food for thought. Having partaken of that food, he has to take several horns to wash it down, and so the world wags on. (Applause.) We all have our good points, but so has a paper of pins. (Laughter.) As Emerson so aptly remarked, 'Hitch your wagon to Three Star.'

"The main cause of drunkenness, Mr. Chairman, in this Canada of ours, is the pathetic tendency most booze-fighters have to taking six drinks before breakfast instead of two. I should like to see some form of legislation introduced whereby it became a crime to take more than two snifters before breakfast. (Hear, hear!) When a man imbibes, say, three Collinses on an empty stomach he gets laid out too soon, having probably to retire to the hay before ten o'clock. Thus your receipts are curtailed for the day and the boss thinks you are knocking down. (A voice, 'That's so!') On the other hand, let your honest booze-fighter confine himself to a couple of snorts in the early morn, just to get the bugs out of his eyes, and then let him make a beeline for the dining room and stuff himself full of ham-and. What must be the natural result, my friends, of such wise policy? That man will last all day and well into the night. (Loud and prolonged applause.)

"Such a concerted movement on the part of the vast horde of rotgut guzzlers would make the wheels of your great and noble industry move the faster, would hasten the filling of your cash registers, give employment to more men in the breweries and distilleries, spread happiness amongst the hotelkeepers, add to the prosperity of the medical profession, fill your hospitals with paying patients, promote the interests of the calomel and bromide merchants, increase the welfare of every gravedigger in the land and cause the marts of the world to hum with the sound of popping corks to the end that the eternal gaiety of nations might not be dimmed by the disgraceful efforts of those who too lightly claim that Adam's ale is more conducive to longevity than Seagram's rye. (Frantic applause, many of the delegates jumping up and waving their handkerchiefs.)

"The economic value of booze is incalculable. Why, for instance, should you pay six bits to go and see the menagerie attached to a circus, when with the simple aid of three bottles of square gin and two of Scotch you can see a far more various and curious collection of animals, and none of them in cages either! You do not even have to leave your place of abode to view them. They come right up to you. (Cheers.)

"Mr. Chairman, I go west tonight. I shall take with me the message to Midnapore that the Pan-Boozological Congress of Demented Bartenders is solid for the unity of the Empire. (Tremendous applause.) I shall convey to the Midnapore board of trade, which consists of myself, my assistant, the local hardware merchant and four cowpunchers, that your congress has declared itself resolutely in favor of free trade in agricultural implements and reciprocity with the United States. I shall tell them that while favoring free trade, you look with grave disfavor on free drinks. (Hear, hear!) Mr. Chairman, and gentlemen, I thank you for your generous courtesy." (Prolonged cheering, followed by the singing of "He's A Jolly Good Fellow.")

After a few words of thanks to Mr. McGonigle from the chairman for his eloquent address, of which only a portion is here given, Mr. Fred Adams of Calgary rose and delivered a monologue on the agitation which was going on out west in favor of five drinks for a half. He said it was an outrage. Mr. Adams also complained that Sir Wilfrid Laurier on his tour through the West had not declared himself on the subject of free drinks for customers before breakfast. (Shame, shame!) Nor had R. L. Borden made any pronouncement on the subject. Whither were they drifting? What did they put these fellers into office for? Mr. Adams concluded by betting his sweet life that he would use his influence next dominion election to put Laurier where he belonged.

The meeting thereafter adjourned—to the bar. The delegates were delighted with their visit to Winnipeg and were driven round the city in automobiles by some of the more prominent local members of the fraternity. It was decided to hold the congress next year in Port Arthur, the city which would not publish its police court records for reasons of state. "What state?" cried the infuriated prophet. "State of drunkenness, you slob." [18]

*

It is with unalloyed grief that we record the untimely death of Mr. Peter J. McGonigle, editor and proprietor of the Midnapore (Alta.) *Gazette*. This also means the demise of the *Gazette*. While examining an ivory-handled revolver which the bartender of the Nevermore House had, during the editor's absence in Port Arthur, accepted from a stranger in lieu of payment for a two-day drunk, the weapon unexpectedly went off and lodged a bullet in Mr. McGonigle's abdomen. A physician was hastily summoned by phone from Calgary. In the meanwhile Jimmy, the bartender, summoned help and had his old friend gently raised from the floor and stretched out on the bar with his head comfortably resting on the slot machine. Mr. McGonigle retained consciousness, but complained of great pain. A tumbler of brandy eased his sufferings somewhat, but he whispered to Jimmy that he feared he had been sent for at last. The tender-hearted mixologist thereupon threw another tumbler of brandy into him, after which, as soon as it had percolated through his system, Mr. McGonigle declared himself as feeling much better.

Pending the arrival of the doctor from Calgary, nine miles distant, Jimmy did all he knew to staunch the flow of blood. Ripping open the shirt and locating the spot where the bullet had entered, he took the glass stopper from a Gooderham and Wortz flask and inserted the blunt-pointed end into the hole, keeping it pressed down with his thumb to stop the rush of blood. The contents of the flask he absent-mindedly poured down his own throat from time to time. No one was allowed to enter the bar except a few specially favored friends, one of whom was despatched over to the *Gazette* office to ease Mrs. McGonigle's mind with regard to her husband's absence. This friend admirably performed his errand, informing the lady that if she didn't see her husband for a few days she was not to worry or feel the least bit anxious, as he was only off on a little bit of a whizzer. Mrs. McGonigle thereupon indulged in some sarcastic remarks about the Port Arthur Jagcureatorium where P.J. had recently blown in a couple of hundred dollars, but finally wound up by asking the messenger to try and prevail on Mr. McGonigle to make it a three-day jag this time instead of a two-week one as heretofore.

On being informed of the success of his messenger the great editor smiled and said he thought they ought to have a drink on the strength of it. One of the men thereupon took Jimmy's place holding down the glass stopper, while that worthy prepared the round. No one took a cigar. At some one's suggestion, the slot machine was taken from under the wounded man's head, as being too uncomfortable, and the cash register substituted. In lowering Mr. McGonigle's head on to the keyboard they rang up $14.65, but P.J. said it was a great improvement on the slot machine and added that he hoped the doc wouldn't be long, as he felt himself getting awful weak.

An auto suddenly pulled up in front of the Nevermore House and out jumped the long-looked-for doctor, carrying a small black case.

"What room is the man in who was shot?" he curtly inquired of the men gathered in the office.

"He's in the bar," was the response.

"In the bar?" ejaculated the doctor, wondering if he had been the victim of a hoax.

A head was poked through the bar-room door, revealing the weather-beaten countenance of Jimmy, the mixocographer.

"Step this way, Doc."

"How is he?" whispered the doctor before going in.

"I'm afraid he's a goner, but I've been throwing the booze into him to keep up his nerve till you came."

"Quite right, quite right."

Mr. McGonigle, on the approach of the doctor, turned his head, ringing up $1.40 in the effort, and greeted the doctor with great cordiality, insisting upon his having a drink before making his examination. Then everybody but Jimmy was ordered to "get out and stay out."

As the doctor bent down to examine the wound he could not

keep back a smile when he ran on to the glass-stopper stuck in the bullet hole. Jimmy gave a pathetic little grin and explained that it would have taken too long to whittle a cork into shape. Then the doctor's face grew grave.

"The bullet must be located and extracted," said he, "and he will have to be taken to the hospital in Calgary by the first train. You can stretch him out comfortably in the baggage car and I'll be at the depot with the ambulance when the train pulls in."

"I'd better go along, eh, Doc?"

"I should certainly like you to accompany him to Calgary, if you can possibly get away."

"Oh, that part of it will be all right. I can get one of the boys to run the joint."

"Have you any one here you can trust."

Mr. McGonigle stirred slightly and rang up 15 cents.

"We can trust 'em all round here. Can't we, Jimmy?"

"Sure we can," said Jimmy, "but not for drinks."

"No, not for drinks," acquiesced McGonigle.

"Then that is settled," said the doctor. "I will hurry back in my car and arrange for a ward in the Holy Cross. Then—ha ha! —we'll do the chloroform stunt, Mr. McGonigle, cut you open, dive into your poor old guts, slosh around among your bowels for the bullet and then—ha ha ha!—sew you up again and send you back here as right as a trivet."

The doctor threw a peculiar glance over to Jimmy, and Jimmy understood.

"Ha ha ha!" croaked that worthy, with a lump in his throat. "As right as a trivet, as right as a trivet, ha ha ha!"

McGonigle, whose eyes were fixed on the ceiling, said feebly, "Doc, you better have another drink before you go. Have one yourself, Jimmy. You two mutts can't fool me with your 'ha ha ha.' This will be the last time I shall ever set 'em up to anybody on this earth. I'll have one, too, Jimmy."

Two days later word arrived at Midnapore that Peter J. had breathed his last on the operating table. The operation itself was declared to have been entirely successful, but it seems that Mr. McGonigle's heart, storm-beaten as it was by many a howling gale of booze, had failed to rise to the occasion when the supreme call was made upon it. The physicians in attendance were unanimously of the opinion that the rather unfortunate and awkward circumstance of his heart stopping beating had not a little to do with his death. In fact, on calm reflection, they were sure of it.

Before being taken to the operating room, Mr. McGonigle, on the advice of the sister in attendance, executed a will. He directed that the printing plant of the *Gazette,* on which he had made only two payments, should, in the event of his death, be shipped back to the Toronto Type Foundry. The bunch of mares, which only last year he was tried for stealing from the Bar U (being triumphantly acquitted on a technicality), he directed to be sold for the benefit of his wife, who also was left the house and lot in Midnapore. Some minor bequests followed. The will, which was quite brief, Mr. McGonigle not having much to leave, ended with the earnest and expressed wish that, should the worst happen, Jimmy would marry his widow, Mrs. McGonigle, after a decent interval of mourning. Say, a week.

Thus passed away a great spirit. The body was shipped back to Midnapore and interred in the little garden back of the printing office. The defunct Midnapore *Gazette* gave comfort, pleasure and instruction to many in its day, its contents being always of an edifying and uplifting nature. McGonigle now belongs to history and the *Gazette* is a thing of the past. Beware of spurious imitations. [19]

*

Mrs. Peter J. McGonigle of Midnapore, relic of the distinguished journalist who passed away six months ago, has given birth to a son with two heads. The youngster is quite lively and healthy and will no doubt prove a source of revenue to the sorrowing widow in years to come. This remarkable curiosity will be on exhibition at the Calgary exhibition in July. [20]

*

The carryings on at Midnapore one day last week were little short of disgraceful. We do not as a rule write unpleasant things about neighboring burgs, but in the interests of common decency and propriety this particular case cannot very well be overlooked. It is hard to understand why the mounted police have not made an investigation into the circumstances.

It appears that last Saturday a week ago, while a group of Midnapore citizens were quietly gathered round the bar of the local hotel discussing the pros and cons of the prohibition bill, a man named Crawley blew in and proceeded to set 'em up. This Crawley is a comparative stranger in the village and claims to hail from Lethbridge. Which is possibly true, seeing that the penitentiary is there. After setting 'em up, Crawley joined in the general discussion and showed no little vehemence in his denunciation of the prohibition bill. So earnest and excited did he become that he inadvertently set 'em up again, forgetting that he had already done so. Crawley may have his faults, but he appears to be no piker.

Mr. Bilkey, one of Midnapore's most prominent businessmen and a leader in church circles, took exception to Crawley's arguments and offered the statement that his books were full of outstanding accounts owed him by men who blew in all their money on whiskey and pin pool. He claimed that the elimination of hard liquor would revolutionize the social and business life of Midnapore, making for the higher life and bringing about a much-needed uplift, and was going on to expatiate about the beautiful, the true and the good, when Crawley hauled off and pasted him in the eye. A roughhouse followed.

When things had quieted down and harmony restored, the proprietor set 'em up and the discussion was resumed along more peaceful lines. It so happened that Al, the barkeeper, butted in with a touching reference to the late Peter J. McGonigle, editor of the once famous *Gazette*, adding his opinion that the bill would assuredly have met with Mr. McGonigle's most vigorous disapproval. This started the conversation on another tack.

Crawley, who claimed to have been an old side-kicker of McGonigle's in the early days when horse stealing was rife, thoroughly agreed with Al's remark and said that he was willing to bet fifty dollars that, owing to threatened prohibition, McGonigle's body, if exhumed, would be found to have turned over in its grave. Mr. Bilkey promptly took the bet and the money was put up with the proprietor.

This was harmless enough if the proceedings had stopped right there, but everybody seemed anxious to see the thing through. Two local bums were quickly requisitioned, loaded up with five or six drinks apiece and despatched with spades to the little garden behind the old newspaper office where Peter J. was buried.

Quite a number of wagers appear to have been made on the side, and before the diggers had half completed their work the whole male population of Midnapore had gathered round the grave. When the spades hit the lid of the coffin Crawley offered to double his wager with Mr. Bilkey, to which that gentleman was quite agreeable. A slight delay ensued until some one had procured a cold chisel with which to pry open the box, the interval being employed to register a few fresh bets at even money.

It did not take over two minutes to open the lid and there, sure enough, stretched out inside the casket was the illustrious editor *lying flat on his stomach.* It was obvious that he had turned over. Mr. Bilkey looked a trifle surprised, but expressed himself as satisfied, after which the crowd wended its way slowly back to the hotel. The paying over of the bets involved a great deal of drinking and long before supper time the village was in an uproar which lasted far into the night. This episode will be an eternal disgrace to the village of Midnapore.

It seems extraordinary that the authorities have not taken official cognizance of this unauthorized exhumation. How often, pray, is the body of McGonigle to be dug up to settle drunken wagers? The whole proceedings were illegal. Permission to exhume a corpse has first to be obtained from the attorney general's department at Edmonton, without which it becomes nothing better than a wanton act of gruesome ghouls. This man Crawley was the instigator and should be arrested forthwith. Where are our police? [21]

*

The woman that maketh a good pudding in silence is better than she who maketh a tart reply. (From the sayings of the late Peter J. McGonigle.) [22]

*

Mrs. Peter J. McGonigle, of Midnapore, who is to be one of the specially honored guests at the Old-Lady-Timers' Luncheon tendered by the Calgary Kiwanis Club, has gone into training for the event. Last week she assembled all the old dames in sight and gave them a blow-out at her home, delivering the speech she is to deliver at the Calgary luncheon and singing her chosen song, "The Land o' the Leal." It was a case of trying it out on the dog, but both speech and song went off so well that Mrs. McGonigle need have no nervous qualms with respect to the main event on the fourteenth. Her song should prove a howling success, anyhow.

For the information of those who have not resided in Calgary very long, we should mention that Mrs. McGonigle is the widow of the late Peter J. McGonigle, the drunken editor of the notorious Midnapore *Gazette* which flourished some eight or ten years ago and kept the countryside to the south of Calgary in a constant uproar. Whenever anybody sued McGonigle for libel he would load up with bad whiskey and go forth and beat the man up. Latterly he had very few libel suits. Curiously enough, the late Peter J. had a host of warm friends who deeply mourned his loss when he passed away at a Calgary hospital in a blaze of delirium tremens.

Mrs. McGonigle, who was deeply attached to her late husband, will give some tender reminiscences at the luncheon, telling of the exciting times when the *Gazette* was going strong and recounting anecdotes of the doings at the bar of the Nevermore Hotel. It is understood that Mr. Inverarity, of the Kiwanis Club, took a run down to Midnapore last Tuesday morning to try and prevail upon Mrs. McGonigle not to sing, but it appears that she insists upon doing so. Otherwise she says she won't come at all, which would make the luncheon look like the play of Hamlet with the role of Uncle Tom left out. By all means let her sing!
[23]

*

An extraordinary scene was witnessed at Midnapore last Tuesday when the body of Mr. Peter J. McGonigle, for many years editor of the Midnapore *Gazette*, was exhumed and finally resuscitated. It reads almost like fiction. Ever since the funeral some months ago the sorrowing widow has entertained grave doubts as to her husband being really dead, and had so expressed herself to friends. Mrs. McGonigle, for a squaw, was a widely read woman, having educated herself by constant and faithful perusal of the lurid colums of the *Gazette*. She had more than once read stories of people being buried alive when in a state of catalepsy, which, in its outward manifestations, closely resembles death. She finally got it into her head that Mr. McGonigle had been buried alive and might even yet, after the lapse of months, be alive. The suspicion gradually grew on her, and became an obsession.

Obtaining an order from a judge of the Supreme Court, Mrs.

McGonigle communicated with several well-known doctors and made arrangements for the coffin to be dug up from the vegetable patch in the little back garden behind the old printing office. Some cabbage and lettuce had been planted over the grave, but the bereft woman was ready for any kind of a sacrifice to have her dear departed back.

The weird scene around the lonely grave would have been more impressive had the sad work been performed in the dead of night, with the moon appearing fitfully from behind the flying clouds, but truth compels us to record that it was pulled off about three o'clock in the afternoon, the hour when the village of Midnapore is beginning to bowl up for the day. Two sturdy yeomen with spades went to work and soon had the dirt flying in all directions. Mrs. McGonigle, ever thoughtful of the comfort of others, had ordered Jimmy, the bartender at the Nevermore Hotel, to have a keg of beer on tap in a corner of the garden. Which, in a manner, accounted for the large crowd present.

It took fully an hour before the spades struck the lid of the coffin. Then excitement ran high. Mrs. McGonigle had to be restrained by physical force from jumping into the grave. At her earnest request one of the diggers rapped loudly on the coffin and cried, "Pete, ho Pete! Are you there?"

There being no response, the heartbroken widow burst into tears and wrung her hands. A sympathetic boozologist offered her a glass of beer, but she waved it aside. The physicians implored her to return to the house, but Mrs. McGonigle was obdurate, insisting on remaining to the end to watch the efforts at resuscitation. In a few minutes the coffin was gently raised to the surface and reverently borne into the old home. Jimmy, the grizzled bar veteran, held the crowd back and prevented all but the physicians from entering the house. Whereupon followed a general stampede back to the garden, there still being about half of the keg left.

The coffin having been placed on the kitchen table, it was the work of only a few minutes to pry open the lid. There, cold and pallid, lay the great editor.

Mrs. McGonigle peered into the face of her beloved Peter and allowed a tear to fall on his rugged features.

"He looks so natural," she sobbed. "He hasn't changed a bit. I'll bet a cookie he's alive and in a trance."

"We'll soon see," said one of the doctors, as he removed his coat and turned up his sleeves as if about to dress a hog. Bending over the coffin, he took hold of the corpse's nose between his thumb and finger and gave it a violent twist.

"Ah," said he, with an air of profound sagacity, "um-um-ha!"

"Cut that out," cried Mrs. McGonigle sharply. "Go ahead and don't look so wise."

"How very statuesque he looks," continued the doctor. And the other two doctors chimed in, "Don't he though! Just as if he had got off a drunk."

"What do you think about it, Doc?" asked the poor woman anxiously.

"Well, he looks to be as dead as a doornail, but, after all, he may be only in a condition of *flexibilitas cerca*. How long has he been dead?"

"About six months."

"Oh, well, there's no particular hurry. I should like to hold a professional consultation with my fellow physicians over at the Nevermore Hotel. We won't be over ten minutes."

"No, you don't!" shouted Mrs. McG. "You'll go over there and stay all afternoon and come back here soused. You stay right here and work on my man to bring him back to life."

"All right," said the doctor, "just as you say. I think, however, it is only fair to tell you that the *rigor mortis catalepticus*, when due to a lesion of the erebrum or the medulla spinalis, presents a heterogeneous concatenation of moribund possibilities which, if you haven't got jacks or better, should be passed up. Do you not agree with me, gentlemen?"

"Why, cert'nly!"

"But why don't you do something?" cried the distracted woman.

"Have patience, my good woman. You remember what Horace says, 'Patientia virtus est.' Now, if you will fill that tub with cold water we will give your deceased husband a shock that will bring him to in a jiffy if he's alive."

Poor Peter was thereupon undressed by the assistants and rudely dumped into a tub of cold water. He looked an odd figure sprawling in the tub, with his inanimate head dangling on his breast.

"Dead as a doornail," pronounced the doctor.

"Doornail," echoed the other two.

The body was taken out of the tub and dried, the assistants

with some difficulty dressing it again in the nice new suit in which it had been interred. Then it was returned to the coffin and the doctors, remarking that nothing more could be done, were about to proceed to their consultation at the Nevermore Hotel.

"Oh, do try something else. Don't go yet!" cried the frantic woman, laying a detaining hand on the doctor's arm. "You haven't tried sticking a pin in him yet."

"By George, that's so!" said the doctor. "Gimme a pin."

The pin produced, Peter was jabbed indiscriminately all over his anatomy.

"Now, ma'am, you see," observed the doctor, as he stuck the pin clear through Mr. McGonigle's nose, "if he were alive the motor centres would be excited by the reflex action. I have no hesitation in pronouncing your husband a gone coon."

The physicians then put on their hats and hied over to the Nevermore Hotel for the consultation, promising to call in before returning to town in their motor. They were soon engaged in the engrossing and popular pastime of throwing the bones to see who would pay for the first round.

Mrs. McGonigle sat by her dead. She studied the well-remembered features of Peter with searching scrutiny. Her head drooped in the attitude of thought, and she looked into nothingness for a long while. Suddenly she arose and went to the door. Giving a peculiar whistle she remained standing on the threshold looking toward the Nevermore Hotel. In a minute Jimmy, the bartender, issued from his den and looked across. A few high signs passed between the two, and Jimmy disappeared inside. A couple of minutes later he walked into Mrs. McGonigle's house and handed her a bottle of rye whiskey, returning quickly to the hotel.

"Those docs are lapping up the booze in great style," said he. "They're sports all right. I wish they'd stay a week. Old Peter still dead, eh?"

Left alone once more, Mrs. McGonigle looked curiously into her husband's face and then began hunting for a corkscrew. This found, she quickly opened the bottle and sat down beside the coffin. With great deliberation she filled a tumbler to the brim and held it beneath the nostrils of her Peter. Nothing happened for several minutes, while the woman could hear her own heart thumping. Then a faint, almost imperceptible flicker of the eyelids appeared. The glass almost slipped from the devoted woman's hand. The next perceptible movement was of the lips, which seemed to twitch slightly. Then the mouth slowly opened. Mrs. McGonigle inverted the glass, allowing half of it to trickle down his throat. A slight shudder and a faint exclamation which sounded not unlike "Wow!" and Mr. Peter J. McGonigle opened wide his eyes.

Mrs. McGonigle, being only a poor squaw, did not faint. On the contrary, she was instantly full of life and fire, and lost no time in tipping the remainder of the whiskey down her husband's dry gullet.

"Where am I?" asked Peter, staring in a dazed way up at the ceiling.

"Never mind where you are, Pete. You're all right, at home with me. I've a whole bottle of whiskey here for you and I'm going to give you another drink right now."

"But, say, look here—my, but I feel weak—I thought you hated to see me drink whiskey."

"Well, Pete, this is your birthday, and I want you to drink it."

"All right, my dear, let's have the hooker. Say, great Scott! What in thunder am I doing lying in a box? Has somebody been putting up a job? I wonder how I feel so weak. I never felt so queer before."

"Here, Pete, after you down this I'll tell you all about it."

Peter downed it and lay back to listen to the tale. Instead of being awed by his narrow escape from a frightful death, struggling for life in a coffin six feet underground, the great editor grinned broadly.

"You can't keep a good man down," said he. "And how is Jimmy?"

"Oh, Jimmy's fine. It was he who brought over the whiskey."

"Good old Jimmy! Let's have another horn."

When Mrs. McGonigle, however, started to relate the efforts of the doctors to bring him back to life, Peter got very hostile. He leapt from the coffin and shoved it off the table, kicking it all over the room.

"They stuck a pin through my nose, eh? The only nose I've got! And chucked me into a tub of water! By gum, wait till I see them!"

"They're over at the Nevermore Hotel, but don't do anything violent, Peter. They did their best and were very kind."

"Oh well, I'm glad to hear that. I'll go right over and thank them, but you better give me another drink—I feel pretty weak."

The three physicians were standing at the bar of the Nevermore Hotel, gaily flopping the dice. One of them had just thrown a pair of deuces and was being urbanely told by Jimmy not to despise them because they were small, when the door opened and in walked the late P. J. McGonigle.

"Have a drink, gentlemen," said he, walking calmly up to the bar.

"Pete—it's Pete—damned if it ain't Pete!" gasped Jimmy, upsetting several bottles on the shelf behind him and wagging his head stupidly from side to side.

The doctors wheeled around and gave Peter one look, just one. Then they jumped for the door, looking back fearfully over their shoulders as they darted through it. A loud honk proclaimed that they were off with a rush for the city, flying like so many Tam O'Shanters from a ghost.

"Jimmy, I want you to come over and have tea tonight with me and the missus."

"All right, Pete, I'll come," said Jimmy fair.tly, "anything you say, Pete."

"And in case the missus runs out of tea you better fetch over a case of extra-special."

"Extra-special goes," whispered Jimmy hoarsely, blinking his eyes and coughing nervously. "Is it really you, Pete, or am I only drunk and imagining it's you?"

"It's really me, Jimmy, returned from the grave. Let us both have a drink for old times' sake."

"I guess it's you, all right," said Jimmy, greatly relieved, as he placed the bottle and glasses on the bar. "I was afraid I had 'em again, that's all. Drink hearty!" [24]

Booze

Every man has his favorite bird. Ours is the bat. [1]

*

Perhaps whiskey really does improve with age, when it gets a chance. [2]

*

The *Eye Opener* has no defence to offer for the booze traffic. It is a bad business; none worse. We've been there. Nobody can tell us anything about it that we don't already know and our frank opinion is that the complete abolition of strong drink would solve the problem of the world's happiness. [3]

*

Some men are hard drinkers, but others find it absurdly easy. [4]

*

Society Note— Mr. Thos. B. McGuigan is suffering from a severe attack of delirium tremens. [5]

*

The genial traveller for Seagram's whiskey concern was in Calgary this week hustling up business for the firm. He presented the newspapers and his customers with a large colored picture of Joe Seagram's race horses. The *Eye Opener* was favored with one of those pictures, enclosed in a $7.50 frame, on the distinct understanding that we were to give Seagram a write-up. We shall do so.

We consider Seagram's whiskey to rank very high amongst the numerous poisons now on the market. Not that it is any worse than other whiskeys, but, being the most drank, it creates more havoc throughout the country. It has put more men in their graves than a corps of census sharps could enumerate in a year and has put thousands upon thousands of good men on the hog. Seagram's wealth is built on the folly of others and each of his race horses represents a hundred or more wretches who have died of delirium tremens brought on by mopping up an overplus of his rotgut. We have no more respect for a man in Joe Seagram's business than we have for Radcliffe or the murderers whom Radcliffe hangs. They are all in the killing business. Seagram's race horses and his wealth cut no figure in our eyes. We have helped him buy too many of his flyers and so has almost every other d——d fool of our acquaintance. [6]

*

Whiskey is all right in its place, but its place is in hell. The liquor traffic hasn't one leg to stand on. [7]

*

The latest stunt is fountain pens filled with whiskey. We have just bought a dozen and expect to do much spirited writing during the coming year. [8]

*

Counsel—Was the prisoner sober?
Witness—No, sir; he was as drunk as a judge.
The judge—You mean as drunk as a lord.
Witness—Yes, my lord. [9]

*

We are sometimes upbraided for featuring booze and the bar in these columns. What would you have us write about? We have to write about what goes on around us and it cannot be disputed that the bar is the centre of social life in small western burgs. There is no town society in the usual acceptation of the term. It is a very extraordinary occasion when a High River young man finds himself sitting in the parlor of a private home talking to the ladies. He is never asked. There is infinitely more hospitality out in the country than there is in the town. Hence the bar becomes perforce the social centre, and there you are, preachers to the contrary notwithstanding.

The bar is indeed a social necessity in western towns. At any rate, the bar is there and the necessity too. Man is a social animal, whether he lives in a Pat Burns baronial castle or batches in a shack twenty miles from town. But the baronial castle has resources; the shack has not. It is a good place to get away from as frequently as possible. The bar is bright and cheery and always on the spot and also touches the spot. The man craving human companionship can always find some of the gang there and the throb of a human heart. He finds, too, in the bartender one who understands his wants and laughs at his jokes. Oh yes, the bar's all right. [10]

*

This report that whiskey drinking is declining in Calgary will cause no surprise. Most of the politicians are out of town telling the festive farmer which way to vote. [11]

*

We take this opportunity of informing numerous friends and admirers who make a point of visiting our place of business when, by some special benignity on the part of Dame Fortune, a flask has been secured by the management, that there are two flasks. One contains the real stuff. The other consists of a blend of acidulated prussic acid and concentrated lye, flavored with just enough whiskey to fool a stranger. It is almost impossible to tell the two flasks apart. Visitors, therefore, during our absence, are implored to leave our whiskey alone. [12]

*

Daily health hint: cut out the booze. [13]

*

You cannot wet your whistle with the whiskey that is past. [14]

*

Jan. 1 : "No thanks, old man, no more booze in mine. I'm off it for good this time, that's straight."

Jan. 2 : "No siree, not on your life. What? Not at all—I don't mind going in and having a cigar with you."

Jan. 3 : "Yes, I've cut out whiskey altogether. It was getting the better of me. A man can't attend to business and drink whiskey, that's one thing sure. Fred, gimme some soda with a touch of John Bull bitters in it."

Jan. 4 : "Aw well, I guess a little claret won't do me any harm. Got any good claret?"

Jan. 5 : Sunday. Safe so far.

Jan. 6 : "Fred, gimme a poney of beer—just a poney. I was eating some salt herring today, etc. etc."

Jan. 7 : "Say, don't put so much froth on that beer. Now shove in a little gin and make a dog's nose of it. Here's how!"

Jan. 8 : "And you call this seven-year-old, eh? It's the awfulest rotgut ever I swallowed. However, here's looking at you."

Jan. 9 : (Morning)—"Make me a Collins."

(Night)—"Say, thish tempransh bishnesh izzalldamnonsense, don't you think? What? Eh? Ain't that right? Course thazzright. Lezzavanother and then we'll call a hack—we'll call-ahack—ain't that right? Betyerlife thazzright!" [15]

*

We held the bottle up and took
A brief and scrutinizing look,
And then we put the thing away
And muttered hoarsely "Not today." [16]

*

Soaking the brain in alcohol does not preserve the mind [17]

*

Our views on the subject of prohibition have undergone considerable change since the memorable days when we worked so hard in favor of it. The whole thing has proved a farce. It may be true enough that the elimination of the bar has brought good results by removing temptation from the path of wage earners with families, who had no moral right to divert their money from proper domestic channels; but in other circles, the damage wrought by so-called prohibition has been something fierce.

We have kept hammering away at those booze parties in the home for a long time now, with no tangible results outside of an occasional knowing wink and smile from the cognoscenti. Everybody knows of the disgraceful orgies that are pulled off nightly in private homes along our quiet avenues which look so innocent, childlike and bland during the day. They form a favorite subject of cynical conversation amongst men during office hours. If the women who participate in these debauches only knew how lightly their names are bandied about amongst the men downtown, they would surely pause and do some calm reflecting for their own sakes.

We do not intend in this issue to refer at length—though many have asked us to do so—to the recent notorious "party" which wound up in one of the saddest tragedies that has yet befallen a Calgary home. Silence is the most eloquent comment on this sickening affair.

The curse of the whole thing—and most men will bear us out in this—is that perfectly decent and respectable women get lured to these parties without knowing in advance what kind of a jackpot they are getting themselves into. They don't realize until it is too late that they shouldn't be there at all, that it is no place for them. It is to be hoped that the case referred to in the preceding paragraph will be a lesson to lots of good women in this city, who quite naturally enough enjoy a bit of fun once in a while, to be mighty careful of the class of bogus-society hoodlums who invite them out to their parties.

God knows, we should be the last one to talk about other people drinking. Our own reputation as a booze artist used to be second to none, but such drinking as we did was always amongst men. In twenty years' residence in Calgary we have never had a drink in a private house, nor have we ever been to one of those drunken parties in the home that we hear so much about. In the hook shops across the river in the old days there was not as much drank in two nights as there is in one night at one of these parties today. While it was part of the duty of the girls to make the men buy as much booze as possible, for the benefit of the house, they themselves rarely got under the influence of liquor. The landladies would not stand for that. One point in favor of the hook shops was that no decent women were present to be dragged down and put on the bum with bad whiskey. For which reason we take it that the much maligned old hook shop was the more respectable of the two.

The explanation of a portion of the above paragraph may perhaps be found in the fact that across the river they only gave you ponies of beer and mere thimblefuls of whiskey, and the champagne only looked like champagne—they called it "wine." The chaps who went over there usually had a good snootful before starting, so did not suffer. The uplifters could greatly improve the morals of this city if they would allow some of these institutions to reopen. It is the uplifters themselves who are responsible for the breaking down of the social fabric with respect to morals in general. No one who has the inside track of what is going on will deny this. [18]

*

There is no use trying to be funny about prohibition. To the wets there is nothing funny about the dry situation and the prohibitionists never see any humor in anything. [19]

*

Bartender (calling down cellar)—"Boss, is Murphy good for a drink?"
Voice—"Has he had it?"
Bartender—"He has."
Voice—"He is." [20]

*

Society Note— Mr. and Mrs. Thos. B. Squirrelle gave an informal drunk at their charming residence in Elbow Park last Tuesday evening. They called it a party. It was some party. [21]

*

Liquor is the nation's worst enemy. It degrades family life, politics and business, causes poverty, insanity and death. It is worse than war and pestilence. It is the crime of crimes. It is the source of three-fourths the crime, and, of course, it takes three-fourths of the taxes to care for the criminals, and to license this incarnate fiend of hell is poor business. [22]

*

Joy is the peculiar feeling experienced by a man after a drunk when he counts his money and discovers that he has all the money he thought he had and a few dollars more. [23]

*

The Moral and Social League of Alberta, alias the Drys, meet at Paget Hall next week for their annual celebration of victory. No, that's wrong. We take it back. The Drys may win a victory but they cannot celebrate it. Their kind of victory destroys the means of celebration. [24]

*

A drink in the hand is worth two in the bottle. [25]

*

Some remark we made in a previous issue was doubtless the cause of a lady jokingly asking us the other day what it felt like to have the jim-jams. We never had 'em. People who have had 'em say nothing about it. But we can tell her about a fellow up in Westaskiwin when Jerry was running the Driard and kept in his backyard a collection of animals in a pen, two pet bears, a badger and some birds. This chap was standing one day in front of the hotel gazing over towards the elevator.

"What are you rubbering at," we asked.

"I'm just watching the animals."

"But they're round in the backyard."

"Not mine," he said, drawing his hand over his eyes. [26]

*

When one is driven to drink he usually has to walk back. [27]

*

It is a curious fact that as soon as a man has made up his mind, or has been induced by his friends, to take the jag cure, he at once proceeds to go off on a terrific bat. He makes a thorough and complete job of it, finally being packed off to the jag-cureatorium in horrible shape. The advanced pupils size him up from the windows as he stumbles out of the rig, but beyond a good-natured remark or two about the dimensions of his jag, make no comment. That is an unwritten law at those places and a very good law too. Talk about your etiquette! We have never been inside one of those institutions, but have heard all about them from those who have. Being a lifelong teetotaller— what ho! bartender. Just fill those up again. [28]

*

Health Hint— When suffering from violent toothache in a hollow tooth, fill the cavity with whiskey and hold there for thirty seconds with your head cocked to one side. Swallow whiskey and refill cavity. Repeat this experiment until you don't give a damn whether you have a toothache or not. [29]

*

Society Note— A delightful tea boozant was given by Mrs. Scufflechopper at her charming residence on Seventeenth Avenue West. The absence of any signs of tea did not detract from the enjoyment of this recherche function and the guests were kept delightfully busy telling each other that they could take a drink or leave it alone. How they all got home, God knows. [30]

*

Booze is a bad thing when it is aboozed. Used in small quantities it is harmless enough. The difficulty lies in using it in small quantities. With those who have a constitutional tendency towards liquor one drink means two, and two means a drunk. Therefore those who, as is often the case, have hereditary tendencies in this direction should abstain altogether. The poisonous stuff will catch them napping at last.

One thing our benevolent government might do is this. They should make the inspectors do a little more to earn their salaries. It should be part of their duties to appear unexpectedly at the various hotels in their district and make a thorough test of the spirituous liquors sold over the bar. This, I gamble, would bring forth some startling revelations. Barney Cooper's first official test of bulk whiskey would read "Muriatic acid one quarter, alcohol one eight, fusel oil one eight, fish-hooks one quarter, hokey pokey one eight, strychnine one eight." Think of pouring that mixture down your epiglottis fifteen or twenty times in a day, trying to make yourself believe that you are having a good time. It is a fool's paradise.

The result? Sore heads, shattered nerves, empty pockets, and worst of all, the loss of the friendship and respect of good men and women. It is the vendor of the booze that wears the diamonds. Once in the maelstrom it is hard to get out, for there is no gainsaying that the booze-life has its fascinations. One hears bright conversations at the bar and some very pretty wit is occasionally slung around. Things are looked at from the roseate point of view. They remain roseate till the following morning, when it takes three or four fish-hook cocktails to get back to par. This is the thorn. Better to eschew the beastly stuff altogether. Don't do as I do; do as I tell you.

I do not believe in that most impracticable piece of legislative nonsense that goes by the name of prohibition. Where prohibition exists the people drink spirits almost exclusively, because it is easier handled by the vendors. Those who formerly drank light lager have to slop up some villainous concoction which they regard as sweet because it is stolen fruit. Make the procuring of booze as easy as possible and there will be less booze drunk. Give every responsible man who has a hotel which complies with the statute a license. The revenues will be increased without any additional drunkenness. A man has only so much to spend on booze anyhow and will spend that much if there are one or twenty bars in his town.

My advice to beginners is to leave it alone altogether, even beer and light wines. In the case of socially inclined young men indulgence in these harmless beverages too often degenerates into a craving for the fish-hooks. The whole traffic only breeds sorrow and ought to be sidestepped.

Temperance is corporal piety. It is the preservation of divine order in the body and diffuses through its innermost recesses a healthful spirit which has no fish-hooks in it. [31]

*

Society Note— John M. Solly has been confined to his house in Elbow Park with delirium tremens for the past few days. His physician states that he has passed the crisis and will soon be around again shaking hands with old friends. [32]

*

The water wagon is certainly a more dangerous vehicle than the automobile. At least more people fall off it. [33]

*

We are sorry, indeed it pains us, to have to lay a complaint against such a well-known hostelry as the Yale, but we are of the opinion that their Scotch contains just a trifle too much sulphuric acid and not enough bluestone. [34]

*

Alcoholism is a disease which no politician or preacher on earth can handle. There are only three people who can—doctors, snake charmers and the cheerful boozers, the latter especially. [35]

*

No power on earth can keep a man from "rustling a bottle" if he is bent on getting it. This booze business is essentially a business of mystery. Booze is always to be had. Prohibition acts may be enforced with a direct form of penalties, distilleries may be shut down and all the whiskey in the dominion confiscated and poured into the rivers, so that not a single drop apparently remains; but do you suppose this would worry your indomitable booze artist? Not a bit of it. As a magician conjures an article from the empty air, so does a drouthy boozer cause a bottle to appear from nowhere in the critical hour of over-mastering thirst.

There is just one suggestion in connection with bootlegging in Calgary which we should like to offer to the magistrate and the chief. It is this: that all bottles or flasks of whiskey sold by bootleggers (at $6 per) which are seized by the police, should be analyzed by the city chemist. Some of this stuff is made by the bootleggers themselves and is sufficiently poisonous to endanger life. Indeed, we have a shrewd suspicion that at least one very recent death in the city was directly attributable to this cause.

We know a chap, long used to his horn, who not so long ago took a couple of drinks out of a bootleg bottle and was confined to his bed for a week. He nearly died. Another man told us of getting a bottle from a bootlegger on Ninth Avenue from which on being opened there issued a bluish gas. What would have happened to him had he taken a snort, he hated to think. It cost him six bones. [36]

*

Gallons of trouble can come out of a pint flask. [37]

*

Yes, we quite agree with you. Whiskey floats more troubles than it drowns. [38]

*

Man is made of dust—which explains why some men are always dry. [39]

*

The more we think of it, the more we are convinced away in the back of our noodle, that this prohibition bill is going to be defeated. As a bill it is a weird and most grotesque affair and the men supposed to be in charge of its wild career are as little children. But, as we said before, we shall support the bill on the off chance of ridding the country of this damned whiskey which has put so many of us on the bum. [40]

*

The Visitor (cautiously)—"Does your husband periodically —er—suffer from an excess of spirituous—er—liquids?"
The Visited—"Ow's that, ma'am?"
The Visitor—"Does your husband permit his appetite for alcoholic beverages to cloud his intellect?"
The Visited—"I don't seem to foller you, ma'am. Can't you say it a bit slower?"
The Visitor—"Does your husband drink regularly?"
The Visited (proudly)—"Reg'lar as clockwork, ma'am, an' twice a week. When he comes 'ome drunk I allus knows it's either a Chewsday or a Saturday." [41]

*

Whiskey is a wonderful drink it is said. It starts for the stomach and goes for the head. [42]

*

After taking a few swallows of rye a man begins to feel his oats. [43]

SEVEN

The Sexes

Woman's inhumanity to man makes countless lawyers happy. [1]

*

The man who hesitates is lost. So is the woman who doesn't. [2]

*

If only men could read women's thoughts they would take many more risks than they do. [3]

*

Call a girl a chick and she smiles; call a woman a hen and she howls. Call a young woman a witch and she is pleased; call an old woman a witch and she is indignant. Call a girl a kitten and she rather likes it; call a woman a cat and she hates you. Women are queer.

If you call a man a gay dog it will flatter him; call him a pup, a hound, or a cur and he will try to alter the map of your face. He doesn't mind being called a bull or a bear, yet he will object to being mentioned as a calf or a cub. Men are queer, too. [4]

*

You hear a lot about "blushing brides," but did you ever see one? [5]

*

A married man never has to waste any time in making up his mind. [6]

*

Mrs. Nellie McClung once took occasion to roast the men for selecting the pretty girls for their wives and leaving the homely ones severely alone. She complained because the preference was for the good-looking girl rather than the intelligent. This would seem to imply that good-lookers are not intelligent, which is manifestly unjust. Their intelligence is surely proven by their singular aptitude for selecting rich husbands who can give them an attractive home in the city, where the movies are, with "somebody else" to wash the dishes and clean up. The pretty girls are quite right to capitalize on their good looks. As regards the men, their choice of a wife is purely one of sex attraction, which puts the homely ones at a disadvantage. And there you are, Nellie McClung or no Nellie McClung.

But will Mrs. McClung kindly explain how it is that when a man marries a nice attractive young lady under the delusion that she will always remain that way, she not infrequently develops into a truculent harpy? [7]

*

Woman may be the weaker vessel, but it's generally the man who goes broke. [8]

*

A girl's kisses are like pickles in a bottle—the first are hard to get, but the rest come easy. [9]

*

The one thing a woman can't understand is how a man can open a telegram without getting nervous. [10]

*

With all their efforts to reform people not so righteous as themselves, the social reformers have never yet made any serious attempt to have a law enacted which will bring to book the man who accomplishes the ruin of a young girl. This seems to be beyond the scope of the reformer's cudgel. A ruined girl has absolutely no protection from the law. She can hale her betrayer into court, but can never make her case stick on account of lack of corroborative evidence. The man's denial is as good as her assertion. And the lawyers and the policemen shrug their shoulders and say to one another that in any case she must have given him encouragement or he wouldn't have done it. And yet this is where the whole sorry business starts.

There must always be a certain percentage of loose women, professionals, floating around in every city. This may as well be admitted first as last. Everybody knows it. Which being the case, it would be to the benefit of society at large if these genial floosies were located in a designated area where they would be subject to medical and police supervision.

The consequences resulting from the dual reform, prohibition and the abolishing of segregated areas, is absolutely appalling. Otherwise law-abiding, decent citizens have become semi-criminal whiskey chasers; respectable women and girls have started the drink game—with what results, time will tell—and the moderate man cannot get his little glass of beer when he wants it. The effect of the other reform mentioned is that men just have to "pick it up" on the street or in blocks, and the amount of ingenuity expended on "picking it up" is astonishing. You'd be surprised. You would, for a fact. Some men chase everything in sight. In this game much smooth work is pulled off, which used to be quite unnecessary in the good old days when all you had to do was "call a hack."

Then there is the type of man, usually married, who, in bygone days never failed to make his occasional trip "across the river" for a touch of high life, but who now specializes in young married women. Afraid of catching something by promiscuously "picking it up" here and there, he deliberately sets about debauching somebody else's wife. He argues to himself that she is bound to be clean and it won't cost him anything. A few "parties," plenty of booze and lo! the trick is done.

Apropos of which, the big hotels that have been built of recent years in our larger cities are (in some cases) very dens of iniquity. They are responsible for much disgraceful goings-on and one of these days when we are in an especially ill humor we shall make some exposures that will create an uproar in the menagerie.

The social reformers have succeeded in forcing upon us an unreal and quite unnatural mode of existence, entirely different from anything we have been accustomed to. By making beer difficult to get, they have made a nation of whiskey guzzlers; by abolishing "the houses," they have made chippy-chasers, girl-ruiners, home-wreckers and adulterers out of pretty decent chaps. We admit that this is not what the reformers intended should happen, but facts are facts. [11]

*

When a gallant man is asked to guess a woman's age, he first makes a silent guess and then knocks off one-third. [12]

*

Anxious correspondent inquires: "Is it proper for a young lady of seventeen to go walking after dark with a young gentleman with no chaperone?"

Yes, perfectly proper, if you keep walking. [13]

*

It's easy for a woman to fool a man who thinks he can't be fooled. What? [14]

*

Answers to Inquiries

"I have only been married a month and I find my husband lied to me. He told me he was well off.—Georgina."

Are you sure he was single when he married you? If so, he was probably telling the truth. Call again, Georgina.

"How many idiots are there in this town?—Calgarian."

We forget the exact number of aldermen just now. Phone the city clerk.

"How do you make a lemon tart?—Angelina."

They are already made tart, Angelina. Ask us something difficult.

"Will you give me a verse to put in my album? Something sentimental.—Maude."

Certainly.

Lives of easy marks remind us
    We can make existence pay;

Let us then be up and doing
   Every stiff that comes our way.

If this isn't sentimental enough, Maude, let us know and we shall take another whack at it.

"Can you explain why it is a dog is such a faithful friend?— Subscriber."

Oh, yes. It is because he never knows when you're broke and don't give a damn. [15]

*

Honest men are as scarce as silent women. [16]

*

Our talented and ready-witted fellow citizen, George Lang, was present at a swell society ball not so long ago, and, while conversing with a lady, noticed a dame go waltzing by attired in a very décolleté costume. The lady he was chatting with caught a glimpse of the décolleté costume also, for she immediately exclaimed:
"Oh, my! Did you ever see anything like that!"
"No," said George, gravely, "not since I was a baby." [17]

*

Men are brave and all that, but when one of them gets sick he grunts twice as much as a sick woman. [18]

*

"So you deceived your husband," said the judge gravely.
"On the contrary, my lord, he deceived me. He said he was going out of town and he didn't." [19]

*

Men are said to be quite as much afflicted with curiosity as women are supposed to be. We can well believe this. [20]

*

Too much distance between husband and wife may result in other enchantments. (This is a deep one.) [21]

*

A man likes a good cook *before* dinner. But after he has eaten his tomato soup he doesn't want a hard-working woman to come around him, tired out, with her hair in a tangle and her eyes and face red from peeling onions and standing over a hot fire. He wants some light, fluffy creature, with the chiffon and lace and all the rest of it, who doesn't know an eggbeater from a carpet sweeper. [22]

*

Widows are successful in handling men because they know exactly what not to do. [23]

*

A woman entered a lawyer's office and said she wanted to get a divorce.
"On what grounds?" asked the lawyer.
"I don't think he is true to me."
"But that is too vague and general a charge. Have you nothing specific against him?"
"Well, I have every reason to believe that he is not the father of my last child." [24]

*

The only thing that beats a good wife is a bad husband. [25]

*

Society Note— The engagement is announced of Miss Josie Sweeney to Mr. James Eccles, the popular undertaker. Mr. Eccles is one of our most notable embalmers and has a bright future before him. His corpses are invariably fresh and lifelike, and always attract a crowd in front of his show windows. [26]

*

It is easy for a man to manage his wife. All he has to do is to follow her instructions. [27]

*

They had quarrelled bitterly and for a month not a word passed between them. Then the girl wrote:
"Kindly return my photograph. I gave it to you in a moment of girlish folly, and now regret that I was so thoughtless in such matters."

She imagined that to part with her photograph would be so painful that the young man would repent and return to her; but she got a severe shock when a bulky parcel arrived in which was a note.

"I regret," it ran, "that at this late date I am unable to pick out your photograph. However, I send you my entire collection and would request that you pick out your own and return the rest to me express at my expense." [28]

*

Twin beds are the abomination of modern civilization. As a young bride explained, they are neither comfortable for two nor satisfactory for one. [29]

*

"Are you sending your wife to Banff this summer?"

"I'm not," replied the man. "If my wife is to break the seventh commandment, she'll have to break it with her own husband this summer." [30]

*

A man's deafness has reached the limit when he can no longer hear a noise like a skirt. [31]

*

A woman seems to think she is a dutiful wife if she pretends to keep on loving her husband after she knows she doesn't. [32]

*

His fellow clerks gathered around him when the news became public property and extended congratulations. "But," said one man, "I understand the girl you're engaged to is a twin. How do you tell the difference between her and her sister?"

"Well, it's a mighty nice family," said the lucky man, "and I don't bother very much." [33]

*

A man always shuts the door when about to be told a secret, but a woman opens it to see whether anyone outside is listening. [34]

*

Why go to California or Victoria summer resorts to get into trouble with a pretty woman? Patronize home industries. [35]

*

Some girls are very touchy. A young chap amused himself by throwing the sun's rays from a mirror into the bedroom window of a young lady who lived opposite, and she promptly brought an action against him for casting reflections on her private life. [36]

*

"Good morning, Mrs. Brown. Did you take your husband's temperature as I told you to?"

"Yes, Doctor. I borrowed a barometer off a neighbor and put it on his chest, and it said, 'Very dry,' so I gave him a pint o' beer and he's gone off to work." [37]

*

When a man tells a joke to half a dozen women and they all laugh but one, that one is his wife. [38]

*

Men and women have little or nothing in common unless they happen to be in love. For company, for straight conversation, for business, for sport, a man would much rather be with men. [39]

*

Few bachelors are as gay as they want women to think they are. [40]

*

Society Note— Mr. J. P. Scufflepanky, the talented plumber, who resides on Sixth Avenue East, has applied to the Supreme Court to have his marriage annulled on the ground that he was crazy at the time the happy event was pulled off. This is pretty tough on Mrs. Scufflepanky, but she certainly is a horrible looking old dame with a mean, evil disposition. Otherwise she is all right. [41]

*

She frowned on him and called him Mr.
Because in fun he went and Kr.
So out of spite the next good night
The naughty Mr. Kr. Sr. [42]

*

A girl may be able to pose as an angel during courtship, but after marriage she sheds her wings. [43]

*

"Do you think a husband and wife can get along happily together?"
"Yes, if they're not married to each other." [44]

*

The woman with the ideal husband very likely wishes she had some other kind. [45]

*

Society Note— E. B. McWhirrie, the charming poker player, gave an "at home" last Wednesday evening to a number of his friends. The host was attired in a chic pair of striped pants and presided at the table in sleeves à la shirt. The decorations involved a pretty color scheme of red, white and blue discs made from celluloid and circular in shape. A delightful evening was spent. Also considerable money. [46]

*

When we hear a woman say that all men are alike we wonder how she found it out. [47]

*

"Teacher, can I be excused for tomorrow?"
"What for?"
"Sister's getting married and she wants me to stay home and mind her baby."
"Why, sure, sure!" [48]

EIGHT

The English

An awful lot of swell Britishers have come across the pond to visit western Canada. We do not know what designs they have on the West, but have a dark suspicion that they intend starting a Belgian hare ranch somewhere. Nobody has started a Belgian hare ranch for some time now. [1]

*

What we need this spring is the advent in our midst of a few healthy young remittance men, armed with fat drafts which they could deposit in our new bank, and cheque out as fast as the exigencies of the local hotelkeepers demand. This would be fast indeed. Did they desire to learn farming they could be shown, as a starter, the great benefit conferred on man through the raising of farinaceous grains. Without leaving the hotel they could study the precious products manufactured from barley, corn and rye, thus becoming imbued with a sense of the nobility and dignity of agriculture as a pursuit.

Our friend the remittance man has had his uses, as many in Calgary, well-off today, can testify. These young gentlemen are deported usually for some small lapse from grace which in the North-West would not afford gossip for ten minutes. The unpardonable sin of preferring a pretty barmaid's society to that of a bespectacled aunt, coupled with a tendency to staying out all night, has been the direct means of enriching our colonies with men and money. They are sent out to be away from fast company, and it is indeed a refreshing sight to watch them making a new start in life amid the ennobling surroundings of the countless drunkeries which, for single men, form the centre of social life in North-West villages.

The day comes, a few months after arrival, when the teller at the bank looks grimly through the little window and tells the youth that his funds are exhausted. Whereupon the youth concocts an ingenious letter home and awaits developments. This, of course, is in the case of the chap who has got his money in a chunk before leaving home.

I remember a chap who had pestered his father and mother nearly to death writing home from some obscure village for more money. Finally the long-suffering parents received an unusually cheerful letter from their son, stating that he had at last succeeded in procuring an appointment with the CPR. He said that he travelled on a special car and lived in the same house with his superior. In order to uphold the dignity of the position he would need at least fifty pounds until he got thoroughly established. This letter brought joy to the household. Out came the money with a letter full of congratulations and inquiries as to how long it would be before the course of promotion made him president of the road.

Needless to say, the appointment was only one tamping ties on the section, the special car was the hand car, and his superior's residence the section house. But the equivoque did good all round. It gladdened the hearts of the dear ones at home and enabled his nibs to quit the section right away and go off on a ta-rara.

What strikes the dullest of remittance men is the extraordinary influence acquired and duly wielded over him by the local hotelkeepers, who with infinite art jolly him along as long as his remittance lasts, give him a job sawing wood when he is busted, and imperceptibly manoeuvre him back into the fold at the first rumor of the arrival of another wad.

There is another class of remittance man who is anxious to keep steady and willing to work. But there are pitfalls for him too. Some wily gentleman—usually a quiet man who does not drink at all—gets him into a business venture, explaining that his experience together with the young gentleman's capital will work to their mutual advantage. The result is catastrophic as usual.

I cannot say that Wetaskiwin has had any remittance men

—at least I never met with what one could call a genuine remittance man here. The places I have in mind are mainly Calgary, Innisfail (that was a hummer some years ago), Strathcona and Edmonton. Lacombe also had her slice.

Dear England, send us out some golden specimens! Send 'em all to Wetaskiwin. Doting parents, do not fire them all out to South Africa to be shot. Send them to us and we will see that they get half-shot, a condition which, if kept up with due persistence, will put them out of your way for ever, if that is all you want. [2]

*

Johnnie Hamilton, the old-time Calgary horseman, has a great stock of yarns about remittance men of the early days, though some of them are too good to be true. Whenever Johnnie and the late Paddy Nolan got together and ran out of true stories about these young English bloods, they proceeded to make up new ones or add fresh bits to the old ones. So that when you hear a funny story along this line you cannot really depend upon the incident ever having happened at all.

However, we will tell you a true one that happened down near High River, where, ladies and gents, the *Eye Opener* first saw the light. It will be vouched for by any of the old-time ranchers of that district.

Jimmy Rossiter was the young Englishman's name. His parents unexpectedly came out from the old country to see how he was getting along, and Jimmy knew nothing about their coming until a telegram arrived saying they were in Calgary and would be down the following day. Luckily, they could only stay over the one day, being en route to California. This placed James in a tight box.

The money this rather wild young scion of an aristocratic house had brought out with him first had long since frittered away, and the numerous remittances received for purchasing additional stock, buying mythical prize bulls, improving his western home and investing in wonderful real estate snaps, were promptly rung into hotel cash registers as fast as they came to hand. He was busted flatter than a pancake, with only a 12' x 14' shack and a cayuse or two to show for it all. The only stock he had was a stock of empty bottles and flasks strewn in every direction round the shack.

But Jimmy was pretty fly. He was not going to be flagged if he knew it. In this apparent dilemma he saw brilliant possibilities for shaking down the guv'nor for more dough. Riding over to a certain well-known ranch he tackled the wealthy owner, whom we may call Fred Manson, a crony of his.

"I say, Fred," said he, "would you mind lending me your ranch for tomorrow?"

"Not much!"

"Look here, old chap, the guv'nor and the mater will be here on tomorrow's train for the day, the day only, mind you, and I really must have your ranch, old top."

"Oh—ah—I see!" cried the genial Fred, a great light breaking on him. "Of course you can have the place, old man. Leave everything to me! I'll be your foreman, Jimmy, and we'll put the boys next. What's more, I'll drive down myself to meet them and you can order me about in great shape. I suppose you intend working the guv'nor for some more dough?"

"Certainly, old chap! What are guv'nors for?"

"That's business. Now you scuttle home and hunt up all your family photos and stick 'em up here in odd corners and I'll take down that picture of "The Nymphs and Venus at the Bath." If you've still got the Bible your mother gave you, fetch it over and lay it open at the Gospel of St. John on the little table, with the leaf turned down."

"You're the stuff, Fred," said the grateful Jimmy.

The following morning an elderly lady and gentleman of distinguished mien got off the train at High River and were courteously approached by Mr. Manson.

"So you are my son's coachman?" remarked the old lady with a generous smile. "I understand his estate is a few miles from here. What a dreadful-looking town!"

When they drove up to the ranch Jimmy was busily engaged issuing orders to a couple of cowpunchers in a very loud voice, feigning to be unaware of their approach.

"Well, well, well!" cried Jimmy in a surprised tone. "Here you are at last! Welcome to my humble home!"

"What a delightful spot!" exclaimed the enchanted mamma.

"I am very gratified, my boy," said the old gentleman, looking around, "to see that you have made such excellent use of the funds placed at your disposal."

"I've not done so badly, have I?" returned the young reprobate.

"But come away in and we'll have a cup of tea. Sorry I haven't any wine to offer you, as we are all teetotallers on my ranch. I never allow any drinking here, mater."

"How you have changed, James! But, dear me, what is the matter with the coachman? He is coughing and choking in a most distressing fashion."

"Oh, he's all right, mater. He is a faithful servant and has doubtless contracted a chill while waiting for your train."

"Poor fellow, I must give him a sixpence. Why, my darling boy, if this isn't the very Bible I gave you at parting, lying open on the table! How good of you to read it for my sake!"

"Yes, Mother, I find it a great support through life. We hold family worship here every night before retiring, and I pray for guidance for myself and my poor ignorant cowboys."

"By the way, James," asked the old lady suddenly, "what is a jaggon?"

"A what, mother?"

"A jaggon. I overheard one of your men say that it was a wonder you hadn't a jaggon."

"Oh, yes, ha, ha! A jaggon is a white shirt. The worthy creatures are no doubt wondering why I did not don a white shirt in your honor."

"What delightful ways you men have out west, to be sure! Now, there is your coachman. Before leaving the little town I noticed he received ever so many invitations to join some shooting party, but he declined them all."

"Shooting party? There's nothing to shoot this time of year, Mother."

"Well, everybody seemed to be wanting him to come and have a shot. I suppose he is an expert marksman."

"Oh, so-so, so-so."

"Yes, my dear boy," said the old gentlemen shortly before leaving, "you have exceeded my fondest expectations, you have done splendidly and displayed remarkable business acumen for one so young. Here is my cheque for another £500 and when you are ready to start that other project of yours for raising gophers, let me know and perhaps I may be of some assistance in furthering the enterprise. There is the carriage. Go and bid your mother goodbye, James. No, don't come and see us off. I know how busy you must be. We return home through the States. Write regularly, James, and God bless you!"

There was a hot time in the old town that night. Jimmy was in great form. He settled up an old bar bill as long as your arm and wept down the neck of the hotel proprietor as he assured that worthy that he was the "finesh ol' shap in Alberra." And where was Fred? Oh, he was there, too. [3]

*

Many readers of our *Summer Annual* seem to doubt the truth of that story of a young Englishman borrowing a neighbor's ranch for a day to palm off as his own, when his father and mother came out from England to pay him a brief visit. Perhaps we had to embellish the details a trifle, but in the main it was true and actually occurred. Old Fred Stimson, who managed the Bar-U Ranch at that period, used to tell this yarn with even more details, especially when he had had a snifter or two. He claimed to have had a hand in it himself. [4]

*

One could go on spinning yarns ad infinitum about the vagaries and pleasantries of the young Englishman of the remittance period. He built Calgary. Without the money he put in circulation Calgary might have withered away on the prairie. He was far more useful to the community than many of those who laughed amusedly at his wild pranks but who were not above benefiting by his reckless expenditures. The hotels, of course, got all his money, which later radiated from the bar till in all directions to keep the local economic situation steady.

Of course the amount of each chap's monthly remittance was known to every bartender and hotelkeeper in town, but it often used to puzzle these worthies how mysterious extra remittances seemed to arrive at unexpected moments when most required. Had they seen Mr. Remittance Man sitting down in the hotel writing room, with just enough horns under his belt to stir his imagination, composing a letter to his dear parents in England, they would have understood. Here is the sort of letter which a combination of fertile imagination and financial desperation was able to create on these occasions.

While reading this letter, you have to keep in mind that the writer of it had no ranch, had no cattle, had no property, had no nothing, except an ever-lengthening bar bill. His daily existence whirled round and round this damn bar bill, which it was vitally important to protect. Otherwise, the world for him was liable to come to an end.

The Raunch, (say) 1902.

Dear Dad,

Can you not use your influence, which I know to be great, with the British government to get the bally embargo lifted on Canadian cattle? I simply won't export any of my steers under present conditions. My cattle are all in prime shape this fall, but by waiting a little longer and seeing what your board of agriculture over there proposes to do, I may be able to sell the steers at an enormous profit and take a run home for a six months' holiday. I need a rest. The work here is very trying.

A neighbor of mine, Claude Fitzmaurice (a splendid fellow —one of the Epileptic Fitzes of Lushingup Manor) has just sold me a purebred Hereford bull, Rudolph III, for $750. He wanted an even "thou" for him, but I did not feel like giving that amount, though the animal is well worth $1,250. I needed a new bull, anyhow, to infuse fresh blood into my herd of purebred cows. It does not do to inbreed.

As I am a trifle short for the moment until my bunch of steers are disposed of, kindly drop me the amount ($750), by return post. Enclosed find my IOU, which I merely send for form's sake, as business is business. Love to all at home.

Your affectionate son,
Percy

Here is another sample, written by a chap who was stony-broke and with an awful bar bill hanging over his head, and the hotelkeeper showing indications of getting peeved. We won't bore you with any more samples, but read this one.

Dear Mother,

The head of the buffalo I shot last month and which I am having mounted for you, to hang in the hall at home, is nearly completed. It is said to be the finest specimen ever shot on the western plains.

Unfortunately, the injuries I received from the infuriated brute when it first charged have laid me up in hospital and I am still far from well. An eminent surgeon came all the way from Toronto to set my fors clavigera and rearrange a few of my bones. There is no doubt that he saved my life. His fee is rather steep, a thousand dollars plus expenses—$1,250 in all, but happily I can well afford it. When I am myself again I may take a run over to England to convalesce. The specialist recommends an ocean voyage. Love to everybody.

Your loving son,
Bertie

P.S. By the way, Mother dear, as I am too weak to leave my bed and attend to the matter myself, would you mind cabling me the specialist's fee at once? I hate owing anybody. When I am allowed to get up, will send you a cheque. May be confined to my bed for six weeks yet. Am having a small silver plate engraved, to place on base of the buffalo head, with date of killing, etc. [5]

*

We were at the depot the other night and saw carloads of Englishmen being shipped to spend Xmas and the proceeds of their last mortgage in the old country. They were going home to lie about the resources of the country and to convey the assurance that the only thing needed to develop the wraunche is capital.

We know of one such who flourished in the neighborhood of Medicine Hat a short time ago. He was a born promoter in the highest and noblest acceptation of the term, and he felt so keenly the necessity for safeguarding the stock interests that he became a member of the local branch of the Stock Association. One of the qualifications of membership is the ownership of a cow and a calf. We discovered on inquiry that owing to the carelessness of the postmaster general his remittance had not arrived in time to enable him to remove his cow and calf (which was all he had) from out of the possession of the vendor, who refused to be comforted even with a lien note pending the arrival of the stuff. Consequently our friend has had to go 'ome to England to see the guv'nor about turning the blooming cow and cawf into a blasted company, and have a prospectus and float shares, don't you know. Make a bally good thing out of it, don't you know.

In the meantime the vendor is watering his stock. [6]

*

The most hopeless case of a green Englishman (of years ago) was one chap who, after blowing his money, got a job in a sawmill. For the first time in his life he was introduced to a circular saw and the foreman, after giving him the necessary orders, left him to his work. He became much interested in the buzzing blade and it was not many minutes before he lost a finger.

As he sat mopping the blood from his hand, the foreman came back.

"Hullo, old man, what's up?" he cried.

"What's up? What's off, you mean," replied the young Englishman.

"And how on earth did you manage that?"

"By Jove, I hardly know. I just touched the bally thing like this with my finger, when—by Gawd! there's another one gone!" [7]

*

A military man was once appointed governor of a crown colony. Among his duties was to preside over the Supreme Court. He went to a very famous judge and asked him how the devil he was going to do that.

"Quite easily," was the answer. "Give your decisions but never give your reasons. Your decisions may be right, your reasons for them are certain to be wrong." [8]

*

Somehow every detail in an Englishman's life seems to unfit him for meeting the slings and arrows of outrageous fortune. If he goes broke away from home he has to fall back on menial employment, because he has no special knowledge of any one thing. Were he good at even one thing, he would be all right. His dilettante training precludes all idea of his getting a job in a store or a bank—he does not know enough even for that. With machinery or mechanics he naturally is unfamiliar, only knows livestock from the saddle of an Irish hunter, couldn't hold a job in a newspaper office longer than ten or fifteen minutes, has not sufficient savvy to go braking on the railroad, is too gentlemanly to canvass books and finally has to seek aid from the local English clergyman as a preliminary to going on to a farm to work for his board.

What can you expect of young men brought up in a fox-hunting and pheasant-shooting atmosphere? It is heresy to say anything against the noble sport of chasing a lone fox and seeing it rent in pieces by a pack of hounds, for fox-hunting is part of the British constitution and consequently sacred; but we are not afraid to express our contempt for their fashionable pastime of pheasant-shooting as being nothing more than a ridiculous and perverted form of alleged sport, sanctified by the traditions of generations of county gentlemen and their city imitators. [9]

*

We have just been reading a glowing description of the—of the—ah—the new school of agriculchah for English schoolboys that is being established south of Calgary. If it is anything like the other school of agriculchah run near High River some years ago, it will certainly be a huge joke. The most amusing part about it (to us) is the fact that the raunche is located close to Midnapore, the home of the Midnapore *Gazette* and Peter J. McGonigle.

The organizer of this school of agriculchah for English schoolboys is the Rev. H. B. Gray, warden of Bradfield College, Berks. This latter name you must pronounce Bahks of Bahkshah, if you want to show good form. His plan is for the training of boys leaving his school in the science of raunching. Their early studies of Ovid and Euclid should help them out a hell of a lot when dunging out the barn at six o'clock of a twenty below zero morning, under the effulgent rays of a lantern hanging up on a nail. What do you think?

The expenses of Dr. Gray's pupils, besides a premium of $500, will be "the cost of passage from London to Calgary, and the fees and boarding expenses of two winter sessions in Edmonton and elsewhere." Edmonton should be a swell place to learn farming.

Judging from the accounts we have just been reading, the chief feature in connection with Dr. Gray's scheme is to be the raising of goats and bees. Of course there will be—are now, in fact, a number of horses and cows, but they already have 240 goats on the raunche. These should properly be pastured further to the west, in the Rockies, where they could leap from crag to crag and where the pupil in charge could go and yodel just like the real thing. And when one of them butted him in the rear he could console himself with the reflection that he had just taken a horn.

The pupils are also to be instructed in bee culture. They will be stung plenty without having to fall back on the bees.

Dr. Gray's ranch or farm consists of 1,920 acres. Those pupils of his will break and plough Dr. Gray's 1,920 acres or a considerable portion thereof, seed it and harvest it and put up all the hay for the winter, milk the cows, look after the horses and do the chores and pay Dr. Gray $500 each for the privilege of doing so.

As you say, there is one born every minute.

The whole thing resolves itself into Dr. Gray getting out a bunch of suckers from England to do his chores and make his property valuable and present him with $500 in return for his kindness in letting them work for him. We thought that pupil farming in the vicinity of Calgary had been faked to death long ago. Even old Fred Stimson used to take pupils from England on the Bar-U Ranch west of High River. When he was at a loss what to give them to do next, he would send them out to herd the horses inside a strongly-fenced pasture. This did not strike the pupils as being at all strange. They rode around fancying they were cowboys. Which, after all, was all they wanted.

Perhaps, however, we are doing Dr. Gray an injustice. But, honestly, we have seen so many fakes and failures in connection with this pupil farm business both in Canada and the United States, that we are naturally extremely dubious about this venture. They all commenced exactly the same way, same optimism, same prospectus, same line of dope. And there always, invariably, inevitably, was an Anglican clergyman tangled up in it to give it a moral tone and help buffalo the dear parents.

The process of sending dear Harry out to "the colonies" seldom varies. Succumbing to one of those alluring prospectuses issued by the promoter of one of those schools of agriculchah, the guv'nor procures an elaborate outfit for his beloved son, gives him his blessing and comfortable cheque, and ships him off.

In taking his farewell of society prior to embarking for Canada and the Wild West, dear Harry promises every dowager-duchess he meets to send her some heads of big game he kills in the Rockies. At dinner parties he is regarded as a boy of "such

145

pluck, don't you know," and is looked upon as a second Shackleton. His mamma tells him to be sure and call on "the dear Greys" at Ottawa and give them her best love.

So off he goes amid showers of tears and good wishes. Mamma tells him to be careful of his health; his sister Violet implores him to write every week, and the guv'nor takes him to one side on the station platform and says, "Look there, Harry, my boy, you have had a good bringing-up and we do not wish our family name to become a byword. Promise me that you will never allow the counsels of evil men to induce you to enter the Canadian parliament."

With this adjuration ringing in his ears, dear Harry departs for the hospitable shores of Canada, wondering what kind of rotters he will find out there. On arrival at Montreal he remembers his promise to mamma about visiting the Greys, but finding that Ottawa is away off in the brush, he decides to go right on to Calgary. He stops, however, a day or two in Montreal in order to get acclimatized to the drinks and the bartenders at the Windsor who, to do them justice, render him every assistance in their power.

Then dear Harry finds himself rushing across vast prairies and gazing out of the car windows upon a magnitude of grass and horizon. He takes great offense because the train conductor laughs in his face good-humoredly when offered a tip, like the "guards" on English railways; and he does not like the gentle snub he gets from the Pullman conductor when addressing him patronizingly as "my good man."

Finally he reaches Calgary, puts up at the Alberta and slowly but surely finds his way down to the Victoria bar. Here he makes friends with Fred Adams who scents the long green. After a good old-fashioned slippy drunk, dear Harry sets forth for the raunche, or rather, the school of agriculchah.

Here he is initiated into the mysteries of agriculchah and does not like it at all. Harry had been given to understand that he was to gallop about all day on a mustang, shoot buffalo and keep off hostile tribes of Indians. He considers the foreman a very rude person and exceedingly vulgar. After a few months of the hardest kind of work he decides to cut it and informs the head of the school that he has just received word that his father is dangerously ill and not expected to live. The head of the establishment is inclined to doubt this, Harry having no letter or telegram to show, but on the astute Harry saying that he is perfectly charmed with the life and would take it as a favor if he could be allowed to invest a portion of the money he expects to be bequeathed by his father in a partnership-interest in the school of agriculchah, he cordially agrees to let Harry leave at once.

So dear Harry finds himself once more in Montreal, waiting for the steamer to sail. He renews acquaintances with the Windsor hotel bartenders, who are unaffectedly astonished at the amount of Canadian slang he has acquired in the meantime. Off he sails for dear old England, flushed with new hopes and Manhattan cocktails.

The guv'nor is much disgusted to see him back, but dear mamma and Violet are overjoyed. As for the dowager-duchesses, they sit for hours listening to dear Harry's adventures in the far West, how he stood off a band of Blackfoot Indians for forty-eight hours till troops arrived from Okotoks, how he was charged by a herd of infuriated buffalo and only saved his life by killing the leader, how he scaled the dizzy peaks of the Rockies and how, in self-protection, he had to kill five men with his six-shooter in a gambling hall in Calgary. Within a week dear Harry is back in his old cigarette and barmaid rut, and enjoying life to the limit.

A goodly proportion of those young English bloods of good family are victims of foolish bringing up in the first place and of classical-Anglican Church-snobbish-useless systems of education in the second place. When they have attained the age of indiscretion, the cigarette and barmaid stage, they can hardly be said to be mentally normal. Every man they meet is either a rippin' good sort or else he is a bounder and rotter, don't you know. All they think about is what they call "good fawm," and it never occurs to them how inexpressibly silly they appear in the eyes of the average person. [10]

*

It is a curious fact that our queen has never set eyes on any of her colonies nor upon any part of the other continents of Asia, Africa, or America. Nor has she been in Russia, Denmark, Austria, Norway, Sweden, Spain or Greece. It seems hard to

believe that Her Majesty has not been in Denmark, but such is
the case. She expressed a wish once to see Okotoks, but was
talked out of the notion by Princess Beatrice. [11]

*

Wonder what ever became of that once famous Barr colony
of Englishmen that started up some fifteen years ago in the
vicinity of Lloydminster? Many an amusing yarn was spun at
their expense. One that went the rounds was as follows:

The young colonist in question was an Englishman who had
quit the colony and struck a job on a sheep ranch. The first
morning the boss told him to saddle up and round up the sheep
into the corral.

"If you don't mind, boss, I'd rather do it on foot. I'm a bit of
a sprinter, don't you know."

"All right, go to it."

The Englishman did not turn up until late at night, completely fagged out. The boss asked him if he had much trouble
with the sheep.

"Oh, not at all, my dear fellow. The sheep were all right, but
the bally lambs were the deuce and all. I had an awful run
after them."

"Lambs?" Where did you find any lambs amongst that bunch
of wethers?"

"Oh, they were there all right. I've got 'em in the yawd right
now. By jove, but they can run fast!"

The mystified boss went out and found over a dozen jack
rabbits lying panting for breath and nearly exhausted. The boss
remarked of the herder afterwards, "He don't know much but
he's willin'." [12]

*

Just one more idiosyncrasy peculiar to the Englishman of
claws. We have often spoken of it before as being his most dis-
tinguishing characteristic. He cannot eat his breakfast without
the adventitious aid of marmalade. Marmalade he must have.
It is distinctly bad fawm not to have marmalade at breakfast,
and your Englishman, no matter what part of the world he may
be in, always insists on the bally waitah fetching some marmalade, don't you know.

When Lord Chelmsford, commander of the British forces in

Zululand, accepted the surrender of Cetewayo, the Zulu king, years ago, he was invited by that dusky old warrior to enter his kraal and join him at his morning meal. The English general courteously accepted the invitation and soon found himself seated cross-legged on the ground in front of a big caldron of steaming food, Cetewayo's wives acting as hashers. Chelmsford stood it as long as he could until, stodged with stewed rhinoceros, he screwed his monocle into his eye and cried aloud to the king,

"Good gawd, my dear sir, have you no marmalade?"

There being no marmalade, the king was formally made prisoner and taken to the coast. He subsequently was allowed to visit England, where he acquired quite a liking for marmalade. Much sympathy was aroused in England on behalf of King Cetewayo, especially in the clubs and the neighborhood of Belgravia, when it was learned that the poor benighted devil had gone fifty years without marmalade to breakfast. When he died, they held a national service in St. Paul's and put up a tablet in the crypt, with the inscription, *Sic transit gloria marmalade.* [13]

*

Slowly but surely the world is putting away its monarchical forms, and when one takes into consideration how little a year counts in history it becomes evident that the process is not so slow, either. [14]

Those Other People

An Englishman, an Irishman and a Scotchman happened to be in Rome and went together to interview the pope. The Englishman told His Holiness of all he had done for the church and the good of the cause generally, whereupon the pope gave him his hand to kiss. The Irishman then stepped forward and gave the holy father an awful song and dance about his piety and so forth, in recognition of which the pope gave him his foot to kiss.

On looking round for the Scotchman, he was gone. [1]

*

It wouldna hae been sae bad had Jenny run awa' wi a chauffoor, but a coachman is oot o' date. [2]

*

After reading further about the Doukobowhatyoucallems, we are beginning to wish that Prince Hillkoff, whom we had the pleasure of meeting in Wetaskiwin last fall, had found a suitable location for a batch of them out this way, if only to give the charm of variety to our region. The form of spirit wrestling as practised on the C. & E. did not appear to commend itself to the prince. To our mind their religion contains no peculiarities any more pronounced than those to be found in other religions. They deny the existence of a personal God and claim that the doctrine of the trinity means memory, reason and will, instead of Father, Son and Holy Ghost. They believe in the immortality of the soul, but assert that a newborn child has no soul, the soul not entering the body until the fifteenth or sixteenth year. This sounds reasonable. [3]

*

Two things are remarkable among the Hebrews—that neither teetotalism nor drunkenness is to be found amongst them. [4]

*

It is not without grave cause that voices are being raised all over the North-West Territories calling attention to the unrestricted flow of undesirable immigration that is pouring into our midst. There are limits to everything, even to Canada's supposed insatiable power of assimilating the fit and the unfit alike; and unless something be done, and done promptly, the North-West will present the shocking spectacle of a hungry, poverty-stricken, skin-clad population of wild-eyed Asiatics and eastern Europeans. It would be better were Bedouins from the Sahara imported along with their camels and turned loose among the rocks and sand hills east of Winnipeg. They could wander about in their usual happy-go-lucky way and would not call on the government for support; the steamship companies' agents would get their one bonus a head; Sifton and Smart would draw up a special report in a blue wrapper, and everybody would be happy. [5]

*

Mrs. Murphy was getting the supper for the children on Saturday night, when a young woman came to her door.

"I'm a collector for the Drunkards' Home," she said, "Could you help us?"

"Come around tonight and I'll give you Murphy," she replied, as she went on with her work. [6]

*

That was certainly a rather astonishing request a deputation (of two) made to the mayor and commissioners the other day, to the effect that a bylaw be passed prohibiting negroes from residing or holding property in their district. They asked that the negroes should be removed to the northeast portion of the city. We were glad to see this deputation sharply turned down by the mayor and commissioners.

In connection with the above matter we have received a letter from Henry A. Stewart, an old-time colored resident of this city whom we are proud to number amongst our friends. He aptly points out that the rough colored element never seek a nice neighborhood to live in, anyhow.

Calgary, April 6, 1920

Mr. R. C. Edwards
Dear Friend:

The enclosed article from the *Herald*, Tuesday, April 6, is very unfair to the few good law-abiding Negro citizens of Calgary in this free democratic country. There are respectable Christian colored people here and it's this class that seek a respectable neighborhood to reside in. The rough element wouldn't care to live in a nice neighborhood. I have lived here twenty years and in business the last eighteen years and I wonder why such ridiculous prejudice at this late date. Knowing you as a friend and broadminded, I beg you to take this up in your next issue.

I thank you respectfully,

Henry A. Stewart [7]

*

The whitefish season, owing to the final disappearance of the ice, has opened again and the Pigeon Lake half-breed is once more in evidence on our streets. The nearest parallel we can think of to the Biblical incident of the changing water into wine is a Pigeon Lake breed changing whitefish into whiskey. [8]

*

It was a Scotch maternity home. A woman acquaintance of the patient sat by the bedside.

"I thocht, Mistress McSorley, that yer mon was awa' in France this lang while back, and hoo' this?"

"Verra true, but we've aye been writin'." [9]

*

A couple of partially crazy sky pilots, to wit, the Rev. Prof. Kilpatrick of Knox College, Toronto, and the Rev. Dr. Sommerville, general agent of the Presbyterian Church in Canada, at a public meeting in Toronto last week spoke in a most disparaging and insulting manner of the Mormons of Alberta. "The greatest grief in Alberta," said Kilpatrick, "was the Mormon settlements."

The Hon. Frank Oliver, hearing of this blatant ebullition of fathead ignorance and collection-plate littleness, came out in the strongest newspaper interview we have ever had the privilege of reading. He stood up for the Mormons of southern Alberta, characterizing them enthusiastically as sober, orderly, law-abiding, intelligent and progressive citizens, and dwelt at length on the splendid results of their industry in the province. Were we to publish all Frank said about them, Dave Elton, of Cardston would get the big head and want to become a bishop right away. [10]

*

Yesterday was Burns's birthday. He was, is, and always will be, to our way of thinking, the greatest of all Scotsmen. And wasn't he treated well by his brother Scots while alive! It was only after he was dead and buried, and there was no longer any fear of being called upon to extend him aid in his difficulties, that they dared to recognize his greatness. They are indeed a canny race. [11]

*

Irishmen are fine people when they have money, but they never have any. Like the Irishman who said it was hereditary to have no children, it also seems hereditary to have no money. [12]

*

It is manifestly the duty of every good citizen of Canada to do what he can to prevent this flood from overwhelming us. If the present rate of immigration from eastern Europe continues, Canada's troubles will soon be increased tenfold, for with a large proportion of the population in a state of semi-starvation, the tax on the working and more prosperous classes will be greater than they will care to stand. The trouble and misery which must follow in the train of so unhappy a condition is as certain as that sunrise follows dawn.

The *Free Lance* cannot be accused even by its bitterest enemies—and even I have mine enemies—of an overweening love for the existing regime in this fair land. But harsh though it may seem to have to say it, this question must be faced on purely selfish lines. What is at stake is our existence and prosperity in this colony as an English-speaking people. For we are to be flooded out by the refuse of Europe or any other continent; the prospect is far from pleasing. No country, however rich—and Canada, acre for acre is far from rich—can afford to become the receptacle for the pauper and worthless off-scourings of another country.

In our immigrants we should demand the best procurable, and also see that we get them. [13]

*

A Hollander addressing his dog, said: "You vas only a dog, but I vish I vas you. When you go mit your bed in you shust turn round dree times and lay down; ven I go mit the bed in I have to lock up de blace, and vind up the clock and put the cat out, and ondress myself, and my frou vakes up and scolds, den de baby vakes up and cries and I have to valk him mid de house round, den maybe, ven I gets myself to bed it is time to get up again. Ven you get up you shust stretch yourself, dig your neck a leedle and you vas up. I haf to light de fire, put on de kiddle, scrap some mit my vife already and git myself breakfast. You play around all day and haf plenty of fun. I haf to work all day and haf plenty of drubble. Ven you die you vas dead; ven I die I haf to go to hell yet." [14]

*

The NWMP are making a great fuss down round Cardston over an alleged case of polygamy and have ordered the Mormon with two wives to pack up and leave the country. This is all right as far as it goes, but, to be perfectly fair, the dominion authorities ought also to get after gentiles who corrupt and lead astray other men's wives. The latter is by far the worse offence of the two. [15]

*

The suggested Anglo-Saxon–American Alliance fills our hearts with gladness and appeals to our best sympathies. Canadians, as a rule, do not seem to regard the idea with any degree of enthusiasm, nor do they appear to love the Americans with an all-devouring passion, judging from their openly expressed sentiments since the war began; but we know why. It is a foolish reason too. It is because the gold brick, shell, brace, bunko, three card, cold deck, and black sand men who come over from the other side find them so very easy. [16]

*

The resourcefulness of the Irish is shown in their method of weighing without scales. "To weigh a pig," said an Irishman the other day, "all ye have to do is to lay a plank across a sawhorse, place a big stone on one end of the plank and the pig on the other, then shift the plank until the two things balance. Then ye guess the weight of the stone and ye have the weight of the pig." [17]

*

An old Scotch woman heard a gentleman ask a station-master in Fife why the train was so late. The answer was: "It has to wait to let the fish train through."

"Fegs," she exclaimed. "Ye get nae consideration on this line unless ye're a haddie!" [18]

*

Pat on his way home from work discovered a basket of eggs in front of a store. Seeing no one around, he swiped them and proceeded on his way. Passing the church he thought of confession. So he went inside, first covering the eggs with a cloth and leaving the basket in the porch. When he had confessed the priest said:

"Pat, this is very wrong. Where did you leave the basket?"

"In the porch."

"Now, Pat, you say twenty-seven prayers before leaving your knees as a penance."

Pat went ahead with his little old prayers until twenty-seven had been said. In the meantime the priest had left the church and when Pat went for his eggs they were gone. He suspected the priest, but dared not say anything. So he went home minus the eggs.

A month or two later Pat was at confession, but this time he had a more serious crime to confess.

"Patrick, my son, you are indeed a dreadful sinner. What did you say the lady's name was?"

"I would rather not tell your riv'rence."

"Why not?"

"Because I haven't forgotten what happened to my eggs." [19]

*

They speak of Englishmen, the remittance chaps, and the bad breaks they make. But to our mind they are infinitely superior in their loose whoop hurrah to the hard, cold, iron-clad, non-souled Scotchmen who are fondly supposed to be the backbone, vertebrae and lights and liver of Canada. We are fully equipped from personal knowledge to meet any discussion on this subject, and will guarantee to get away with any one who cares to take issue with us on the above remarks. [20]

*

A lady heard that her two sons were in the habit each, at separate times and quite unknown to each other, of taking one of the maids "out for a lark." Fearing to bring down on their devoted heads the wrath of their father by making a bother about it, she asked them quietly if it was true, but could obtain no satisfactory reply. It occurred to her that by a little strategy she might get the truth from the girl, so she said in a jocular manner, "Now, Mary, I want you to answer me candidly. Which of my two sons do you like going out with best—George or William?"

"Weel, ma'am," replied the girl, reassured by the lady's manner, "if ye maun ken, o' the twa I like Maister George best; but for a rale dounricht guid spree, gie me the maister!" [21]

*

The following libretto, set to music, is respectfully submitted to the choirs of the Wetaskiwin churches. The composer has just about completed the score. Land seekers of various nationalities are supposed to be grouped on the sidewalk, as we see them every day, chattering at the top of their voices like a flock of magpies. In singing this anthem the choir must shout it out in the most discordant tones possible, each member singing independently of the others: "Oh ah slupinsky skoll jopplunky kerplunk sniftersky sacre nom de dieu pas moyen le terra est mauvais I don't mind if I do kachorka dvorak ski say that old crock I bought from Young is mais ecoutez donc le quartier sw 14-44-14 est le meilleur morceau de slopmagulcher kamarachinchoo svi da I took it up last fall and the old stiff came along and breektonka rinski squak allons prenez un coup gimme a little Scotch slambango good and quicksy!" [22]

*

Which reminds us of the following story.

A small Scotch boy on returning home from school in Aberdeen proudly exhibited a book which he triumphantly declared he had won for natural history.

"Natural history, laddie? Losh, you're far ower young for natural history. Hoo did it happen?" asked his mother.

"Well, the teacher asked hoo mony legs an ostrich had, and I said three."

"But an ostrich only 'as twa legs," said the mother.

"I ken," said the urchin, "but a' the rest o' the chaps said four." [23]

Show Business

All the world's a stage, and the majority of us sit in the gallery and throw things at the performers. [1]

*

The best show of the season was that Ponoka conjuring entertainment last week. The eminent conjurer could make anything disappear he wanted to, especially booze. His gifted manager, Ole Roth, also disappeared with the gate receipts while the performance was in progress. A fashionable throng was present. Mr. and Mrs. Joel Slop were present in a box, or rather a dry goods box, and seemed to enjoy the entertainment. Mrs. Slop was tastefully dressed in fur-lined shoes. Miss Flora Selwyn was in the paraquet wearing little else but a bland smile. Mr. Selwyn, her talented father, was becomingly attired in the suit of clothes he had taken from the corpse of the man he murdered last fall who was known to be a good dresser. Those Ponoka society events are great features up north. [2]

*

A machine to deal cards has been invented. Now, if the inventor can only produce machines that will play poker, many a needed night's rest can be secured. [3]

*

If you want anything done well, do it yourself. This is why most people laugh at their own jokes. [4]

*

Our Canadian vaudeville managers would make a big hit with their Canadian patrons if they were to prevail upon the performers to give us fewer of those melancholy, dried up, shop-worn jokes about Taft and Roosevelt. Surely vaudeville artists have wit enough to adapt their alleged jokes to the country in which they are performing. If not, any one of the ushers, or even the caretaker, could provide them with a few fresh witti-cisms to go on with.

We notice, also, that musical performers seek cheap ap-plause by everlasting grinding out "Dixie" and the "Star Spangled Banner," and they invariably get it. Punk performers for pale people usually have something in their act calculated to drag and wrench applause from the American portion of the audi-ence, not having talent enough to get it any other way, and being mortally afraid of losing their jobs on the circuit if they fail to get a hand.

Calgary is not very strong just now in high-class entertain-ment. Indeed, a No. 5 Uncle Tom's Cabin troupe, or a stranded East Lynne layout, would receive a hearty welcome. Thank God, the baseball season has started! [5]

*

"Now," said the great magician, rolling up his sleeves to show there was no deception, "I shall attempt my never-failing experi-ment."

Taking half a dollar from his pocket, he said: "I shall cause this coin to disappear utterly."

So saying, he lent it to a friend. [6]

*

Harry Lauder would have been a greater success in Calgary if he had sung more and talked less. [7]

*

An old hotel clerk was telling us the other day of his experi-ences in the early days of this province, when he used to clerk at Tom Wilton's place in Macleod. Except for the fun associated with booze the life was pretty monotonous. Few shows struck town, but when they did everybody attended who was not broke.

One day at noon a funny looking old geezer with long whisk-ers drove in from Pincher. He was a phrenologist and proposed giving a lecture and reading heads. The main hall of the burg was already engaged for that evening by a small theatrical company which was expected by the afternoon train, so the professor had to hire a smaller place for his show. Later in the afternoon, before the arrival of the counter-attraction, the professor said to the clerk:

"Say, I'd like you to come to my show tonight. Your coming may draw others. Step up to my room after supper and I'll give you a couple of tickets and read your bumps free of charge."

"All right," agreed the clerk.

When the theatrical company arrived on the scene and had registered their names, the soubrette, a somewhat brisk looking proposition, lingered for a moment at the desk and said:

"Say, they tell me there's an old bumpologist here tonight. Now, you must know everybody around here. You come to our show—our show, not his, savvy—and it will draw the crowd."

As if struck by an afterthought, she turned back and said, "You come up to my room after supper and I'll give you a couple of tickets."

"All right," agreed the clerk.

As soon as supper was over and the dining room closed down, the clerk began to remember his two appointments upstairs. He had to keep one of them at least, but which one?

"Ha!" thought he, "I'll toss up a coin. Here goes—head or tail."

Our friend the clerk remarked sadly that it came head and he put in a perfectly rotten evening at the phrenological entertainment. Some men are conscientious to a fault. [8]

*

Visiting comedians at the Empire have been complaining that Calgary audiences lack a sense of humor. The reason Calgary people don't laugh at their jokes is because they have heard the jokes before and are through laughing at them. [9]

*

Could not somebody persuade Charlie Chaplin to pay us a visit, on the understanding that he adhere strictly to his silent drama methods? He would create intense excitement in the community. Charlie no doubt would also have enough sense not to deliver a severe lecture to Canadians who have already done much and are continuing to do their level best in the war effort.

A popular character should never take undue advantage of his fame—that is if he wishes to remain a popular character. [10]

*

They talk a lot these days about the bad effect of crime pictures upon boys. There are ample grounds for these objections, it is true, but it has always struck us that the careless moralities observable in the private lives of some of those beautiful movie stars, who are so enthusiastically admired by our young girls, must have an equally injurious effect. The barnyard morals of a certain movie colony in southern California have become a regular joke. The pity of it is that our own flappers seem to enjoy reading about their pranks. They think it cute.

There is hardly a movie star of any note but what has been through the divorce mill. They marry in the most casual fashion, get tired of one another quickly, get divorced, marry again, chuck it and get divorced again, and so on. And yet these people are objects of the most intense and sincere hero-and-heroine worship to millions of impressionable young people all over the world. Can you beat it? [11]

*

In the last issue we happened, by some coincidence, to write something about the barnyard morality of the Los Angeles movie colony, but had not figured on rape and murder trimmings. The fact is, most of these movie stars are in the same category as "beggars on horseback." They find themselves in sudden possession of much wealth, and have inevitable periods of idleness between pictures, when they don't know what to do with themselves. This is where Satan comes in. The male stars are bright, live men, full of pep and deviltry, and the women are invariably good lookers. They mix together on terms of professional familiarity. Every blessed one of them has a swell car and, needless to say, they all drink. Further explanation is superfluous. Immorality, under these alluring circumstances, becomes almost automatic.

Only a couple of weeks ago a couple of famous movie stars appeared in person at the Orpheum in Calgary. They put on a dandy little one-act play, acted it splendidly, and were greatly admired. And yet one could not help remembering, while looking at them on the stage, that the man had obtained a divorce, abandoning a wife and five children, in order to marry the good looker who was then with him. They are a strange breed. [12]

*

That movement to uplift the movie shows has only got as far as the price of admission. [13]

*

Hoity! Toity! Read this, will you? It is from Mr. Chalmers, the hypnotist.

To the Editor of the *Free Lance:*

Sir, I have no hesitation in informing you that none other than an unprincipled cur would treat others as you have done me through the medium of your contemptible dirty rag. You are aware that I did not endeavour to deceive any in your town, and that subjects who I tried to hypnotize under unfavorable circumstances admitted that they did feel my influence and that one of the subjects was put to sleep. If you cannot find more interesting matter for your readers better for you to take a mile race and bunt your idiotic brain against a stone wall. I can assure you there would be no loss. It would only be the death of another jackass. You may publish this if you wish. If you do not send me an apology for your ungentlemanly act I shall hand a copy of this letter to be published in the *Herald* or *Tribune.*

JAMES G. CHALMERS

Now what do you think of that! Oh McChalmers, McChalmers, how could you! [14]

*

Society Note— Miss Eugenie Champneys has returned home from Paris, where she has been studying music under Madame Marchesi. Miss Champneys has a beautiful contralto voice and has been assured by John de Reske, Mascagni, Hammerstein and others that by carefully cultivating her voice with a hoe there is no telling but that some day she may become a prima donna in a moving picture show. Her mother, Mrs. Champneys, poured tea. [15]

*

Some years ago we went out of our way to write a special criticism in the *Eye Opener* of Olga Nethersole, when she presented "The Redemption of Evelyn Vaudray" at the Grand. This must have been a damn fine piece of work on our part, because it was reproduced in *The Bookman* of New York, an ultra-highbrow publication of tremendous authority, as a "specimen of dramatic criticism that might well serve as a model for some of our more pretentious critics on the New York press."

We have this copy of *The Bookman* in our possession.

The writer went on to say that "Over the literary quality of this sample of dramatic criticism, there can be no quibbling, no dispute. And, in spite of the traces of colloquialism that may be observed, it may not be fairly urged that it is not without proportionate traces of clear judgment and common sense."

The only thing that annoyed us about these flattering remarks in *The Bookman* was the appalling sentence: "The criticism appeared in the journalistic organ of Calgary, a small mining town in the western section of Canada." [16]

*

It is charged that "jazz" music causes warts on the feet. The trouble lies in lack of gray matter above the cervical vertebrae. [17]

*

Great Scott, if there isn't another palmist come to town! This time it is a woman named Madame Bayla. Calgary hasn't had a palmist now for six months. The last one, it will be remembered, was a man, and he broke his leg in a scuffle while being chucked out of the Queen's Hotel dining room while drunk. There have been a pretty tough bunch of lady palmists in Calgary during our time, the smoothest being Mlle. Rhea. This lady was up before the police magistrate on a charge of fakery or obtaining money under false pretences, but R. B. Bennett put up a strong defence and got her off.

Calgary is a good place for palmists. They have always done well here, there being so many suckers. Room 7 in the Alberta used to be their usual headquarters and the fee for being told that you were coming into a fortune and that a dark man, with a swivel eye would cross your path, was a two-spot. Chappies drinking down at the bar would hilariously announce their intention of having their fortunes told and, after three or four more Scotch and sodas, would mosey upstairs, returning ten minutes later looking very mysterious and calling for more booze.

"Wunnerful! Wunnerful! She tole me losh 'bout myself—most 'strawd'nary, sir, most 'strawd'nary! She tol' me I had been drinking—wunner how she foun' that out. Fred, just fill those up again."

Palmistry is firmly believed in by many good people. So is fortune-telling by cards, and there are quite a number of otherwise sensible people who believe in "reading the teacups." While not wishing to do Madame Bayla the injustice of suggesting that she is a fakiress, we cannot refrain from expressing our own opinion that all those money-making mysteries are the grossest kind of frauds, supported by simpletons of a perverted, imaginative and superstitious turn of mind. [18]

*

"This large bump running across the back of your head means that you are inclined to be curious to the point of recklessness."

"I know it. I got that by sticking my head into an elevator shaft to see if the elevator was coming up, and it was coming down." [19]

*

Society Note— Mr. and Mrs. James B. Buffkins of Okotoks are in the city taking in the fair. Mrs. Buffkins had her palm read by Madame Jumperine Thursday, the while Mr. Buffkins was gorging himself with hot dog on the midway. A pleasant time was had. [20]

*

The following story is told of a ventriloquist, now famous, but at the time of this incident he was so poor that he used to walk between the places where he was to appear. On one of these tours he picked up a miserable little dog because it looked so much like he felt. The story will explain what became of the dog.

The first house he came to was an inn, and, of course, he wanted a drink. He had no money, but went in anyhow to see what he could do.

The proprietor said, "Well, what will you have?"

He said, "I'll take a little whiskey." And then, turning to the dog he asked, "What will you have?"

The answer came promptly: "I'll take a ham sandwich."

The publican was so surprised he almost fainted. He looked at the dog a moment, and then asked, "What did you say?"

The dog replied, "I said I'd take a ham sandwich."

Mine host thought it wonderful that a dog should be able to talk, and asked who had trained him, how long it had taken, and wound up with, "How much will you take for him?"

"Oh," replied Mr. Ventriloquist, "I wouldn't sell him at any price, but I am a little hard up and if you will lend me $50 I will leave him with you until I bring back the money."

"All right," was the reply. "I just want him for a little while, so I can show him to some people I know around here."

So everything was settled, the money paid, the dog left with the proprietor, and as the ventriloquist went out he turned and waved his hand to the dog and said, "Well, good-bye, Jack. I'll come back soon."

The dog looked at him and said, "You mean, despicable man, to sell me for $50 after all I've done for you? So help me, Moses, I'll never speak another word as long as I live."

And he didn't. [21]

ELEVEN

Morality

Miss Maude de Vere, of Drumheller, arrived in the city Wednesday and was run out of town the same night. It is a pity that Miss de Vere is not a racehorse, for she is very fast. [1]

*

A young lady recently wrote to her fiance: "I dined out with some friends last night and had three glasses of wine. Did I do wrong?"

The reply came back: "How can I tell? Can't you remember?" [2]

*

There has been considerable talk lately about underpaid girls going wrong. Of course poor pay has a good deal to do with many a girl's fall, but only in cases where the girl's love of finery and pleasure is stronger than her moral sense. There is also the girl who possesses physical attractions and is disinclined to employment, choosing the easiest way of escaping the drudgery of life. Oddly enough, although for centuries Ireland has ranked amongst the poorest countries and France amongst the richest, yet Ireland is noted for the purity of its women and France for the opposite. [3]

*

While wondering why the ladies have such a liking for

Scotch it has occurred to us that someone may have told them that it was a great bust developer. [4]

*

There is considerable talk just now about the social evil in Calgary. The solution is simple. Segregate the fair ladies away off where they will be out of sight and beyond the ken of decent women. It may involve the blowing in of an extra dollar or two on a rig, but the boys don't mind a little thing like that. The houses across the river might also with advantage be moved further north to some more remote spot, for it is somewhat embarrassing for a gentleman to take a drive with his wife or a party of ladies out to the celebrated irrigation ditch and have to pass in quick succession the Mascot, the White House, the Chicken Ranch and the Jap houses. Outside the latter there is usually a geisha girl in short skirts standing on the porch, hailing passers-by. If you have your wife with you, it is all the same to Mimosa San. This is rather rotten, don't you think? What?

We will say this, however, for the "houses" across the river. They are unusually well conducted, quiet and orderly. Nothing tough about them at all. No one gets rolled and no rows ever take place. This is a great showing. The landladies and the inmates are a good-natured lot, quietly accepting their losing numbers in the lottery of life with submissive fortitude and fitful hilarity. They are a great study to the student of human nature and not half as black as they are painted.

In this connection we should like to remark that the ones whom the police should get after are neither the inmates of those places nor their occasional visitors. The ones to whom the police should show no mercy are the men who live on the earnings of those unfortunate women, those men whose correct title rhymes with the word "imp." All such despicable characters should be run out of town or thrust into the jug for vagrancy. We could point out one or two with little difficulty. [5]

*

Etiquette— On no account start a discussion on prison reform in the presence of a lady whose husband is in the coop for keeping his store open after hours. Have a heart. [6]

*

Without money the doors of society are shut. That's a cinch. If you have money, just lose it and see what society will do with you. Even the doors of the churches do not welcome so enthusiastically the cheaply clad man as the big man in broadcloth with the dough. This is a comfort-seeking and luxury-loving age, when men are ready to do anything—anything, we repeat—for money. Nowadays men—we refer more particularly to men who make a profession of politics—will sell their souls and their government and rob the people whose interests they are fondly supposed by their constituents to be looking after, for one bright smile from the goddess of graft. Honor? What's that? It's only the dough they're after. That is all. Surely this is simple enough for your comprehension. [7]

*

Society Note— Mr. Percy Redingot, who was recently caught in flagranto deplunko with a careless dame, has gone east for his health. Mr. Redingot has been suffering from his lungs for some time past, but there is nothing the matter with his gall. [8]

*

The floozies of the city are to hold an indignation meeting in Paget Hall next week to protest against the activities of west-end society-fringe alcoholics who are encroaching on their business. [9]

*

Who was the Calgary dentist who insulted a girl employee of a certain hotel in Edmonton, not far from the CPR depot, some time ago? This man asked her to bring some ice-water to his room and when she did so grabbed her by the leg, with the remark, "You're some chicken!" It is gratifying to know that she instantly smashed him in the face. Can you guess who the man was? Yes, that's just who it was. [10]

*

Society Note— Mr. Fred B. Sprawley of Edmonton, accompanied by his alleged wife, registered at the King George Wednesday. [11]

*

There appears to be an impression that this week's *Eye Opener* is to be full of a lot of salacious stuff about that alleged assault on a girl by a well-known gentleman in town. Those who have been expecting this will be disappointed. It might be as well to say, however, that we don't believe a word of the girl's story. She strikes us as being batty. [12]

*

A recently-married young couple were dining in a restaurant, when a tall, handsome blonde entered and passed their table, giving the husband a glance of recognition and a dangerous smile.

"John," said the young wife, "who is that woman?"

John's brow contracted.

"Now for goodness sake," he said, "don't go bothering me about who she is. I shall have enough trouble explaining to her who you are!" [13]

*

Sensible divorce laws (similar to those in England) already exist in Nova Scotia, New Brunswick and British Columbia. If you reside anywhere else and catch your wife in flagrantico delicatessen, you have to bring the whole matter before the divorce committee of the Senate and then, if you make your case stick, they bring in an act of parliament granting you your divorce. When they have got through with you, you haven't any money left to marry again and probably have to go to work on the section.

There is so much failure about marriage that a reasonable divorce law would be nothing more than a simple act of humanity. Lots of women wonder why men are so chary about getting married. We can tell them why, easy enough. As it is now in Canada, a married woman is responsible to no one. She knows that her husband cannot afford a divorce and has to keep her anyhow. The marriage contract has made her irresponsible. At marriage the man becomes responsible for an irresponsible being. It is this that makes marriage a bit of a snare in this country.

A young man, for instance, is in love with a woman and thinks she is an angel, so he gets married without further investigation. The poor idiot takes it for granted that as he is

169

responsible for her to the world, she will surely fulfil her obligations to him. He assumes vaguely that there must be some way of holding her faithful to the terms of the marriage service. He discovers later that there is none. He comes to realize in time that he is married with a vengeance, bound hand and foot, while his wife need play her part as a true wife only so long as it suits her.

A woman can pass up the marriage contract for a multitude of reasons, all good enough to satisfy her alleged conscience. She may not love him so well as she did before they were married; she may think that, after all, she likes an old sweetheart better and it was only spite that made her marry this one; she may not be having the "good time" her fancy led her to expect; he may not be giving her enough dough to fool around the Hudson's Bay store with; she may decide that she does not like children after she has had two or three and may feel that she is altogether too bright to be delivering children and getting her figure knocked all out of shape; or she may conclude that her husband looks quite a slob in comparison with the gay dogs of bachelors she meets at dances. So discontent with her husband grows on her and she does the other thing.

Perhaps once in about 4,000 years there is a woman so much in love with a man that she never outgrows it.

A man cannot leave his wife unless he wants to be jailed for desertion. The married woman's power is practically unlimited. Good women do not abuse this power, but the bad ones all do. If we could have a sensible divorce law that holds both man and woman equally responsible, women would rise to the situation and would often be saved from themselves.

We hesitate to speak of men in their capacity as husbands. They are usually infinitely worse as husbands than women are as wives, so we will leave them at that. They are a bad lot, take it from us. [14]

*

"Oh, Maw! Maw!" shouted the little boy some time during the day of the first of April. "There's a man in Bridget's room!"

"There is, eh?" said the lady grimly, making a break for Bridget's room and preparing to burst in the door.

"April fool! April fool!" cried the little rascal. "It's only paw!" [15]

*

170

Most people who are old enough to know better often wish they were young enough not to. [16]

*

Society Note— Mrs. William Buckle, of Seventh Avenue West, was hostess at a luncheon last Wednesday in honor of her nephew, who has just been liberated from jail. [17]

*

We have been informed that in one of the houses in the south coulee, which, be it again emphasized, is inside the city limits, there is a young girl apparently not much over fifteen years of age, with her hair hanging down her back, more like an innocent school girl than a sporting woman. If our informant be speaking the truth, this savors not a little of white slave traffic and should be looked into. [18]

*

When you get into trouble most of your friends will say: "It's too bad." And let it go at that. [19]

*

Society Note— Miss Evangeline Golightly gave a charming musicale down at the police station Wednesday afternoon. She was screaming to beat the band and had to be given a shot of snow. [20]

*

While standing on Eighth Avenue the other day chatting with a well-known detective of the RNWMP, a couple of giggling flappers passed by. They were apparently about fifteen or sixteen years of age, extremely pretty, daintily dressed and with dam-short skirts. These two giggling darlings were so attractive and so reckless-looking that every man in their path had to pause and turn around for another glance.

"Looks like two new flappers in town," we observed.

"Looks as if they were pretty well hopped up, too," said the detective cynically, as he went on with the story he was telling.

Yes, there is a lot of this drug-taking going on in Calgary right at the present moment amongst young girls, right under the nose of these fearful and wonderful women's uplift societies, of which there are about a thousand, more or less. There must also be considerable drug addiction up in Edmonton, to judge by Magistrate Emily Murphy's recent articles on the subject in *Maclean's Magazine*. And if the underworld and the lower strata of flapperdom have taken to this deadly form of excitement, it stands to reason that a corresponding number of men are also hitting up the cocaine, morphine, heroin or opium or whatever it is they take around here. "Snow" seems to be the popular stuff, injected with a hypo syringe or snuffed up the nostrils.

And all because there is no beer to be had!

The professional reformers should all be lodged in jail. Judged by results, they are exercising a most demoralizing and pernicious influence throughout the country. [21]

*

Zinn's Dancing Girls, who occupied the boards of the Lyric all last week, did big business, especially after the show. The charming creatures were the means of introducing metropolitan customs into our benighted midst, the spectacle of Johnnies waiting at the stage entrance being quite like old times in other climes. Although the wages of Zinn is death, many of the girls with this company seem to be laying up treasure in their stockings where neither moths nor flies do corrupt. Call again. [22]

*

Just as we prophesied, the ladies of uneasy virtue, driven from their suburban haunts, have spread all over town and are now comfortably ensconced in blocks and in cosy cottages along the avenues right in the midst of the gillies who have been making such a roar about them. Only a day or two ago a well-known real estate man rented two cottages to a couple of workingmen who claimed to be employed in the town and discovered that, on the very same day, the cottages had been handed over to scarlet ladies. He is now in a quandary what to do about firing them out.

We are now in a position to offer the only sensible solution to the social evil problem in Calgary. Let the city set apart the island on the Bow River below the barracks, build a bridge and charge toll over same till it pays for itself, segregate the ladies on this spot which is "out of sight" in more senses than one, let them build their own houses with a promise of permanence and have the whole bunch under direct city supervision, police and medical.

It is absolutely ridiculous for parsons to attempt to handle a question that they know nothing of. They only make a bungle of it, as they have done in the recent instance. The proposition herein set forth as inoffensively as possible, should be considered not with levity but with dispassionate recognition of the inevitable presence in our midst *always* of this so-called evil. Reformers who think they can stamp it out are crazy. [23]

*

Society Note— The proceedings against John F. Broadfoot have been withdrawn. Mr. Broadfoot has agreed to marry the girl. [24]

*

Wot's that? Oh yes, why certainly we beheld Maude Odell, the $10,000 beauty. Maude was all she was cracked up to be and appeared to be rather a ladylike proposition when she first stepped on the stage with a fair amount of clothes on. Later, however, when she posed in the picture frames, she was practically naked. But that is none of our business, and if sitting and gazing at studied nudity is considered the correct thing in Winnipeg, why, it's all right. We are the last one to kick at this sort of thing, only we fancied, from the recent uproar about segregation, that the authorities were hell on morality.

The nude, after all, is a relative term, and really implies and emphasizes the existence of clothes. Without clothes, there would be no nudity. For example, no one would speak of a nude cow, a nude elephant or a nude hippopotamus, and yet these creatures go around stark naked. Nudity implies that one has a wardrobe somewhere.

We have seen ladies in lofty circles of society appear in the ballroom and at the theatre with almost as little on as had Maude Odell, and far more suggestively attired so far as immodesty went. There really is nothing suggestive in the altogether.

The art of going nude is, of course, like any other art—it depends upon the judgment used in doing it. There is a time and a place for everything. No self-respecting lady moving in the highest circles would come down to breakfast in a French bathing suit, for example. To be semi-nude morning, noon and night without regard to one's religion or standing, would be fatal to the most exalted position. No woman would gain much by walking semi-nude along King Street, Toronto. But upon arriving in a ballroom it is quite the proper thing for your refined, cultured and even, maybe, religiously-inclined lady-fair to throw off her clothes, leaving them with the boy at the door.

The line between morality and nudity has never been defined correctly. The best morality, of course, wears no clothes at all. Doubtful morality is usually half-naked. This comes from living in a chilly zone. If it were too hot to wear clothes, studies in the nude would be so common that they would no longer be high art. [25]

*

A buxom young woman charged an aged doctor before a magistrate with having assaulted her.

"But how was it," said the magistrate, "that being strong and vigorous, as you happen to be, you could not successfully resist a feeble old man like the accused? Had you not strength enough to protect yourself?"

"Oh, sir!" said the girl, "I have plenty of strength when I'm angry, but when I laugh I'm as weak as a cat!" [26]

*

Well, they got Moose Baxter at last. It is an old story by this time. We are not surprised that Moose got it into his nut that he was immune, for was he not permitted to run the second-worst dive in the city with comparative impunity for nearly a year? The illegal sale of liquor was the least of the evils at this joint. Every man in town knows that. Like the first-worst or red-ribbon dive, the one reposing innocently beneath the shadow of the court house, it was nothing but a common hookery, where booze was sold at regular Nose Creek rates. The landlords of these buildings are well-known local millionaires, and, apart from certain wolfish instincts, men of high personal character. Why they never ejected their objectionable tenants has been a mystery to the citizens of Calgary for the past year or two. A lease can always be cancelled for cause. [27]

*

And so Chief Mackie is going to close up the dives at Nose Creek and gambling joints in town, and make Calgary the cleanest city in the whole of the dominion. Well, well, if that isn't just fine! By the way, when do the municipal elections come off? In

a month? As soon as that? Well, well, well, what a curious coincidence!" [28]

*

Anxious Inquirer: No. A floozy is not a person who has the
floo. Your informant has been stringing you. [29]

*

Modern civilization has many amusing kinks. It is generally
regarded as immodest for girls to appear on our streets in skirts
that are too abbreviated. People pretend to be shocked. They
aren't really, but civilization demands that they should pretend
to be. And the uplifters fear that public morals may be corrupted
by these exhibitions of female nether limbs. It is all right, however, to go to the theatre and sit in a comfortable chair gazing at
some dancing girl capering about the stage in bare legs and
practically naked. This is licensed by the authorities and nobody
feels shocked. Not a bit of it. What ho! [30]

*

The recent brutal assault on a woman by a strange man who
obtained entrance to her home under some plausible pretext
while she was alone in the house with her little child, again
draws attention to the fact that women always get the worst of
it. Things have indeed come to a pretty pass when, in addition
to the drudgery of housework, the woman has to undergo the
daily risk of criminal assault.

We should like to see a jury of women sit on the case when
the brute who committed this cruel outrage is up for trial. Men
always seem too prone to protect their own sex when offenses
against women are on the tapis. In the recent instance, however,
the facts are too patent and glaring to be overlooked. Public
sentiment will not stand for any bogus plea of extenuating circumstances here. It is a dead open-and-shut case.

Did you ever hear of a man losing out on a charge of rape
in this country? No, you never did. They all get off. Why? Because of lack of corroborative evidence and because at least four
of the six jurymen are sure to take the cynical view that the
man would not have committed the offense if he hadn't received
some encouragement from the girl.

Offenses against women should be tried by women. Not only

that, but offenses against young girls should be investigated and the cases heard in camera. A poor creature who has been wronged by some libertine should not have her misery augmented by being compelled to enter a witness box before a crowded court of rubbernecks and made to tell her tale, being further subjected to the browbeating of some flip lawyer. Instead of getting the redress sought, the chances are that she leaves the court overwhelmed with shame, and her reputation all shot to pieces.

There is really no law for the protection of women in this country, much less is there a law for the protection of the honor of the family and the home. There is, it is true, a law to meet such crimes as the one committed on Tenth Avenue this week, but only because the assault happened to be accompanied by extreme violence. Otherwise, the only punishment the scoundrel would have to fear would be shooting at the hands of the husband. [31]

*

Etiquette— When a young society man is present at a pink tea, it is considered a grave breach of manners on his part to start up a conversation relative to the white slave traffic. He will do well to confine his sparkling remarks to the splendor of the weather and the atrocities of the early closing bylaws. [32]

*

One of the foulest exhibitions of man's inhumanity to man is on the eve of being pulled off in Calgary, with the full knowledge and connivance of the council and commissioners, and the *Eye Opener* hastens to make the matter public before it is too late. The aggregation of so-called Christians—or bunch of rummies, whichever you prefer—whom you elected to run the city, are busy constructing a stronghold of police tyranny and cruelty compared with which the Bastille and the Black Hole of Calcutta were joy palaces.

If you don't believe this, go down today, as soon as you have read this, and look over the dank, dark, dismal cellar-basement of the new police station where they are installing the iron cages, and see what you think of it. It is a disgrace and will grow into a foul scandal if not knocked on the head. There have been a number of scandals in Calgary in bygone days, but they all pale before this one.

This unspeakable hole in the ground is being packed jam-full of small iron cages, with narrow alleyways between the rows. In winter, when the windows are shut, this dungeon will be in total darkness unless artificial light is brought into play; and such air as they can pump in will neither relieve the physical distress of the unfortunate prisoners nor modify the horrible stench which must obviously permeate the place during the hot days and suffocating nights of summer.

It will be no time at all before this black cellar is swarming with vermin. No real fresh air can ever find an entrance here. Not in winter anyhow. Abandon air all ye who enter here. It seems incredible that preparations for the infliction of such monstrous cruelty upon human beings should be allowed to proceed. The people of Calgary did not vote money for the reproduction of the Black Hole of Calcutta. Prisoners are human and entitled in a Christian country to human treatment. If this dark, unhealthy, sickening basement is actually put into operation as a local prison, the *Eye Opener* and the *Eye Opener*'s friends will undertake next fall to sweep out of official existence every alderman whose term then expires and who has shared responsibility in this diabolical crime against humanity. [33]

*

Society Note— The many friends of Peter F. Scratchley, the popular oil broker, will be glad to learn that he is rapidly recovering from a severe cold contracted while making a somewhat hasty departure, via the window, from the elegant mansion of the charming society matron, Mrs. J. T. Blinkbonny, at an early hour last Sunday morning. [34]

*

It is usually the fast young man who is left at the post. [35]

*

Society Note— Miss Lottie Migglethorpe, whose hosiery is almost as remarkable as her voice, has accepted an engagement of thirty days at the Edmonton police station. When going full blast, Miss Migglethorpe can be heard for miles around and many people at the beaches think that the weird rumblings come from the Fabyan oil well. She read an interesting paper on Gordon gin at the meeting of the Leduc YWCA last week, giving some wonderful demonstrations to illustrate her remarks. It is hardly likely that this talented lecturer will appear again in Leduc for some time. [36]

*

A well-known tailor in this city had a handsome young lady in his employ and she, in the ordinary course of events, succumbed to his balmy influence and was ruined. A month or two ago he took her to the private maternity home on Fifth Avenue and left her there for the confinement, paying the matron some cash in advance. Shortly after the kid was born the unfortunate young woman became violently insane and her friends from the north came down to fetch her to her old home, leaving the baby at the hospital. They evidently didn't want it. Neither did the matron. A lady was found who took away the child with a view to adoption, but she changed her mind shortly afterwards and brought it back, saying she didn't want it after all.

"Neither do I," said the matron.

The lady then took the baby from the perambulator, entered the house and laid it on the table, saying, "Now you've got it, you'll have to keep it."

Well, the upshot of this shocking circumstance is that the police came and took the child away, turning it over to the good old Salvation Army Rescue Home, where it is now.

The city is paying for the child's keep.

Will Alderman Stuart kindly tell us why the tailor is not called upon for some explanation? The chief of police, no doubt, can give him full particulars. [37]

*

Society Note— Peter F. Ayer, who has been absent from the city for over a year, returned home last week to find himself the proud father of a bouncing boy just a few weeks old. Mr. Ayer is instituting inquiries. [38]

*

A painful case has been brought to our notice during the last week or two.

In a certain block on First Street West lives a woman who has kept a house of ill-fame for the last four years, having been moved about from one block to another. She calls herself "Mrs." and is reputed to be supported for immoral purposes by a professional man of the city. That part of her life is of no consequence, but she is dragging innocent young women down with her. Into her net they go, one by one. That is of very real consequence.

This is her modus operandi. She will meet some attractive looking girl in a store or at a dance, and make friends with her victim, for she has a very smooth way. Then she will say, "Oh, do come and have afternoon tea with me." Of course the poor victim goes like a lamb to the slaughter. On the victim leaving, she will say, "Oh, do come up some evening and have a game of cards." And, of course, the girl goes.

At this stage of the game two men are introduced. A pleasant evening is spent and the girl goes home all right—this time. The next week she is again invited and the same two men again appear. This time brandy and milk are introduced, and before the poor victim realizes her danger she has lost control of herself, and you can guess the rest.

We have this information at first hand, and have been asked by one of the victims to do something in the matter. The girl says she would give all the world to recall what passed during one month in this woman's company. We know who this woman is and also know the two men referred to. If they repeat this offense and we happen to hear about it, their names will be published in big type in this paper. This woman especially had better take a tumble to herself. The punishment for procuring is a fairly long term of imprisonment.

This is a most unpleasant thing to write about, but it may serve as a warning to young girls to be equally as careful with respect to the acquaintances they make amongst their own sex as they do amongst the other. [39]

*

Living up to one's reputation for respectability is awfully monotonous. That is why so many Calgary men like to get away from home occasionally. Indeed, there is always one section of our male population away off in California or in Europe or the Mediterranean, or sloshing around the East somewhere. When they have blown off enough steam they return and another section of the populace hotfoots it for parts unknown, where a pleasant time may be had. Thus our purely local respectability is preserved untarnished. We are a remarkable people. [40]

*

Etiquette— Should a lady enter your office during business hours and cock her feet up on your desk, give her a drink out of your private bottle and show her out as quickly as possible. Tell her to come back later. Get her to leave her 'phone number. [41]

*

If Mayor James Findlay, of Vancouver, has any political ambitions he may as well pigeonhole them. His career as a public man was nipped in its bud two Sundays ago by the blighting agency of his own pigheadedness. Acting presumably under his orders, the police undertook to prevent a demonstration of Vancouver's unemployed on one of the open spaces of the city. Not only did the police smash innocent onlookers over the head with their batons, knocking some of them senseless, but a bunch of mounted police charged into the terrified crowd acting like drunken Cossacks. One report says:

"The horses plunged into the heaving human mass. Men were knocked senseless by the indiscriminate use of the policemen's batons and whip-stocks by the onslaught."

Reactionary methods such as these are not to be tolerated for a moment in Canada.

Not satisfied with turning the police loose on the harmless demonstrators and innocent bystanders, the Seventy-Second Highlanders were under orders with twenty-five ball cartridges for each man! The question agitating the minds of Vancouverites is, who issued the mobilization orders for the troops? If it was Mayor Findlay, then it may be presumed that he was panic-stricken and lost his head. Which is not a very creditable performance for the chief of a great city like Vancouver.

For the general information we should explain that there is a large number of unemployed in Vancouver this winter and the meeting was called by the local labor delegates who had attended the recent labor congress at Victoria and incidentally interviewed Premier McBride with a view to seeing what measures the provincial government would take to provide for the commencement of public works in order to ameliorate the condition of the unemployed. The premier had intimated that immediate steps would be taken with this end in view.

It was to deliver this message of hope to the hungry that R. P. Pettipiece and J. H. McVety called the meeting. Such a gathering should have called for kindliness and sympathy on the part of the authorities, not blows and curses. When Mr. Pettipiece got up to revive their hopes of obtaining employment by telling them of his satisfactory interview with the premier, he was promptly pinched. A bunch of prominent labor men were taken into custody at the same time.

This unparalleled treatment of the labor element will rankle for many years. It will not help the Conservative cause in the province either, to any alarming extent, for Mayor Findlay, who was at the bottom of it all, is head of the Vancouver Conservative Association. His political finish has been accomplished by a blunder which he will never be able to live down this side of the grave. He ought to be heartily ashamed of himself.

Even in London, the centre of the Empire, parades through the streets and public demonstrations on the part of laborites, of unemployed, and of strikers, are freely permitted by the authorities. Trafalgar Square and Hyde Park are the favorite points of rendezvous. Of course, the metropolitan police are on hand to prevent obstreperous conduct, but their methods of handling large crowds are characterized by skill, good temper and a trained intelligence which is lacking in the ignorant slobs who get on to the police force in Canada. [42]

*

This business of young girls staying out late of an evening hinges entirely on the kind of company they are keeping while out. It is not always the young men who are to blame if anything goes wrong. There is a certain type of middle-aged women in this town who drink like fish and who like to encourage others of their own sex, especially the young and lively ones, to drink also. These are a tremendous source of danger to our girls, because once these youngsters get to like the taste of whiskey, it is all off. This is official. [43]

*

There will always be a certain percentage of fallen women in every large community. This being so, the question resolves itself into this: is it better that men should allay their grosser passions in the occasional company of these women who have already fallen and who earn their livelihood that way, or is it preferable that the men should break the hearts of mothers by ruining their daughters or that they should wreck homes by corrupting honest men's wives?

These are the alternatives. Which do you choose? [44]

*

Etiquette— When attending a dinner party it is considered bad form to slip from the parlor a few minutes before the gong and secrete yourself under the table, later on arching your back suddenly while the guests are lapping up their soup, thus tipping over everything in sight. Most hostesses hate this sort of thing. [45]

*

The license department in Winnipeg is a funny outfit. They have a department to censor moving picture films. Every now and again in Winnipeg some picture gets in that needs clipping. It is clipped. The clipping goes on for a year, and all the clippings are kept.

Then what happens?

The city hall sanctions a private view of the pictures. Now, the fun lies in the fact that the people who have been railing against improper pictures are the very ones who attend these private exhibitions! When the private show was pulled off recently in Winnipeg at the Bijou Theatre, the place was jammed to overflowing with the moral lights of the city. Representatives of the best-known charitable organizations were also present, gloating over pictures of the hootchee-kootchee and all the rest of it. They are a bunch of libidinous hypocrites. That's what they are. [46]

*

The maid had conscientious scruples against telling visitors that her mistress was "not at home" when she really was in the house. The minister had sent a message to say that he would call early in the morning, and the mistress told the maid that if he came at any unreasonable hour she need not say "not at home," but could explain matters, and ask him to wait.

When the mistress came down to breakfast the maid was waiting for her with a distressed face.

"Please, ma'am," she said, "the minister came, but he went away angry."

"What on earth did you say to him?"

"I said, ma'am, as you said, you were in your bath, but that if he liked he could come in and see you." [47]

TWELVE

Life & Death

Life has many shadows—but most shadows are due to sunshine. So buck up! [1]

*

Make the best of your life. You will never get another chance to be happy. [2]

*

Obituary— The many friends of Martin M. Bingham will be sorry to learn that he fell down a steep flight of steps Wednesday a week ago and broke his neck. Mr. Bingham was in the act of lowering a case of Three Star Hennessey into the cellar when his foot slipped. It is understood that the Hennessey was three-year-old and will revert to his widow. The bereaved woman is receiving many callers. [3]

*

Just about the time a man gets comfortably fixed in this world it is time for him to move on to the next. [4]

*

Few of us in the North-West can be judged by ordinary standards. In too many cases Nor'westerners have in former days and in other climes been weighed in the balance and found wanting. Many of us are here in the same sense as the Spanish fleet is supposed to be in Santiago de Cuba—bottled up. And some are here because they have bottled up not wisely but too well. As the storm drives the wings of the petrel over a measureless sea till it falls limp and tame on some passing ship, so are —at least a few of us—run to earth, tired out, in a western burg.

Yet we are fairly happy. Our boyhood visions of cabinet positions are exchanged for amusing little anxieties about securing jobs that will bring in $40 or $50 a month. Often, often are we bewildered with dismay at the recollection of lost opportunities, and sometimes when we are in the blues, memories crowd upon us that make us turn hot and cold by turns. But past experiences cut little ice out here. One gets out of the habit of thinking deeply on grave subjects, and few people take themselves seriously. Reflections on the immortality of the soul are ruthlessly pushed aside to make room for speculations on the next horse race. [5]

*

Happiness has a peculiar way of coming and going without any warning. [6]

*

James T. Postlethwaite of Hillhurst had the misfortune to break his neck last Wednesday and will be buried this (Saturday) afternoon. Deceased had suffered a sharp attack of sciatica between the shoulder blades and his wife, under the doctor's instructions, had applied alcohol lotions to the spot. It was while trying to lick it off that Mr. Postlethwaite dislocated the medulla oblongata. Not lost but gone before. [7]

*

The things that come to the man who waits are seldom the things he has been waiting for. [8]

*

We regret to record the sad death of poor Mrs. J. B. Warble, of Seventeenth Ave. W. It is said that she died of despondency and worry. When the sun didn't shine, deceased was miserable, and when it did she said it faded the carpets. In the midst of life we are in death. [9]

*

Don't sneer at the man in a hole. He may climb out and kick you in. [10]

*

Did you ever get so lonesome that you wanted to howl like a dog? [11]

*

An old Wetaskiwin acquaintance, Charles Dunlop, has died and was buried last week. During our residence at Wetaskiwin Mr. Dunlop was one of our bitterest enemies, and there was no love lost between us. In the shadow of the tomb all is forgotten. Deceased had his faults. Besides being an inveterate rustler of young cattle, he made more than one mysterious shipment of horses. But the good traits of deceased greatly outnumbered his faults. We have long since overlooked his theft of a posy of flowers from a grave to give to the dining room girl of the Driard, and trust that no vandal will play the same mean trick on his own resting place. There is little likelihood, however, of there being many flowers placed over the tomb of such an ornery cuss as Dunlop. With a cold wintry spring like this he is probably happier in hell than in Westaskiwin. Rest in peace. [12]

*

In order to enjoy life a man must be a little miserable occasionally. [13]

*

A light-hearted jest may be empty enough, yet we are all the better for it. [14]

*

James T. Richardson of Edmonton, who claimed to be the inventor of two percent beer, expiated his crime on the gallows at Fort Saskatchewan last Tuesday. His screams for mercy while the noose was being adjusted under his left ear were heard as far as Cooking Lake. [15]

*

Time is said to magnify our good deeds and diminish our naughty ones. (Important, if true.—Ed.) [16]

*

The buds on the trees are hesitating. Trees usually wait until they receive certain assurances of spring before permitting their sap to rise. Of course the human saphead is on the job all the year round. [17]

*

No man is so religious that he considers dying a pleasure. [18]

*

The sad death is reported of Mr. Benjamin F. Blink, a promising young businessman of Calgary. It appears that Mr. Blink, who had been induced to purchase some lots out in Calgary Junction a year ago, drove out last Sunday to have a look at them for the first time. He was found dead on his property, with his throat cut from ear to ear. His pocketknife lay by his side, showing that it was a case of self-destruction. A look of intense disgust pervaded the face of deceased. Mr. Blink was an expert billiard player, being especially adept at cushion caroms. Mr. B. was married, but looked remarkably cheerful up to the time of his death. Much sympathy is expressed for Mrs. Blink and the little Blinks whom this tragedy has put on the blink. In the midst, etc. [19]

*

Hope for the best and then hustle for it. [20]

*

A man begins to get life in its proper perspective when he quits expecting to find pearls in his oysters and is extremely gratified when he gets the oysters. [21]

*

So what, after all, does it matter how you act or what you do in this world, so long as you keep out of jail? You may have lived a most virtuous life, denying yourself many kinds of worldly amusements and enjoyments, because you were told by the preachers that true virtue lay in self-abnegation; but after you're dead, the community at large won't think any the more for it. Not they! They will shrug their shoulders and say, "that mutt didn't get much out of life anyhow."

The man who economizes his emotions, his money and his pleasures during youth and middle age gets about as much satisfaction out of life as a man who is dieting does out of his dinner. Some clever man has said that the cost of living is just a little more than you can earn. It is beginning to dawn on people that the successful—worldly—man commands just as much respect as the successful businessman who is trustee of a church and therefore, very solemn. Even the young folks nowadays cannot fail to observe the silent admiration of the world for the successful scoundrel, the debonair master of craft who is morally, financially and perhaps politically opaque, but who floats on the crest of the wave to the golden shore, living on the fat of the land, whirling about in motor cars, and ordering pints the live-long day. When the first mentioned and second mentioned are laid away in their graves, they are both at a par, their bones will rot and crumble into dust "just the same" and they are known no more. [22]

*

It is a waste of life to be sensible all the time. [23]

*

Obituary Note— John M. Crawley, of Seventeenth Avenue, one of our best-beloved Rotarians, was found dead in his bedroom early Wednesday morning, hanged to the bedpost by his suspenders. At the inquest the coroner's jury decided that Mr. Crawley, whose sad demise has cast a gloom over the community, met his death by coming home full and mistaking himself for his pants. Not lost, but gone before. [24]

*

One can always tell when one is getting old and serious by the way that holidays seem to interfere with one's work. [25]

*

No man ever does as much today as he is going to do tomorrow. [26]

*

Wealth is not his who gets it, but his who enjoys it. [27]

*

There is no doubt but what the lack of a marked individuality leads to a happy, peaceful and contented life. Those of a passive temperament who humbly follow a simple unobtrusive routine in their daily lives, who never get into snaps, jackpots or tight boxes, never commit themselves, who say nothing but saw wood, whose coming and going is not noticed, whose presence or absence is not marked, who never made much money, and yet, are never in debt, they are the happiest of us all. By never leaving the harbor they escape the rocks against which more active and aggressive members of society bump their heads. Men of weakly defined character, good-natured nonentities with no fiery impulses or nonsense of that kind, who cut little figure in their native towns, to whom the usual objects of existence offer no attractions, these are the lucky ones. To them belong the steady honest jobs, to them three squares a day and innocent slumber. Would we were like them. It would be money in our pocket. Instead of being in debt about fifty, we would probably only owe about five or ten. [28]

*

When Misfortune reaches a man's door she walks right in without knocking. [29]

*

Did it ever occur to you that now is the future you longed for several years ago? [30]

*

Fewer flowers for the dead and more flour to the needy living might help some. [31]

*

Keep on trying. It is often the last key of the bunch which opens the door. [32]

*

Poor old John McSwalligan, beloved by many friends and

old-timers, is the latest victim of the flu. Before passing away, Mr. McSwalligan divulged to his broken-hearted family a secret cache in the house where ten gallons of F.O.G. were stored away. The sorrow engendered by the visitation of death was thus tempered with joy and gladness. The Lord tempers the wind to the shorn lamb. The number of people who have called to express their sympathy has been something fierce. [33]

*

You can learn a little each day—unless you are one of those persons who know it all. [34]

*

Here is a yarn sent to us from Banff. We don't believe a word of it, but you can have it.

One day week before last, at the Cave and Basin swimming pool, a timid and retiring looking man waited until that good old Scot, Mr. Galletly, the boss in charge, was disengaged, and then said to him:

"I do hate to give anyone trouble, but have you got a long stick or a pole of any kind you could lend me?"

"No, sir, I have no pole. I told you so ten minutes ago," snapped the busy Galletly.

"So you did," replied the man, "but I thought I'd ask just once more. I think I've done my duty in the matter. Don't you think so?"

"What matter? What in thunder are you talking about?"

"Why, you see, my mother-in-law dived off there at the deep end about half an hour ago and as she hasn't come up yet I thought I would like to tell my wife that I had jabbed around the bottom for her for a while, anyway. But if I can't, why, I suppose I can't, that's all."

And pensively writing her address on the back of an old envelope, to be pinned to the old lady when she came up, the conscientious man shook hands with Mr. Galletly and walked thoughtfully away. [35]

*

Most of the entries in the human race are also-rans. [36]

*

The fool takes things as they come, but the wise guy lets a good many of them pass on. [37]

*

The remembrance that comes to us all once in a while, especially during a fit of the blues, of how soon we shall cease to be young, is no pleasant reflection to man or woman. More especially is the thought depressing when one is conscious of wasting one's time in an ineffectual existence on the outskirts of civilization. There are certain moments when the time, the lapse of which we have been forgetting all about, makes itself suddenly apparent to our eyes; when the change we had not been noticing stares at us suddenly from a looking glass. The lines and drawn marks on the face might have been planted in a single hour, so unnoticed have they been.

Birthdays are just as annoying recurrences to men as to women. When it comes to the age feature, men are as vain and sensitive as women. Indeed, we believe them to be even greater storytellers in this respect than the fairer sex. Usually we can gauge the correct age of a girl pretty accurately from a knowledge of the various members of her family, but with the lone man who has been knocking about the world you cannot tell a thing about him in the age line. When he says he is twenty-five, he is liable to be thirty; if he claims to be thirty, put him down at thirty-five; and should he admit forty or over, then you may bet heavily he is sixty or seventy. [38]

*

It's easy to be happy. All you have to do is to be foolish. [39]

*

To the question "How much did Pierpont Morgan leave?" the answer must continue to be "all that he had." [40]

*

The proof of success is the ability to deliver the goods. [41]

*

Did it ever strike you—you, gentle reader, who have lived in Calgary for say ten or twelve years—what a lot of our old friends with whom we used to joke and carouse are lying cold in death out in the cemetery? We made up a list of them the other day and have been in the blues ever since. What strikes us most forcibly is the quickness with which the dead are forgotten in this western country. "Old Jorkins has gone toes up." "Too bad—booze, I suppose?" A string of buggies, filled with men talking real estate, follow his remains to the graveyard, and pouf! he passes completely out of memory. Were we to die tomorrow the only remark passed would be—"When are they going to plant the ———? I wonder where I can rustle a buggy."

Which of us will be picked off next? [42]

*

The shadow of trouble is usually blacker than the trouble itself. [43]

*

Remorse is memory that has begun to ferment. [44]

*

He who tries to be all things to all men usually ends by being nothing to nobody. [45]

THIRTEEN

Sports

A man never loses money on fast horses. It is the slow ones that cause all the damn trouble. [1]

*

"Eureka!" exclaimed the shade of Darwin. "I have discovered it at last!"

"Discovered what?" asked the shade of Huxley.

"The missing link that makes a man out of a monkey," answered Darwin. "It's the golf link." [2]

*

A knockout in the ring is not as black as it is painted. They all recover their senses in due course, some more quickly, some more slowly, but it is usually only a matter of a few minutes before the defeated gladiator is inquiring of his seconds how it all happened. If you see a fighter copped full on the jaw, fall straight backward from his heels, don't think for a moment that fellow is out. Unless he has hit his head on the floor he will be up before the ten is spoken.

Now and then when a man has been battered about a lot in previous rounds and is all in, and falls backward after a stiff punch, he may not be able to summon energy enough to his legs. Then he'll have to take the ten count, but he'll be wriggling and flopping and his brain will be perfectly sensible.

But when you see a fighter pitch forward, landing face downward on the canvas—that's all. Ring the gong, toll the bell, drop the curtain, carry him away and pour cold water on him. He is finished for that evening. This style of fall is an infallible sign of a knockout punch, and there is little need for the referee to bother counting.

Of course there are variations of the knockout fall. Some men stay on their knees, unable to clear the fog from the head in time to rise. Now and then they sit down heavily and stay on the canvas. But the vast majority of boxers who are smitten squarely on the chin fall either straight backward or straight forward—and they will get up if they fell backward, while they'll stay down if they fall forward. Curious, but true. [3]

*

We read a lot about expert baseball pitchers at fabulous salaries, but we will bet a hundred dollars that not one of them could take a wad of paper and land it in the wastebasket three feet distant, twice out of five attempts. We have yet to see the man who can. [4]

*

Some one has remarked that heavyweight champions are rarely knocked out before they are thirty-five. Well, how can they be? They never do any fighting after they become champions. At least, not if they can get out of it. Willard boxed ten rounds between the time he whipped Johnson in 1915 and the day he fought Dempsey in 1919. Ten rounds—thirty minutes—in four years and four months.

And Dempsey, at twenty-four, has quit the fighting game for the movies. It has been nearly ten months since he trimmed Willard, with no match in sight. You can't get knocked out in the movies—not if you are the hero, anyway. [5]

*

A friend who recently popped down to Spokane popped back with the following delightful experience:

He met an American gentleman, "one of the finest chaps you ever met," who was brimful of novel ideas. One of his novel ideas was the reconstruction of the national emblem to conform with the spirit of the times. He said:

"I would have the national flag, of course, but on each corner I would put a baseball, a golf ball, a tennis ball and a football, in order to immortalize the glories of outdoor sport. Then, instead of having the eagle on top spreading her benign wings over the flag, I should have a stork, as emblematic of what I believe may justly be regarded as the king, if not the pioneer, of indoor sport." [6]

*

This is a good opportunity to tell our readers of how foot racing—more especially sprinting—was brought into disrepute in Canada. The sprinters were the crookedest bunch that ever came down the pike, ever ready to double-cross their own friends and backers at the first favorable opportunity.

About twenty years ago there was a bunch of fakirs who made their headquarters at Chatham, Ont., that certainly were the limit so far as crookedness in the foot racing business is concerned.

They ran more crooked races and skinned more suckers for bigger wads than any other gang that ever operated in that line. The men who did the running were Ben Coyne, of Chatham, Wm. Boyd, of Woodstock, and James Quirk, of Brantford, Ont.

Any one of these three could do a hundred in ten seconds flat, and in a pinch, Coyne, who was the youngest and speediest of the trio, could do a fifth of a second better. Later on these men were joined by the celebrated English runner, Fred Vokes, and the four were in the profitable business (to them) of relieving suckers of their money for years.

The manner in which Vokes joined the gang shows the methods this bunch were in the habit of using to get the money from the unwary.

In the year 1890 Coyne went to Detroit during the week of the Grand Circuit Trotting Meeting and secured a job under an assumed name at the old Hamtramack racetrack as a stable boy. In the evening he would run a race with some of the other boys, and, of course, beat them. Before the week was out he showed the horsemen a ten-second clip, and they thought they had a world-beater. About this time Boyd, who was well known in Detroit, came along and made a match with the stable boy, and to make it even gave him a start of ten yards in a hundred. Of course, the horsemen speedily made the match and staked considerable money on the result. Boyd won the race and he and his pal, Coyne, divided the spoils.

One of the men who lost considerable money on this race, was a well known saloonkeeper, who owned a swell saloon on Woodward Ave., Detroit, and he thought of a plan to get even.

Fred Vokes was the fastest runner in England at that time and had just won the famous Sheffield handicap, the blue-ribbon event in English racing circles. The Detroit crowd sent over for Vokes and offered him a good thing to come to America and run. He accepted, and the saloonkeeper at once went to Chatham and arranged a race between Coyne and the "unknown," the latter to have a start of two yards.

The Detroit man's scheme would have been successful, for the man never lived who could give Fred Vokes two yards in a hundred and beat him, but the Chatham crowd got next to the scheme of bringing Vokes over. They saw they were up against it unless they could buy Vokes to lose the race.

One of the gang accordingly met Vokes upon his arrival in New York and made the proposition to him and he accepted so readily they thought he was trying to give them the double cross.

To make sure of the race the Chatham bunch held him at Chatham and sent a loyal bartender named Smith on to Detroit, where he represented himself as Vokes.

This Smith was a fast man all right, but he was an easy mark for Coyne, and being a member of the gang, would not beat him if he could.

The supposed Vokes made good with the Detroit sports and they backed him to the limit, the saloonkeeper even going so far as to mortgage his business to get more money to bet on the race.

The race was run one Saturday afternoon at the track in Windsor, Ont., and was a cinch for Coyne. Smith did not stop running at the tape, but kept on at a speedy gait until he reached a cab that was waiting for him at the track gates. The Canadian sports cleaned up about $12,000 on this race, and it is probably the largest amount ever made on a race of the kind.

Boyd, who was the brains of the bunch of sure-thing men, is still alive, although he must be about sixty years old. During the great St. Louis exposition the papers gave him credit for beating some sucker out of $5,000 in that city. Vokes died in Buffalo in 1890. Before his death he became famous as a trainer of bicyclists. Quirk was murdered by some unknown in an outhouse in the rear of his hotel in Brantford, Ont., several years ago. Coyne, if still alive, makes his home in Toronto. [7]

*

Society Note— Mrs. Eugene Fosburg will give an informal luncheon to a select party of Rotarians at the country club tomorrow (Sunday) on the occasion of the opening of the golf season. Miss Brackett will pour the tea and Miss Farnum cut the stymies. If old man Fosburg will keep out of the way, this affair will be a success. Fosburg is a damn nuisance and might well be disposed of in the city incinerator. There is no justification for this man being allowed to live. When he applied for membership in the Rotary Club last fall, the available black-balls were all used up and they had to send the steward out to buy a crate of blackberries before the voting could proceed. [8]

*

Here is a rich one:

On the fourth of July, the year of the big fight, Franklin P. Adams, the paragrapher, and a friend named Mercer, also in the business, went to the Polo Grounds to see a ball game and sat in the press box.

There was a big crowd present, all anxious for news of the prize fight at Reno. No bulletins were read at the game, but before the clubs went on the diamond Adams and Mercer, sitting near the telegraph instruments, began to read fake bulletins of the fight to one another, as though they were taking them from the telegraph instruments used to send out the news of the ball game.

They read the reports of the preliminaries and soon had four or five hundred men who sat nearby straining to hear what they said. Finally they began the fight and read, for the benefit of the listeners, a record of eight bloody rounds, in which Jeffries knocked Johnson down repeatedly and Johnson knocked Jeffries down an equal number of times. Just before the ball game began Adams read: "Ninth round. Both men very weak. Fierce fighting. Jeffries knocks Johnson down with a left hook to the jaw. Johnson clambers to his feet and knocks Jeffries against the ropes with a tremendous body blow. Both men fighting desperately all over the ring. The knockout blow is delivered. Tex Rickard, the referee, counts ten. The insensible man is taken to his corner and the referee proclaims the other the champion of the world!"

Then he stopped.

"For Heaven's sake!" yelled the excited men behind them. "Who won? Who got knocked out? Who won the fight?"

Mercer turned calmly to the howling mob and held up his hand. There was instant silence.

"The despatches do not state," he announced, and then the ball game began. [9]

*

The boxing game seems to be all shot to pieces. The trouble is that the boxers themselves and their managers are "sports" when they ought to be "sportsmen." The greed for money has spoiled them. Like the beggar who was placed on horseback, they have ridden to the devil. The simile of the goose and the golden eggs is also applicable. The game has become nothing more nor less than a coarse money-making device, very little fighting is actually done, and the people have become heartily sick of the whole business. [10]

*

It was Deacon White
Who went over to the library
In the parliament buildings
One day before the war
For a book on baseball
And picked out
The second volume
Of an encyclopedia
Because it was labeled
"Ata-Boy." [11]

*

As for the old-time sport of wrestling, that faked to death years ago. Nobody bothers his head about a wrestling match nowadays. One time while we were living in Winnipeg, Dr. Roller, the famous Seattle wrestler, came to the Walker Theatre to wrestle the equally famous Pat Connolly. Dr. Roller won after what appeared to be a terrible bout. A couple of years later, while in Calgary, Gotch and Mahmoud the Turk appeared at Sherman's Rink. We forget with whom Gotch wrestled, but the man who wrestled Mahmoud (and of course lost) was the same man we saw wrestle Roller under the name of Pat Connolly. His name was something else this time. A year or so after that again, while on a visit to Vancouver, we went to see Szybysco (Stanislaus) who was billed to wrestle "the famous Pat Connolly." This Pat Connolly bore not the slightest resemblance to the Pat Connolly whom we saw wrestle Dr. Roller and to this day we are in the dark as to which, if either, was the genuine Pat Connolly, who—the real one—is a man of undoubted renown in the wrestling world. [12]

FOURTEEN

Purely Personal

Don't you think "absolutely" a much overworked word?
Absolutely. [1]

*

If money talks, all it ever said to me was goodbye. [2]

*

The other day we ran across a copy of the old *Free Lance*, a
weekly journal published by ourself in Wetaskiwin some
twenty or more years ago. This particular number is dated
May 6, 1898. Wetaskiwin at that time had a population of
about 300 and everybody was busted higher than a kite. Our
office was in a butcher shop which had just been vacated by the
butcher who had gone broke. His sign remained over the door
and we wrote our stuff on the counter where he had been wont
to chop meat. Great place for inspiration. The following paragraph will explain itself.

"We take this opportunity of announcing that the beautiful
painting of a bull's head over our new office does not signify
that it is a meat market. It was once, but not now—not now.
People wandering through our portals in search of pork chops
will have to go empty away. Our patience, as it is, is well-nigh
exhausted by little children coming in and rapping on the
counter with a dime, while we are dashing off an editorial on
CPR atrocities, and calling for ten cents' worth of liver."

We said we were all broke in Wetaskiwin in those days.
This is quite true. The butcher had providentially left us a stove

and a chair, but the difficulty lay in getting wood for the stove during the winter. It so happened that Constable Ketchen of the NWMP had his barracks next door and all his wood was provided by the government. This wood he got sawed to the proper stove lengths by stray prisoners or half-breeds. Our neighbor on the other side was an Englishman named Keble, who bought and sawed his own wood. Well, we didn't do a thing to those two woodpiles. Many a dark night when the town was asleep, also Ketchen and Keble, we sallied forth and laid in a supply of fuel. Neither of our genial neighbors caught on to our depredations until we mentioned it ourselves, when spring arrived, in the following paragraph:

"Now that the winter has come to a close we beg to thank the various owners of woodpiles in the vicinity of our office for all the wood we have stolen. Although not caught on any occasion, we consider it our duty to express our grateful appreciation of the wood. It was all right. The only improvement we can suggest for next winter is that Mr. Ketchen get his wood cut a little shorter and Mr. Keble, his a trifle longer."

Nowadays a man would be sent to jail for this sort of thing. Ketchen, the Mountie, not having had to saw his own wood, was easily placated. All we had to do in his case was to set 'em up a few times down at the hotel. Keble, on the other hand, who had had to saw his own wood and didn't drink, was rather inclined to grumble at first, but beyond remarking that he thought it d——d cheek on our part, he soon got over it.

These certainly were happy-go-lucky days. Whenever a new subscriber drifted into the office with a dollar, we instantly abandoned all business for the day and convoyed the subscriber down to the hotel, where the dollar was duly blown in. Did a man, through some happy streak of fortune, come into possession of, say, five dollars—which was damn seldom—it became known all over town immediately and the local sports could be seen converging towards the hotel from all directions at an exceedingly rapid gait. Many of those to whom we are here referring as "local sports" are today prominent businessmen in various parts of the province and well-blessed with this world's goods, to say nothing of overdrafts at the bank. As for ourself, we should worry! [3]

*

Veritas, Regina: Yes, there are other animals besides camels that can go a considerable time without water. Newspapermen, for example. [4]

*

The *Eye Opener* had a slight ginning up from the postal authorities last week on account of the irregularity of its publication. It appears, according to regulations, that a paper which poses as a weekly and receives postal privileges as a weekly, must come out weekly and not semi-occasionally. Our infuriated subscribers thus have cause to rejoice, for we shall have to come out once a week now whether we like it or not and whether there is anything to write about or not. It is a confounded nuisance, but it can't be helped.

If the postmaster general could only see our staff we feel sure that he would not insist on us coming out regularly. Those of our assistants who are not off on a drunk are in temporary confinement down at the barracks. Even the society editress has begun to drink more than is good for her and has taken to laughing boisterously at pink teas. In other respects she keeps fairly straight, but it is mortifying to the management to have ladies on the staff who don't know how to behave themselves in a drawing room. [5]

*

Acting on the advice of our lawyer we have cut out half of our stuff this week. Perhaps it is just as well. [6]

*

A correspondent from Olds writes to say that he went into a store there the other day to ask for an *Eye Opener* and was told that they did not sell such papers, as it would corrupt the morals of the town.

From the fact that one of Olds' ministers of the gospel some three weeks ago eloped with a young lady of that burg, he already having a wife and child in the States, we may be justified in presuming that the morals of Olds need no further corrupting just at present. This scandal should hold them for a while. [7]

*

It has often occurred to us that the name of this paper is an unfortunate one. There is nothing dignified about the title "Eye Opener." Public speakers who occasionally would like to quote some of our wise remarks, hesitate to do so, because they know full well that the moment they start to say, "I have it on the authority of the *Eye Opener*," or "only the other day I saw in the columns of the *Eye Opener*," the audience forthwith begins to grin and some d——n fool with a jag on sings out, "Wot's the matter with the *Eye Opener*?" There is, as we say, no dignity to the name. People are used to the old standbys, *Gazette, Herald, Review, Star, News* and so forth. Village weeklies are usually called the *Clarion*, the *Bugle* or the *Voice of the People*, but they are neither here nor there. It is too late now to change the name of the Calgary *Eye Opener*. [8]

*

An editor who started about twenty years ago with only 55 cents is now worth $100,000. His accumulation of wealth is owing to his frugality, good habits, strict attention to business and the fact that an uncle died and left him the sum of $99,999. [9]

*

Thanks to the courtesy of Superintendent McCall and Mr. Bob Lett, of the GTP, we were given the opportunity (since last we met in these pages) of taking a trip into the Yellowhead Pass as far as Fitzhugh. Jim Cornwall, M.P.P., O. Happy Day, near-M.P., and Pat Welch, one of the builders of the road, formed the balance of our little party. That is, not counting the excellent chef, Li Hung Chang. Now, look here, don't get scared. We are not going to bore you with descriptions of scenery. All that we will say about it is that it was O.K.

Real estate victims all over Canada will be interested to know that we spent an hour or more in the townlet of Edson. This little burg of one short, straggling street, is the scene of one of the awfullest real estate impositions ever pulled off upon a gullible public. The city limits extend four miles in one direction and four and a half in the other. On all sides of this lone street is a forest of trees, and as for muskeg—why, it's all muskeg. Down around the GTP station and yards, the land has been drained. Those who have purchased Edson lots from real estate agents in Toronto, Winnipeg, Vancouver, Seattle and other distant points, will have one devil's own time locating them, unless they happen to be within a few yards of the aforementioned street. By the time their great-grandchildren are old men, however, these lots may be quite valuable. Why hurry? In the meantime they may consider themselves stuck.

Between Edson and Fitzhugh we ran into a magnificent timber belt, and paused for a few moments at a big sawmill whose capacious yards were packed with millions of feet of the finest kinds of lumber. We gazed around in awe and rapture.

"To whom belongs this great timber property, stretching as far as the eye can reach, apparently spread all over God's creation, and who owns this wonderful sawmill?" we inquired of a native.

"Theodore Burrows," was the reply.

"And who might Theodore be?"

"Clifford Sifton's brother-in-law," responded the native, with a droop of his left eyelid and a faint grin.

The town of Edson, which contains about 800 souls and is not as big as Claresholm, with nothing to make it much larger than it is at present, takes in no less than fourteen and a half sections of land within its city limits. We have no hesitation in making the statement that Edson has been made the goat by unscrupulous sharks for the most preposterous real estate fraud that has ever been perpetrated in this country.

The GTP runs through the beautiful Athabasca Valley until it reaches the mountains, the most prominent of which are Roche Perdrix and Roche Miette. These two giants guard the entrance to the pass. The scenery around here is wildly picturesque, and almost lives up to the literary spasms of the little GTP booklets—which is saying a good deal. It would be hard for any kind of scenery to quite live up to the following verbal convulsion:

"Gradually those phantoms take definite form, out of their shimmering, prismatic, gauzy haze, until the first escarpment of the Rockies is thrown up, well-defined, mighty and defiant— transcendently beautiful with its battlemented heights, castellated towers, ramparts and beetling ('beetling' is good) precipices, filling the range of vision."

Jasper Park, the new national playground, rich though it be in scenic grandeur, cannot compare with the Banff Park, except in one respect—a very important respect. In the Jasper Park there is to be found the finest fishing in the world. Around Banff there is no fishing to speak of, although there used to be lots of it before certain people took to catching the fish with dynamite instead of flies. With good fishing added to the scenic attractions, Jasper Park will be able to hold its visitors for protracted periods after once getting them there. They also have hot sulphur springs and all that bally rot, you know. In fact, Jasper Park will be a replica of the Banff National Park, and every bit as attractive.

We only went as far as Fitzhugh within the park, which in due course is bound to become a favorite summer resort. This is really a delightful spot, located in an amphitheatre of mountains with chains of lakes and fishing streams all around and of easy access. The townsite has not yet been surveyed into lots, but will be this summer. Further west where an army of men are laying track, one runs into a more wild and rugged type of mountain scenery, the famous Mount Robson being their one best bet. But, as we remarked, Fitzhugh was as far west as we went. Mr. Cornwall and the writer hurried back to Edmonton to be in time for the fight that never came off.

As everyone knows, the Grand Trunk Pacific between Edmonton and Winnipeg is a model of what a smooth, solid-built railway should be. Well you can take it from us that the road west of Edmonton is equally smooth and solid, though there are many construction difficulties not to be met with on the prairie section. Some time in July the GTP is going to put on a fast passenger as far as Fitzhugh. Better take the trip and see something of this wonderful new country which is being opened up. Go, if only to have a hearty laugh at the Edson town lots.

On the trip, we forgot to mention, one passes the site of Jasper House, an historical landmark of the early days. It would have been an historical landmark yet had not some chump come along a year or two ago and pulled it down to make a raft to float down the Athabasca River. This vandal was arrested for stealing the logs and fined $50. He should have been shot. This historical house was built about the year 1800 and was an important post of the Hudson's Bay Company. It was a famous landmark of old days. [10]

*

When a man begins by saying, "Of course it's none of my business, but . . ." he is getting ready to butt in where he doesn't belong. [11]

*

There is absolutely no truth in the malicious report that a file of the *Eye Opener* was publicly burned by the common hangman in front of the parliament buildings at Ottawa last month. Parties circulating this report, which is calculated and probably intended to prejudice the moral status of this paper, will be prosecuted. It is inconceivable to what lengths some people will go. [12]

*

Last Wednesday being a lovely day we took a stroll out in the country and visited the charming Miss Louise Hinks. After a pleasant tête à tête with the lady we were driven home by her father, with a club. [13]

*

A certain curiosity having been expressed as to how the editor of the *Eye Opener* spends his time in High River, we beg to state that he rises every morning contemporaneously with the opening of the bar. After partaking of a jolt, he communes a while with Thomas Behan on scriptural subjects, and then has another jolt. This makes him a new man and he has to stand the new man a jolt for luck. After a few more desultory jolts he goes into the dining room and throws in a little breakfast, not infrequently throwing it up afterwards. Thereafter he secures a cigar and takes a walk across the bridge to the Paw Squatch to give good advice to the features. A few more jolts and luncheon comes on. After this function he takes a siesta and as many jolts as happen his way. At three o'clock the school children gather below his window and sing the national anthem. A jolt carnival follows, and if he has time to spare he writes stuff for his great moral journal. After a hearty supper he engages in a few games of seven-up, followed by family worship and a salubrious succession of jolts. Seven or eight nightcaps bring the day's labor to a close and the editor retires for the night. It is a strenuous life. [14]

*

We hear through a private letter that Joe Pringle, who ranches east of High River, has been calling us all sorts of names since we came east. All because, early last April, we put the rightful owner next to the whereabouts of a horse Joe had been using all winter to drive into town when he wanted to get drunk, which was pretty nearly every week. Joe should thank his stars he is not in the jug. We could have put him there had we felt inclined to be mean, but having once enjoyed his hospitality overnight, we prevailed on the owner to let the matter slide. And now here he is calling us all sorts of names.

The day we visited Pringle's house last winter, he was stretched out comfortably on a sofa, smoking a pipe and reading a comic supplement. In the course of conversation he said in a querulous tone:

"Do you know, my wife's the most helpless creature on earth, simply can't do anything without bothering me to help her."

"Is that so?"

"Yes, that's so. Only last night I had to reach up and get a lantern off the nail for her so she could go down cellar and bring up a scuttle of coal."

That's the kind of man Joseph Pringle is. If he does not shut up we shall have to tell how he got that cauliflower ear. [15]

*

Again, once more, for the hundredth time, we warn our readers in Vancouver not to pay more than 5 cents for copies of the *Eye Opener*. We learn that the kids out there are at their old tricks of selling this paper for 10 cents. Kindly notify us if those little imps are continuing to pull off this holdup game. This sort of thing queers the paper and makes our readers sore. Our agent gets the papers at the same price as all other agents, who seem to make plenty of profit at the regular 5-cent price. [16]

*

One of the reasons why the *Eye Opener* has so many high ideals is that Calgary is over 3,000 feet above the level of the sea. [17]

*

Saturday Night is good enough to say that "the Calgary *Eye Opener* has done more single-handed to expose western townsite fakes than any other western publication."

(Why, cert'nly!—Ed.) [18]

*

Our genial but cautious publisher writes advising us to use the word "alleged" more, as being safer in case of libel suits. We'll use it right now. J. W. Pringar of Cayley, with his alleged daughter, paid High River a visit last week. After putting his alleged horse in the barn Mr. Pringar filled up on some alleged whiskey which seemed to affect his alleged brains. It was alleged by those who saw him capering about the burg that he is under ordinary circumstances an alleged man, but few who saw him climb our flagstaff backwards will believe that he is other than a monkey. Mr. Pringar and his alleged daughter, after making extensive purchases of alleged pork sausages from George Meyer, returned home the same evening, Miss P. driving. [19]

*

The *Eye Opener* thinks that it is due to itself to announce that all advertisements which appear in these columns are the advertisements of reputable people doing a reputable business. We have lately declined quite a number of ads from firms whose business methods struck us as being on the shady side or as being detrimental to the interests of the investing public. [20]

*

While gazing out of one of the back windows of the old Walker House, where we are boarding, wondering where the next meal was to come from, our hungry eye lit on a bunch of forty or fifty tame pigeons perched on top of the barn. We at once decided to have pigeon pie for dinner.

The only hitch lay in the catching of the birds. Luckily our pardner happened in, and he, being also very hungry, solved the proposition in no time. There is nothing like having a good pardner. He ran out and borrowed a loaf of bread, came back, crushed it into crumbs, saturated it in the last of our whiskey and chucked the mess out of the window. In an instant the whole flock had pounced upon it, and it was with no little anxiety that we watched them as they acquired a jag. The rest is soon told. The pie was all right. As long as we can rustle enough whiskey to soak the crumbs, we need never go hungry till the last pigeon is gone. Come and dine with us some day. [21]

*

During a stormy career of close on to ten years the humble individual who runs the *Eye Opener* has accumulated a bunch of enemies who, if stretched out lengthways on the ground, would reach from Calgary to Banff, and back again as far as Morley. We now wish all such enemies to be our friends. Let us call it a stand-off. If those whom we have lambasted hell out of will forget it, we shall freely forgive all those who strove so vainly to put us on the bum. In effect, the *Eye Opener* celebrates the great Conservative victory by granting a general amnesty to all its enemies and will be glad to receive the same generous treatment in return. There is only one man barred, and you can guess who it is. Every one else we wish to regard as a friend, and it is our heart that speaks. This goes. [22]

*

Many a great man's reputation for wit is due to his having been interviewed by a bright reporter. [23]

*

We are delighted to learn that some awful stories were circulated in High River about the editor of this truly Christian organ before he arrived on the scene of his present labors. It proves the old axiom that the more virtues a man has, the more glaring are his shortcomings. One might well reason that the possession of as many virtues as we have, while no doubt exciting envy, should excuse in us certain faults. But it is not so. Of those who have, much is apparently required. Yawp! [24]

*

The latest sensation in literary circles in London is the claim that Bacon wrote the King James' version of the Bible. Oh well, so long as it wasn't Bernard Shaw. [25]

*

Love is the wine of life and old bachelors are prohibitionists. What, ho! [26]

*

A recent number of the *Daily Sketch* (London, Eng.) contained a paragraph about Calgary, with the added explanation, "where the *Eye Opener* comes from." Oh, well, if the E.O. has helped put Calgary on the map we shall not have lived in vain. [27]

FIFTEEN

Personalities

Seagram and Gooderham are regarded with feelings of intense admiration and awe, on account of the millions they have derived from rotgut whiskey that has put more people on the bum, wrecked more homes and killed off more men than disease or war in the same space of time. They belong to the élite of the cities wherein they reside.

Some people's idea of a great and virtuous man is a man who has secured as much as $10,000,000 without ever having been put in jail. [1]

*

Society Note— Lt. Col. James Walker is in the city today having been here for the last thirty years. He will likely be here tomorrow also, and the day after. [2]

*

R. B. Bennett has been relieving his feelings by telling his friends that he will run the editor of the *Eye Opener* out of town. [3]

*

Every man in these parts who gets found out and is conscious of being in the wrong, instinctively turns for aid to P. J. Nolan. This keen-witted lawyer immediately proceeds to prove the entire innocence of his client, getting unfavorable witnesses all balled up so that they don't know their own names, playing on the jury box as if it were a jew's harp and finally pooh-poohing the prosecution into a condition of manifest imbecility. It has not infrequently occurred to us that it would be better for the sake of the country at large if P.J. was not so diabolically expert at his business. [4]

*

Sir Frederick Borden is being sent by the dominion government to England. This is the beginning of the new era of reciprocity between the mother country and her chief colony. Canada has been importing studs from England for years, and it is gratifying to find that the government has at last decided to do a little exporting on its own account. [5]

*

The statement attributed to Mr. W. R. Hull in a recent interview that he intended purchasing the late pontiff's herd of papal bulls to put on the range adjacent to the New Oxley ranch for the purpose of improving the breed, is entirely without foundation. Mr. Hull has no such intention. [6]

*

Clifford Sifton has resigned, ostensibly over the school question. This implies a conscience on the part of Clifford. The idea of Clifford resigning on the ground of conscientious scruples is laughable to the extreme. What has really made him resign is the trouble he has gotten himself into over a married woman in Ottawa. It is a Sir Charles Dilke case over again.

Now then, take a long breath and prepare for the little telegraphic despatch announcing that Clifford is about to take a trip to Europe for his health.

The story of Sifton's escapade, wherein he seems to have been ministering to the Interior in great shape, reads like some of the spicier cantos in *Don Juan*. The outraged husband is Walter Mackay, son of the late millionaire, William Mackay, the old lumber king of Ottawa. It appears that Mackay started for Montreal one night, but for some reason turned back and spent the evening at the club instead. Returning to his residence about two o'clock in the morning, he tried to open the front door with his latchkey, but the latch was fixed on the inside so that he could not get in. So away he went round to the back door of the house to see if he could get in that way.

Approaching his back door, what was his surprise to see it cautiously opened from the inside and a big, tall man issuing therefrom. "Burglar!" thought Mackay, and quickly seized hold of the mysterious unknown. It was pretty dark at the time, and the two of them tussled and rolled all over the backyard. Finally, to Mackay's astonishment, a ray from the moon revealed the sinister features of the minister of the Interior.

"Hello, Sifton! What are you doing here this time of night?"

"Oh," quoth Clifford, panting, "your wife was in trouble over some legal matters and sent for me to discuss them."

"Well, that's strange," said the husband, scratching his nose dubiously. "I suppose it's all right, though."

Next day, however, Mackay put on his thinking cap, and rather foolishly aired the story downtown, telling all his friends about it. Their ill-concealed amusement showed him but too plainly that they had for some time been alive to what he, husbandlike, had been blind. Then the row began.

A private conference was held at the Mackay home, among those present as conciliators being Father Whalen, Archbishop Duhamel and Sir Wilfrid Laurier. Father Whalen next day took the lady to her former home in Quebec. Sifton just about this juncture left for the West, this stirring incident having taken place shortly before the elections. Ye Gods, and we didn't know about it!

By the time he returned the scandal had become the property of the politicians and of the inner circles of society, though no newspaper dared breath a word.

What between the uproar in his own family and the demands for reparation on the part of the husband, Clifford thought it was up to him to duck his nut. He left for parts unknown, and remained away from his seat in parliament, neglecting his duties and pretending he was in a sanitarium somewhere for his health. His health must have been all right about this juncture, if we know anything about this line of business.

Sifton returned to Ottawa a discredited man and handed in his resignation. That is the whole story. For the benefit of his dupes, the public, it was arranged that he should retire with dignity under the benign wing of the school question. This, in sporting parlance, is a stall. In connection with it, we rise to remark—"Rats!"

That is the plain, unvarnished tale. Not unlike one of Balzac's droll stories, eh? There are one or two other versions, one in particular which is far racier than the foregoing, but we prefer to confine ourselves to what we know to have actually happened.

In the meantime, we understand, hubby has filed a suit for divorce. The governor general, we presume, could not stand for his most important minister being co-respondent in a divorce case, though certain of the other cabinet ministers are not a whit more virtuous than Cliff. We are ruled over by a fine gang at Ottawa. [7]

*

It is discouraging to learn that several respectable, honest-minded persons in this town were highly indignant last week over the *Eye Opener's* frank exposure of the toodledyumpty-ido pranks of the ex-minister of the Interior, the representative of the North-West in the cabinet. They are apparently of the opinion that there is nothing particularly undesirable about having our destinies, the destinies of the Territories and indeed of the whole interior of Canada, placed at the mercy of a wily reprobate who has debauched the wife of his friend, wrecked a home and dishonored himself in the eyes of right-thinking people. If they think it is all right, then their moral code needs a thorough overhauling.

It is furthermore right and proper that the common people of our land should know these things. The public should be told all about the type of men whom the fortunes of politics have placed in charge of the affairs of this nation, and, as their virtues—if they have any—are extolled, so should their vices—if flagrant and dangerous to society—be exposed.

We have no apology to offer, nor retraction to make. [8]

*

Judge Beck was a Tory and he turned Grit to get his present job on the bench. He was a Mason and turned Catholic. Judge Beck is first one thing and then another, but is always the same narrow, prejudiced, fanatical Beck. [9]

*

Society Note— Bishop Pinkham, of the Calgary diocese, was down in Okotoks the early part of the week holding confirmation services. Superintendent Horrigan of the mounted police says he is unable to connect his lordship with the bank robbery. [10]

*

"Did you ever hear," began Dave McDougall, the Calgary old-timer, "about the winter I put in on my ranch near Morley in '67? It was what a man might be excused for calling some winter. That is to say, it was cold.

"We began to notice unusual symptoms along in November. To begin with, the creeks all froze solid—clear to the bottom, you understand—and instead of water flowing along in the creek beds there was ice moving along about the same speed. Regular glaciers.

"The creeks where I was emptied into the Bow and of course the Bow was as full as the creeks. So there was nothing left for the creek ice to do but hump up when it reached the river and double back on itself. Then when it got back to headquarters it had to double up again and go down to the river.

"All the creeks kept up this process until they were piled on top of themselves four or five times, or even more than that. Calgary folk looking west thought that the mountains were walking into town. They did, for a fact! We had to tunnel through those creeks to get from one place to another. And we had to keep making new tunnels, too, as the old tunnels kept moving up above our reach, where we couldn't get at 'em. You never saw anything like it, believe me!

"But the worst was yet to come. The first cold snap lasted until along in January. Then we had the usual January thaw. But this thaw hadn't got good and started when a big freeze set in one night and froze the ground so quick and so hard that it popped the rabbits and the gophers up out of their holes the way a little boy pops a pea out of its pod. I tell you it was a corker."

"It must have been," said J. J. McHugh, regarding the speaker darkly.

"You bet it was," said Dave. "Every one of those rabbits and gophers just stayed there in the air—frozen stiff, some of them six or eight feet above the ground. There were so many of them that a man couldn't go out without bumping his head. It was much like walking in a dense forest, only the animals were

214

closer to our heads than the branches of the trees would have been."

"Certainly," said Colonel Walker, with a strained look.

"The only way we could get a glimpse of the sun was to take an ice axe and climb up the side of one of the creeks. I never expect to see the like again."

"It must have been bally cold," ventured an Englishman.

"It was," said Dave.

"Well," put in J.J., "I suppose that when you wanted dinner all you had to do was go out and build a fire anywhere and the dinner would thaw out of the air and fall down into the pot, eh?"

"Not on your life! It was so cold that whenever anybody tried to start a fire the air melted and put the fire out. Every time. But that's not all—,"

"Oh, yes it is!" cried J.J., as he and the colonel reached for their hats and hastened over to the Alberta.

The Englishman remained behind. When he showed up at the Alberta an hour later, he looked pale and his eyes were popping out of his head.

"Make mine fairly strong," said he to the bartender. [11]

*

"Yes," said Mr. McDougall, reminiscently, "I remember one very hot day in the summer of 1854. I was asleep under a tree not far from where Banff now stands and awoke to a bear watching me. You ought to have seen me getting out of that! I ran so fast that I had to go sideways to keep from flying. When I struck the Belly River I knew I could get away if I only could get across. The water was frozen over, but I took out a hatchet I had in my pocket to cut the ice. What's that? Oh, you see, the bear chased me from July until well on in December. Yes, I got clear away after all, but I've had closer shaves than that. That's nothing.

"Perhaps the most exciting chase I ever had," continued Mr. McDougall, "was in 1847, when travelling in a sleigh between Morley and the Blackfoot reserve. While driving along I discovered, to my intense horror, that I was being followed by a pack of wolves. I fired blindly into the pack, killing one of the brutes, and you bet I was relieved to see the others stop and devour it. After doing this, however, they came on again. I kept on repeating the dose, with the same result, and each respite gave me an opportunity to whip up my team. Finally, there was only one wolf left, yet on it came, with its fierce eyes glaring in anticipation of a good hot supper. What's that? The last wolf must have had the rest of the pack inside him? By gum, that's so. Now I remember it did wobble a bit. Oh, yes, I killed the monster and pursued my journey to the reserve, where I found a movement on foot among the Blackfeet to take my scalp. But that is another story." [12]

*

An eastern despatch informs a startled world that Harry Corby, of "Corby's Whiskey," has been made a member of the Canadian Senate. If Corby only made better whiskey the appointment wouldn't be so bad, but we never fancied "Corby." It tastes too coppery. If Mr. Corby would rectify this he no doubt would make a fair senator as senators go. [13]

*

With all due respect to the memory of the late "Judge" Travis of Calgary, we have often wondered what that man got out of life. When he died Judge Travis was a very old man and had just reached the million mark. In spite of which he was up to his neck in real estate deals and busy from morning till night raising his rents and engaging in altercations with the assessor. The paralytic seizure which carried him off occurred in a real estate office where he was fixing up a deal. [14]

*

The late Paddy Nolan used to tell this story about a man whom he had just got off on a charge of horse stealing:

"Honor bright now, Bill, you did steal that horse, didn't you?"

"Now look here, Mr. Nolan," was the reply, "I always did think I stole that horse, but since I heard your speech to that 'ere jury, I'll be doggoned if I ain't got my doubts about it." [15]

*

The inevitable has happened. The sheet known as the Calgary *News*, of which that old liar McGillicuddy was put in charge for the purpose of sandbagging western people who had the courage to expose Clifford Sifton and other members of the rotten Ottawa gang, has gone up the flue. It is now in the hands of a receiver and L. F. Clary, solicitor, has been appointed liquidator. The old hypocrite, of course, was not fitted to conduct a newspaper, but was admirably equipped to run an obscene and libelling sheet for shameful purposes. Incidentally we may say, in writing the obituary of this bloodsucking fraud, that he has for years lived on pap handed out by politicians. We write "30" to this old dog's career with a great deal of satisfaction and had it not been for the favoritism of the judge before whom he was convicted of libelling us, he would have been wearing stripes in the penitentiary two years ago. Wonder how his imbecile son, Owen, the Train Dog, is taking the family misfortune? [16]

*

With McGillicuddy in hell and ourself in the legislature, why worry. [17]

*

There is a man whose career we shall follow with interest in the house of legislature, for the reason that from what we have observed he is destined for higher honors on the political battle-field in days to come. We allude to R. B. Bennett. Let him not, however, antagonize his opponents overmuch, as he is prone to do. The sly old politicians never do that. The soft word which turneth away wrath does not necessarily eliminate the fortiter in re feature.

Regarded from various points of view, Bennett is the best-equipped man for the fray of the whole galaxy of M.L.A.s going east from these regions. Mentally and by study he is the peer of any one in this country and although he don't drink, is not a bad fellow.

We don't want to keep harping on Bennett, but his platform is one which should be kept uppermost in the minds of all the members from this part of Alberta. Let them not forget it either. Alberta a province; Calgary a capital; railroad connection with the transcontinental American lines to the south; irrigation works constructed by the government; and one or two other minor matters. Bennett is essentially an initiative man. In him and Rosenroll we place our trust. Let them never be confounded. [18]

*

In the king's New Year honor list will probably be found the name of Senator Lougheed. Besides being thoroughly representative of the West and one of the most prominent upbuilders of the western metropolis, the senator is leader of the government in the Senate and a minister of the crown. Being a public-spirited millionaire, he can well maintain any dignity that is bestowed on him by the king. [19]

SIXTEEN

Rural Life

Prairie fires.
And
Measles.
Both running on time. [1]

*

A man was trying to sell Johnny Hamilton a windbroken
horse and was trotting him around for Johnny's inspection. He
stroked the horse's back and drew attention to his lovely coat.

"His coat's all right," said Johnny, "but I don't like his pants."
[2]

*

Most men who live in a city have a hard time proving to their
country acquaintances that they are strictly honest. [3]

*

We were glad to notice by the papers that "a hired man on a
farm" has at last won a wage case against a farmer. This is
indeed a change from the old days when the "honest farmer" used
to pay $25 a month, tell the hired man that he couldr't pay
him "until after threshing," and then, when the crop was
threshed, wind up by paying him his money in the most grudg-
ing manner or by not paying it all. These days are over.

It was a Lethbridge magistrate who decided that the hired
man on the farm was worth $75 a month. With wheat prices as
high as they are, $100 should be the wage. As it is, the farmer

hates the $75 touch, but has to come through. It has taken a long, long time for farm labor to meet with adequate wage recognition.

The worst characteristic of the farmer, especially the old-fashioned farmer with the whiskers, on both sides of the line—we speak from the experience of our hobo days—is his rapacity and greed. There are very few farmers but what begrudge paying the hired man his wages when due. He wants all the money received from the elevator to be "velvet."

We don't know how it is now, but when we were a good deal younger than we are now the hiring out process went like this: You asked how much he was paying.

"Oh, twenty-five to an experienced hand."

Then in your innocence you would ask, "How late do you work here?"

"Oh," would come the careless reply, "we unhitch at six o'clock."

The inexperienced one naturally jumped to the conclusion that all work therefore stopped at six. Poor fish!

What happened? It is worth recalling. Up in the morning at five, cleaning out the barn, feeding the horses, milking the cows and chopping a cord or two of wood, all before breakfast. Should it happen to be Monday, washday, you pack about twenty buckets of water into the house to fill the boiler. Then the breakfast and the l'il old bacon and eggs.

While gobbling away at the mess, the farmer tells you all about the hog the bacon came off, when he killed it and how much it dressed, and which particular hog he intends to kill next. Thereafter you sally forth with your team and put in a hard day's lick. For the first week the farmer is rather sociable and communicative, getting a line on what kind of a chap you are and how much you will stand for. If you are big enough to beat his head off, he is liable to continue being quite sociable. If not, look out!

Yes, you unhitch at six o'clock all right enough. That was no lie. But it is for the horses' sake, not yours. Having fed and watered the equines, you respond to a noisy summons made by the rattling of a baking pan with a big spoon at the half-opened kitchen door. Then more bacon and eggs, and then—O accursed memory!—the chores.

All those bloody cows to milk over again, the horses to bed

down and feed, wood to chop and water to fetch into the house for the morning. Between eight and nine, nearer nine, you enter the house for a smoke and a rest. The literature with which you may regale yourself and refresh your weary mind is hanging up on a nail over the wash basin in the form of a Hood's Sarsaparilla Almanack, a delightful work containing illustrations of the signs of the zodiac (Gemini and Sagittarius and the rest of 'em), together with an assortment of testimonials from people who were cured of the botts by taking copius doses of the sarsaparilla.

Having conned over this magnum opus you climb a steep flight of stairs to your room and drop off into a deep sleep. Within an incredibly short space of time the farmer's raucous voice is heard hollering up the narrow stairway, and lo! it is another day.

In the old days—not so long ago, either—where the Canadian farmer got in his really fine work on the hired man was in the winter. Manitoba farmers were especially guilty in this respect. There used to be hundreds and hundreds of busted young Englishmen in this country, green as grass and innocent as little children. They made great pickings for the "honest farmer" in winter time. Here it was not a question of wages at all.

The cold days and lengthening nights of late fall usually found the improvident young Englishman busted flat, with perhaps an insufficient outfit of clothing to face the rigors of a Canadian winter. He could not stay bumming around the little burg, and the hotelkeeper with whom he had blown in his pitiful summer earnings did not want him hanging around absorbing the heat of his stove and standing him off for grub. Enter the "honest farmer."

The "honest farmer" allows his baleful eye to rest for a moment on his victim. He passes the time of day and stands him a shot of booze, possibly two shots, not impossibly five or six shots. Then he says, "If you like, you can come out to my place and stay the winter. I guess I can find some odd jobs for you to do around the place to pay for your board. It will be better than hanging around this blamed old burg, and in the spring you can start in regular work and draw wages."

"By Jove," says the delighted young Englishman, "that's awfully decent of you, old chap! It will be quite a godsend. I assure you."

A few weeks later a sad-looking young man might be seen meandering down to the barn about six in the morning, carrying a lantern, snow knee-deep, wind blowing and thermometer 30 below freeze-out. Having fed the stock, he starts cleaning out the frozen barn with a pickaxe. After a couple of hours choring around milking a row of cows among other things, he carries the milk into the house and hits up the inevitable bacon and eggs and koffy.

This over, the unfortunate youth hitches up the wagon, on which is perched an enormous hay rack, and drives off through the biting cold to a distant haystack. Returning, he feeds the cattle and waters them. If there is a creek handy, he chops holes in the ice, if not, he pumps water into a trough until the thirst of the bovines is thoroughly quenched. Each bovine drinks about a barrel. Then he chops or saws a cord of wood to get up an appetite for dinner.

Afternoon, lots to do, lots to do, any God's amount of it. Come what may, the folks won't have that lazy Englishman loafing about the house and he must be kept busy outdoors. Evening comes, with its interminable chores. Chores, chores, chores! "Chore, boys, chore! My mother keeps a mangle!" Then the Sarsaparilla Almanack and to bed. Blessed sleep!

Once the "honest farmer" got this type of English youth out on to his farm to "help around during the winter for his keep," it was all off with that youth, who would have been much better off in jail. The farmer had him where he wanted him. The unfortunate young man could not walk into the neighboring burg penniless, for he would only starve there and be compelled to pass the bitter cold nights in the hay loft of the livery stable. And the cold blasts of winter prevented him from risking the danger of beating his way to the nearest big city, where he would only be vagged anyhow.

No, he had to tough it out with Mr. Honest Farmer till spring, and Mr. H. Farmer knew that he had to tough it out, and meant to see that he earned every mouthful of his damn old bacon and eggs and koffy and soggy bread.

There is happily none of that in Canada today. If there is we have not heard of it. Indeed, it is years since we met a green Englishman at all. They all seem to have got wised up. In any case, there would be none of him just now during these war times. If this type still exists, he is fighting for his country. Although a bit green, he was never yellow. [4]

*

Society Note— J. B. Huxley, well-known horse thief, is in the city for a few days shaking hands with old friends. J.B. predicts a bumper crop again for next year. His own crop this fall thrashed out nearly sixty bushels to the acre. [5]

*

Westward the course of empire takes its way, veering slightly to the north in the direction of Athabasca Landing. [6]

*

"That horse knows as much as I do."
"Well, don't tell anybody. You may want to sell him some day." [7]

*

City people envy the farmer—but not to such an extent that they take advantage of the continuous opportunities to be one. [8]

*

I have sometimes while following my vocation of rustic josher found myself poking feeble jokes at the honest farmer and his calling. *Qui rit le mieux rit le dernier.* The farmer has the laugh on his side in the long run. What I chiefly envy him for is that he does not have to solicit patronage from anybody. He doesn't need to enter into competition with any of his neighbors like a merchant. He does not have to wrangle and play foxy for a living like a lawyer whose bread and butter comes out of the misfortunes of others, and doesn't have to depend on collections reluctantly doled out as country editors have to do. Thrice blessed farmer!

Granted that he manages his business in a business-like way and does not play sucker to the town shark, the farmer can be the most independent mortal on the face of God's green earth.

When I say he is independent, I do not mean that he is independent of the elements. With them he has to be meek and humble, and take what they give him. It is like a basket social. You don't know what return you are going to get on your investment. [9]

*

Hobo—"I've walked many miles to see you, sir, because people told me that you were very kind to poor chaps like me."
Householder—"Oh, they said so, eh?"
Hobo—"Yes, sir. That's why I came."
Householder—"Are you going back the same way?"
Hobo—"Yes, sir."
Householder—"Then will you be good enough to contradict this rumor?" [10]

*

On Thursday of last week a lunatic—another lunatic—was brought down from the North by Sergeant Charlie Phillipps of Wetaskiwin. On Tuesday of this week yet another lunatic from the North was brought down. This steady shipment of lunatics from the North is getting beyond a joke. [11]

*

When a farmer is drilling a well for drinking water it must make him hopping mad to run into a great deposit of oil. [12]

*

Duhamel, 1st November, 1898.
Sir: What is a good thing to fix a dog that rushes out at you from a farmhouse and bites you in the leg?
Yours truly,
CITY

There are several ways of fixing it. One is to take a small lump of lard, bore a hole in it, insert some strychnine and place in the dog's path. When the dog swallows it he is permanently cured of this obnoxious habit. Another favorite way is to secure a billet of wood and batter the animal's head into a jelly. Yet another way is to kick the dog in the stomach, and then go in and hammer the stuffing out of the owner. This latter method is the one we would recommend if you think you can get away with it. But there is yet another way of killing the animal. Climb a tree and commence reading aloud a copy of the South Edmonton *Plain-dealer*, when the dog will be pretty sure to kill himself laughing. [13]

*

Though Calgary is in the midst of a great cattle region, it is almost impossible to get a tender bit of meat from the local butchers. The explanation is that all the good beef, the top steers, are reserved for export. All the beef left unsold in the Calgary meat markets by Saturday night is bought up by the boot and shoe trade. Many a man is walking about our streets today in shoes manufactured from rib steaks. They are said to be more durable than the ordinary tanned leather. [14]

SEVENTEEN

City Life

When Solomon said there was a time and a place for everything he had not encountered the problem of parking his automobile. [1]

*

The millennium has came.

The cities of Edmonton and Strathcona are going to celebrate Coronation Day by amalgamating the two municipalities and uniting under the name of "Edmonton." This happy union means that Edmonton will have three breweries instead of only two as heretofore. In breweries she will lead Calgary by one. [2]

*

The devil is surely looking after Calgary. Mount Vesuvius has had a frightful eruption, with great loss of life, and San Francisco has put up a strictly first class earthquake, destroying hundreds of lives and burning up four square miles of the best part of the city; and yet, through all this period of calamity, through all this turmoil of stress and suffering there was not a single life lost last week at the railway crossing on First Street West. [3]

*

With the advent of the automobile Calgary advances another stride as the logical leader in all that is good, fashionable, immoral, gay and joyous in the Territories; and by way of further justification for the auto's introduction we have only to mention the two hospitals, the coterie of skilled surgeons, the coroner and the police magistrate, and the patriotic, progressive, prosperous, perspicacious, popular, potent, powerful politicians of that beautiful and lovely city who will now have the honor of passing bylaws regulating the auto's speed and incidentally fixing the fines. [4]

*

Society Note— Mrs. Peter McSnorter gave a brilliant party this week in honor of Miss Sweeny, who is on a visit from the coast. The guests wound up a delightful evening at the police station, bail being fixed at ten dollars a plate, and were thereafter driven to their respective homes in the comfortable limousine of one of our most talented bootleggers, whose native modesty would be outraged if we mentioned his name. [5]

*

One of the saddest cases of suicide within our recollection occurred last Sunday evening when James L. Cameron, an old friend of ours and for years a respected citizen of Calgary, hanged himself from a tree near the south end of the C. & E. railway bridge. Mr. Cameron was around his usual haunts Saturday and appeared well and hearty. He was naturally of a jocular turn and had many friends. His untimely death will be widely mourned.

His body swaying in the early morning breeze was discovered on the Monday by the crew and passengers of the Calgary and Edmonton northbound. The train was brought to a standstill and the conductor, followed by a number of passengers, hastened to the scene and had the body borne on a handcar to the station, whence it was removed to Shaver's Undertaking Parlors for the inquest. The news quickly spread over the city and the members of the lodge to which deceased belonged took charge of the remains and undertook arrangements for a suitable funeral.

Coroner Costello summoned a jury, of which Alderman T. A. P. Frost was foreman, and a rigid inquiry was instituted as to the causes leading up to the act of self-destruction. Several witnesses were called who testified that deceased was a bachelor in good circumstances, living in an apartment block with little or no worldly cares or worries. He was a man of cheerful disposition and was known to be kind to his mother, who resided in Brockville, Ont. A letter found on his person, addressed to the coroner, was finally opened in the presence of the jury and partly explained the rash act. It read as follows:

Dear Sir— This letter will be found on my person and should reach you in due course. I am taking my own life, not in a moment of passing insanity, but in a fit of terrible depression. My naturally cheerful temperament precludes any idea of degenerate mentality, my mind as a general rule being absolutely normal. So pray direct the jury not to return a verdict of suicide while temporarily insane. No man is saner than I.

Today is Sunday. When I arose this morning the Salvation Army band was passing my windows playing a frightful tune. This was a bad start. The Hudson's Bay restaurant, where I usually feed, was closed, and I partook of an exceedingly bum breakfast at a joint on Ninth Avenue and was overcharged by the waitress. On returning to my rooms I found I had nothing to read, so went out again to buy some papers and magazines. The hotel book stores were shut down tighter than Billy be damned. I then decided to get a box of cigars and pass the day in calm reflection and quiet contemplation. The cigar stands were also closed.

Returning to my rooms I took a seat by the window and watched the dreary groups of men who gathered on the street corners and huddled in doorways with nothing to do and nowhere to go. Pretty soon the church bells began to ring and I beheld a man who had flimflammed me out of $500 the previous day walking down the street with an immense Bible under his arm. A feeling of intense irritation came over me, and I felt in all my pockets for a cigar to sooth my feelings. Nothing doing. I then put on my hat and sallied forth to see if the drug stores were open. Perhaps here, I thought, might be found some relief in the cigar line and peradventure the obliging clerk might even be worked for a glass of spiritus fermenti. Vain hope! The obliging clerk explained that while he was distressed beyond measure that he could not accommodate me with either of these commodities, he would be delighted to let me have as much calomel and Seidlitz powders as I wanted. He said he had a fine lot of those delicacies. I then decided to take a brisk walk. No sooner had I made a fair start than I ran into a flock of people, all dressed in black and looking very lugubrious, on their way to church. I crossed the street and ran into another bunch. Turning down an alley I regained my rooms by a circuitous route and decided to go to bed. When half undressed I changed my mind and reclothed myself. It then occurred to me that a bachelor friend who had rooms on the same flat might possibly have a bottle of beer to spare, or perhaps a shot of booze. This man usually keeps a small assortment for emergencies. But when I entered his room he was fast asleep in bed and when I woke him up the first words he uttered were, "Say you haven't got such a thing as a drop of whiskey, have you, or a bottle of beer? I had a thick night last night." So that settled that.

The Salvation Army again passed my windows, the drum making a most diabolical noise and the trombone going oompa-oompa in great style. Once more I put on my hat and sallied forth. Groups of homeless men were collected in the entrances of moving picture palaces, looking at the gaudy pictures of the films to be put on the following day. What struck me more than anything else was the absence on the street of any one I knew. None of my social or business acquaintances were to be seen. They were no doubt comfortably ensconced in their cosy homes in the bosom of their families, or what is more likely, were playing billiards and quaffing goblets of Scotch and Polly at the club. Not being a club man, I felt lost indeed.

Lunch time came around and I entered another Ninth Avenue joint and downed a cup of unspeakable coffee and a chunk of apple pie with leather underpinning. On my way back I ran into the black-robed crowd returning from church, some of whom I knew and had to bow to. One man in particular I tried to stop, because I knew that he seldom, if ever, was without a flask in his hip pocket, but his wife was with him and he passed on. Ships that pass in the night.

A furtive visit to the various hotels produced nothing but disappointment. The proprietors, most of whom I knew, were all out driving in their automobiles, the outward and visible result of 15 cent beer, and I did not happen to know any of the clerks. At any rate, they all said the same thing, that "they didn't have the key."

The gloom deepened. A man for whom I have an intense dislike, and whom I knew but slightly, stopped me on the street and began explaining to me why Billy Manarey should be elected commissioner. That settled it. This was the last straw. I decided to go to some remote spot and in the cool shades of the evening end it all. Hell were a paradise to such a Calgary Sunday. True, Monday is tomorrow, but Sunday will come around again and I dread to face it. I am not a coward.

> What man dare, I dare:
> Approach thou like the rugged Russian bear,
> The arm'd rhinoceros, or the Hyrcan tiger;
> Take any shape but an Ontario Sunday,
> And my firm nerves shall never tremble.
> Unreal mockery, hence!

In my rooms I found a suitable length of rope, such as had enwrapped my trunks on many a well-remembered holiday, and wound it round the belt inside my coat. Then I sat down to pen this letter, my last farewell to the world. It will be found in my pocket. My affairs are in good shape and I am addressing a letter to my banker to act as my executor and devote the whole of my current account to the poor. This should buy at least three turkeys. Goodbye. Tell the Rev. Marshall and his co-stiffs that my blood is on their heads.

Sadly yours,

JAMES L. CAMERON

After a brief consultation the jury returned a verdict of "Death due to neurotic effect of a Calgary Sunday," with a rider to the effect that Calgary Sundays should be modified in their severity. The coroner agreed with the verdict and invited the jury out to have a drink. The funeral was largely attended and many wreaths were placed on the coffin as a tribute of affection and esteem. A message of condolence was forwarded to the sorrowing mother in Ontario, who, it is said, is prepared to bring an action for heavy damages against the Rev. Marshall and his co-stiffs. [6]

*

The first thing a man with a new automobile runs into is debt. [7]

*

Edmonton is not really larger than Calgary and Winnipeg put together. It only feels that way. [8]

*

A handy nightlight can be made by putting a small candle-end into a hole in a potato, the bottom of which has been pared flat to keep it steady. If the candle is so short as to burn down to the potato before seven o'clock in the morning, you find a freshly-roasted potato ready for your breakfast. [9]

*

We hate to say anything about it, we do for a fact, but how in thunder did the new city hall of Calgary come to cost $350,000 when Pat Burns' splendid residence, which everybody knows well by sight, was erected for less than $25,000? This is a profound mystery—one of the seven mysteries of the world, in fact. [10]

*

What a number of people there are in Calgary who abhor one another. Good God! What is the matter with them? Are they bereft of their senses or are their better selves lost in a maze of selfishness and self-absorption? There is hardly a man but what pretends to be better than his neighbor; if not financially, then mentally; if not mentally, then morally. They've got to be better somehow.

For instance we become acquainted with James Reilly, a strong personality and we get to like the man. Another man comes along and says, "You ain't on to Reilly yet, he's . . ." and so on. Somebody introduces us to Lougheed, and we come away impressed with that gentleman's courteous and business-like ways; a chap meets you half an hour later and says, "Say, you ain't on to Lougheed, now there's a man who will . . . , etc." Mention Paddy Nolan, Bennett, Sifton or any prominent man in the community and there is certain to be some member of a class, a sect, or coterie standing around who will at a moment's notice tear his character to pieces. And yet everybody, but us, attends church. [11]

*

Edmonton now estimates that it has a population of over 4,000. Estimates are easy to make. Calgary with her bona fide population of 11,000 is seriously thinking of estimating her population at 25,000 just to prove that its imagination is not inferior to Edmonton's. [12]

*

Society Note— The family and relatives of Henry M. Beaglet, of Fourteenth Ave. W., are rejoicing in his death by being run over by an automobile at the Bank of Montreal corner last Saturday night. Old Beaglet had lived long enough and won't be missed. There should be a law compelling drivers of automobiles to run over men like Beaglet when they catch sight of them. It was rather a bum funeral. The corpse was not the only stiff present, there being three or four weird-looking bums, friends of deceased, who appropriately enough sang a wreckquiem at the graveside, in which the driver of the hearse lustily joined. Later in the evening they all repaired to the Plaza. [13]

*

It is said that one-third of the people who go mad recover their senses. The other two-thirds locate in South Edmonton. [14]

*

Who is responsible for choking off our Calgary newsboys from crying their papers on the street? This surely is a trifling, paltry, trumpery piece of business. There are altogether too many mischievous little busybodies round that city hall, who seem to have nothing else to do but search around for openings to "place" novel and vexatious restrictions. Those brisk young merchants who peddle papers should be left alone. They are an agreeable necessity to the public. [15]

*

Yes, house-hunting in Calgary is some job. It seems to have driven some people to adopt desperate measures.

Mr. Bott was wending his way home after a tiring day, house-hunting with no result. Passing by the river he heard a splash. Horrors! There was a man struggling in the water. Could it be?

Yes—it was his friend Mr. Jopkins. Disregarding his appeals for help, Bott made a rush up town for Jopkins' house agent.

"Excuse me," he said, breathlessly, "but can I have Jopkins' house? He has fallen in the river and is drowning."

"Sorry," said the house merchant, "but you're too late. I've already let it to the man who pushed him in." [16]

*

"Look here," shouted the Calgary householder to one of Coste's gas men, "there's a leak somewhere and a lot of gas is going to waste."

"No, sir," replied the man, "you are mistaken. Maybe there's a leak, but there ain't any gas going to waste. You'll find it all in the bill." [17]

*

It takes all kinds of people, as Adam remarked to Eve, to make a world. For example, there is the man who comes out of the dining room picking his teeth. [18]

*

Don't envy the fellow that has a big automobile and lives in a big house. If you only knew that guy is just as hard up in a big way as you are in your little way. [19]

*

Like Hootch and other unspeakable prairie burgs, Edmonton has been having trouble with its fire brigade. Edmonton, after all, is still the same dear old frontier town it ever was. Subjection to municipal discipline is abhorrent to its soul. It is still in the reeve stage, with town marshall and calaboose, barber who organizes local band and the inevitable enthusiastic hook and ladder company to give the burg something to be proud of. They are still advertising "Good opening in Edmonton for a blacksmith shop."

The one redeeming feature of Edmonton is its old-time spirit of hospitality, friendliness and camaraderie. This has always been Edmonton's most lovable trait. And when you want a drink, you can get it. What, ho! [20]

*

233

Did you ever pause to think that about ten years ago automobiles were about as great a curiosity as airships are in the present year of grace? [21]

*

This is the season of the year, Christmas coming on and so forth, when we most envy the folk with nice cosy little homes of their own. You who have your own fireside do not realize what you possess. You do not know what it is to go without having anyone to say to you, "Goodbye, will you be gone long?" or to come back without anyone to welcome you and say, "Oh, how late you are!" Think at this time of the year of the many young men far from their own homes back east, living in Calgary with no place to go of an evening, moping in their $8 a month rooms reading *Frenzied Finance* or hanging around hotels hitting up the booze. Give them a thought.

It needs only a little friendly interest to make better and happy the solitary individual who lives near you, who is abandoned to himself and to the inspiration of his unutterable ennui. The solitary youths, far from their paternal hearths, have a rocky old time struggling with the discouragements of their existence here, exposed to the temptations of the booze shops. There are evenings upon evenings that they are at a loss where to go or what to do, evenings that they make bad use of for want of a better. Perhaps they are nothing to you and you are under no obligation to them, but—put yourself in their place. [22]

*

Next to running the affairs of the city as they ought to be run, a man is seldom quite sure what he could do best. [23]

*

When the train pulled into Hamilton, Ont., a passenger put his head out of the window and asked a native:

"My friend, what is the name of this dismal, dried-up, heaven forsaken hole?"

"That's near enough," answered the dejected native. "That's near enough. Let her go at that." [24]

*

234

The most distinctive attribute of a large, bustling city are streetcars, crooked gamblers, confidence men, and a "complacent" police force. Hurry up with those streetcars, will you? [25]

*

The provincial parliament will assemble at Edmonton on the 15th. This solitary annual attraction should draw the usual number of visitors to the capital, unless the novelty has worn off. Calgary sits serenely and by virtue of its manifold attractions smiles indulgently at this lone event in the Uncle Tom-East Lynne beleaguered city up north. Dear Edmonton, will that hold you for a while? We are not sore. We do not need the parliament. There will be an occasional visitor straggling in without it. Have a drink on the House. [26]

*

Believe us, gentle reader, whatever we say and whatever we do, is said and done with a single eye to Calgary's welfare. The citizens of this town are all too good-natured and easy-going. They are prone to think that if their own private businesses are running smoothly, everything is hunky-dory. Everything is far from being hunky-dory when, through their own neglect, indifference and habit of electing popcorn vendors and peanut-roasters to run the town (to say nothing of the inevitable contractors skirmishing around for business advantages thus obtainable), they allow the civic pot to boil dry and crack.

It is gratifying to note the revival of popular interest in matters affecting the present and future welfare of Calgary. When the people at large become as little children and permit themselves to be jollied along in the dark by a handful of piegrabbers it is time to give them a ginning up and make them alive to their individual interests.

There are three matters of supreme importance to be decided upon within the next few weeks—the mayoralty, the personnel of the next council and the lighting question. On the first point we feel very strongly and so expressed ourself last week.

Puerile personal predilections should cut no ice. Were we to allow ourselves to be influenced by purely personal leanings, first thing we know we would be recommending the ratepayers to make Jack Moseley mayor on the ground that he was a h—ll of a good fellow. No, no, good masters, we have to look further afield. Remember it is Calgary first, last and all—the time. [27]

*

The scenery round Edmonton is lovely. It doubtless inspired the bard who sang "Ye Banks and Braes of Bonny Rat Creek." The view from the Edmonton Club is superb, looking down the valley of the Saskatchewan on to the dilapidated gold dredges and battered grizzlies of days that are no more. After a few horns inside, the gorgeousness of the scene becomes more and more impressive. It looks especially fine after two stiff Collinses. [28]

EIGHTEEN

Frenzied Finance

The size of a dollar depends entirely upon how many more you have. [1]

*

Before congratulating yourself when you come out on top, bear in mind that the froth of a glass of beer does the same. [2]

*

Calgary is fortunate for having had all its real estate and oil scandals while young, as children have the measles and other diseases while young and are then shed of them forever. [3]

*

Society Note— Mr. and Mrs. Orville Roy Browne sent out cards this week for a reception in honor of their son, Percy, who has just returned from New York. Percy's career is of more than ordinary interest. He started life in the big city, unknown and practically penniless, being too proud to borrow from his parents. He stood off a merchant for a basket and then obtained credit for enough tinware to fill it. With this he started peddling. That is ten years ago. Today, Percy ain't worth a bean and still owes for the basket. [4]

*

The CPR, like most corporations, is a cold-blooded outfit. When there is a bad wreck the conductor, engineer and the whole bunch, barring the newsy, are hauled onto the carpet and put through the fourth degree. One gets fired, another suspended, and there is hell a-popping.

But let an engineer, by cool-headedness and presence of mind, stick to his post regardless of imminent danger to himself, and do the right thing at the right moment and thereby save the company hundreds of thousands of dollars, to say nothing of saving human lives, the company never lets loose a word of appreciation. It would be undignified. And besides, engineers and firemen are well paid to jeopardize their lives for the company. Oh, certainly.

What prompted us to write the above was the quick work of Engineer Pratt the other night while rushing passenger train no. 3 into Calgary at a thirty-mile clip to make up time. Through the negligence of a switchman, who has since ducked his nut, a switch was left open in the east Calgary yards at the curve just east of the bridge. Into this dived Mr. Passenger train, the light of a switch engine less than a hundred yards away! The fireman and a helper jumped, the former being killed trying to make his friend, who was a green hand just learning the work, jump first. The engineer must have done some lightning thinking, for when the two engines came together the speed of his train was less than six miles an hour and the headlight of his engine was not even smashed. This is what baseball fans would call "pretty work." The fact that Engineer Pratt stayed with the job, with death a four to five favorite in the betting, cuts no ice with the company. [5]

*

Say, you jolly Canucks, how do you like the prospect of becoming hewers of pulpwood and drawers of waterpower for the Americans? [6]

*

The path to success is paved with good intentions that were carried out. [7]

*

Things are very quiet in the East just now. Molson's Bank has not been robbed or bunkoed for two months. [8]

*

One trouble with being efficient is that it makes everybody hate you so. [9]

*

The lawyer took his wife to court. After she had looked around a minute she gave a sudden shudder.

"My," she whispered, "what an awful creature the prisoner is."

"Sh-h-h!" her husband hissed. "The prisoner hasn't come in yet. That's the judge."

(Must have been Beck.—Ed.) [10]

*

Of course we are all great believers in the magic number seven. "Success" has just seven letters. But then, again, so has "Failure." [11]

*

"You will admit that doctors sometimes make mistakes, won't you?" suggested the cross-examiner.

"Oh yes, the same as lawyers," was the cool reply of the medico.

"And doctors' mistakes are buried six feet under the ground?"

"Yes, that is right, too," said the other, "and the lawyers' mistakes often swing in the air. How does that strike you, you bottle-nosed old shyster?" [12]

*

Contentment is sometimes the result of being too lazy to kick. [13]

*

The income tax returns would indicate that there is untold wealth in Canada. [14]

*

That was a wise guy who said that a lawyer is a man who gets two men to strip for a fight and then runs off with their clothes. [15]

*

The gross inhumanity of some Canadian employers is a disgrace to civilization. The case of Miss Olive McCarty *vs.* The Moose Jaw Steam Laundry Co. shows up the latter outfit in a very bad light. Miss McCarty had been employed by them to work as a fancy ironer at the rate of $6 for fifty hours. (Wonder how much the plain ironers receive?) Owing to being physically unfit to stand the work, through heat and other causes, having been in a railway wreck some time previous, she told them she would have to quit.

She had worked forty-five of the fifty hours.

The company refused to pay her unless she worked out the other five hours. The poor girl went three times to try and get her pay for the forty-five hours, with no success, so she laid a complaint with the police.

Magistrate Dunn, after hearing the evidence, gave judgment for the girl with costs against the laundry company.

We have often wondered how honest working girls stand for the raw deals handed them by rapacious sweatshop employers. The cue usually adopted by employers of cheap girl labor is to frighten the stuffing out of them by a policy of gruff talk and coarse bluff that a male employee wouldn't put up with for a moment. Had it been a man instead of a girl in this case, the manager would probably have had his face beaten in. It is always the honest girls who get sandies run on them by the bosses, for the latter know full well that honest girls are dead scared of finding themselves out of work. The bosses don't bother the flossy ones very much, because this sort is never in any alarming danger of starving, even if they never work at all, and are ready to quit at the drop of the hat.

Now, about this $6 a week. The cheapest you can get a meal ticket for in Moose Jaw is $4.50 and the cheapest room is $1.50 a week. There's the six dollars gone to blazes right there. Not a bean left for clothes, shoes and sundries. Not a bean. Industries like this Moose Jaw Laundry Co. are a veritable curse to a town of Christian people. The life of penury and constant struggle that is forced on girls who wish to keep honest and good, is a moral disgrace and a grave danger to society. God knows, these laundry sharks charge their customers enough. It is a pitiful state of affairs which should call for the attention of men in authority, with a view to prohibiting the employment of any girl labor except at decent living wages.

Right here lies the basic cause of the sadly frequent downfall of young women. Every man who has knocked around much knows that. [16]

*

Oil! Oil!! Oil!!!
Let 'er gush!
Wow!
This is the life!!! [17]

*

Society Note— The many friends of Alex B. Munson, who amassed a comfortable fortune in Calgary during the oil boom, will be glad to learn that he is still out of jail. [18]

*

People are always ready to admit a man's ability after he gets there. [19]

*

The following seems like a sound proposition:

Calgary, Alta., February 20, 1920

Dear Sirs:

Knowing that you are always interested and open for an investment in good live business propositions, I take the liberty of presenting to you what seems to me to be a most wonderful business, and in which, no doubt, you will take a lively interest; and perhaps write me by return mail the amount of stock for which you wish to subscribe towards the formation of this company.

The object of this company is to operate a large cat ranch in northern Alberta, where land can be purchased cheaper for the purpose. To start with, we will have about one million (1,000,000) cats. Each cat will average twelve kittens a year. The skins run from 10 cents each for the white ones, to 75 cents for the pure blacks.

This will give us twelve million (12,000,000) skins a year, to sell at the average of 30 cents a piece, making our revenue about ten thousand dollars a day gross.

A man can skin fifty cats a day at $2, and as it will take

100 men to operate the ranch, therefore, the net profit will be about nine thousand eight hundred dollars ($9,800) per day. We will feed the cats on rats, and start a rat ranch next door. The rats multiply four times as fast as the cats. If we start with one million (1,000,000) rats, we will have, therefore, four rats per day for each cat.

Then we will feed the rats on the carcasses of the cats, from which the skins have been taken, giving each rat a fourth of a cat. It will thus be seen that the business will be self-acting and automatic all the way through—the cats will eat the rats and the rats will eat the cats, and we will have the skins.

Awaiting your prompt reply, and trusting that you will appreciate this opportunity to get rich very quickly, I remain,

Yours very truly,
J. G. Cattaratt.

P.S. Eventually we will cross the cats with snakes and then they will skin themselves once a year, and thus save the cost of the men's wages for skinning them.—J.G.C. [20]

*

A man's ability should be rated by what he finishes and not by what he attempts. [21]

*

When a man begins by saying you are too wise to be caught for a sucker, look out! He is going to try a new kind of bait. [22]

*

A man in Calgary had been beaten out of his money by a real estate shark. So he hurried to a lawyer. He explained the case and told the lawyer he had a reasonable sum of money for retainer and subsequent fee.

"All right," said the lawyer, "I'll represent you."

"No," said the man, "I've a proposition. I have a little money, as you see, but not enough to interest you greatly. My idea is this: you get the job of defending that swindler when I sue him, and divide with me after you get all his money, because I am getting you the case."

"I'll do better with you than that!" exclaimed the delighted lawyer. "I'll make you my partner at once."

This, of course, is manifestly impossible. If the man had been so sharp as we have made him out to be, he would have done up the real estate shark himself in the first place. [23]

*

Many a man's failure is due to the fact that he bit off more than he could chew. [24]

*

COME TO CALGARY, The Aquarium City, Full of Sharks! Boozorium Park!

Seize your opportunity! Do not delay!! Come early and avoid the rush!!! Yellow ball in the corner pocket!!!! Boozorium Park is the future residential district of Calgary, beautifully situated in the midst of the unparalleled scenic beauties of the baldheaded prairie, on a site famed for its badger and gopher holes and renowned in song and story for its entire absence of water. A pleasant place for a murder. Rural mail delivery service promised before close of century. Boozorium Park, owing to prevailing tranquillity, is specially adapted as a place of residence for those learning to play the violin and for those who may be desirous of studying the habits of range cattle. It is within the thirteen-mile circle. Ample room for a Carnegie library and bowling alley. Two lots have been donated by the owners for church purposes. Next ecumenical conference will be held at Boozorium Park. A school is also in contemplation. For higher education come to Boozorium Park. Choice site for a home for inebriates. An automobile will convey you to Boozorium Park any day, provided you have the price to pay for it. Make your reservations tomorrow. An hour's delay may lose you a choice corner lot. BRING A FLASK!

Prices range from $175 to $350. TERMS EASY. One-fourth down, balance three, six and nine months.

BUNK, SOAKEM & CONTOK, Real Estate Agents, Calgary. [25]

*

"Here's poetic justice for you. One of these oil-stock promoters married a woman for her money."

"Yes?"

"Only to discover that she had invested it all in oil stock." [26]

*

243

The Family Doctor

This department of the *Eye Opener* has been opened to meet the wants of those who cannot afford to pay the fees of a regular practitioner. They cannot arrest us for this, can they? Many queries have already been sent in and we shall do our best to answer them satisfactorily.

J.B.S., Red Deer, Alta.—Is strychnine efficacious in stopping ailments of the heart?

Ans.—If taken in sufficient quantities, strychnine will stop almost anything.

A.F., Edmonton—A man in this town is suffering from phlegm. He owes me five dollars, and seems unable to cough it up. What would you suggest?

Ans.—Give him a stiff dose of salts and he'll soon loosen up.

F.O.B., Okotoks—Am afflicted with prairie itch. What is a good thing for it?

Ans.—Try scratching.

Miss F.M.G., Lethbridge—I yawn frequently when commencing to sing. What will prevent this?

Ans.—Don't sing.

Mrs. J.F.M., Vancouver—A wealthy uncle of mine, aged ninety-two, is run down, has poor appetite and takes very little exercise. Sleeps a great deal. Has hallucinations that his end is not far off.

Ans.—Make him hop into a cold bath every morning and run five miles before breakfast. If his will is made out in your favor, throw three or four whiskies into him and he will forget about the breakfast. Prepare a nice dinner for him and see that he gets enough whiskey so that he won't want to eat it. Between dinner and supper throw half a dozen more under his belt and after supper, which by this time he will have forgotten all about, give him a ten-spot and start him off downtown. Phone a bootlegger to meet him at the corner of Hastings and Granville and when he comes home roaring and shouting at 3 A.M., put him to bed. Keep this treatment up for three days and then make your arrangements to winter in California. [27]

*

If one-half of a man's schemes turned out according to his preliminary figures, he would have nothing to do but spend his money. [28]

*

"How about that horse you sold me last week," said a man to Johnny Hamilton last Saturday in the Alberta Hotel dining room. "It's as blind as a badger. I thought you said it had no faults."

"So I did," replied Johnny, gazing at the bill of fare. "But blindness is not a fault. It's a misfortune. I'll take some corn beef and cabbage, please." [29]

*

Make money, and the whole nation will conspire to call you a gentleman. [30]

*

The Natural Gas Company, of which Eugene Coste is manager, is probably the most unpopular and most badly managed industrial concern in western Canada. This outfit have their offices on Sixth Avenue and what the clerical staff don't know about running a business would fill every shelf in the Carnegie Library. For arrogance and over-bearing methods these people are in a class by themselves.

The chap deputed by this company to receive complaints on the part of their victims is an especially objectionable person. He adopts the timeworn attitude of "Well, what are you going to do about it?" The result has been disastrous to the company. At least half their original customers have cut out the gas and gone back to good old reliable coal. The idea of there being such a thing in business as give-and-take seems to have no place in the ivory noddle of this concern. The luxury of being grasping and disagreeable is one that even the wealthiest of companies can ill afford these days. [31]

*

It's no trick to be a successful salesman if you have what

the people want. You never hear the bootleggers complaining about hard times. [32]

*

A lawyer asked a man who had at various times sat on several juries, "Who influenced you most, the lawyers, the witnesses or the judge?"

He expected to get some useful and interesting information from so experienced a juryman. This was the man's reply:

"I'll tell yer, sir, 'ow I makes up my mind. I'm a plain man and a reasonin' man, and I ain't influenced by anything the lawyers say; no, nor by what the judge says. I just looks at the man in the dock and I says: 'If he ain't done nothing, why's he there?' and I brings 'em all in guilty." [33]

*

Somehow the man who attends strictly to his own business never acquires a reputation as an entertaining conversationalist. [34]

*

Every successful man knows more about his own business than he does about other men's. [35]

NINETEEN

Pure Philosophy

Taking things philosophically is easy if they don't concern you. [1]

*

Never exaggerate your faults; your friends will attend to that. [2]

*

A man seldom attempts to escape any temptation that looks good to him. [3]

*

Never trust a man whose dog crawls under the house when it sees him enter the front gate. [4]

*

Have you ever noticed how much larger your troubles appear at night than during the day? [5]

*

At any rate, prohibition has made Alberta safe for hypocrisy. [6]

*

If things were reversed so that we could all start at the top, it would only be a matter of time until there would be just as big a crowd at the bottom. The same crowd too, probably. [7]

*

What a slovenly old world this would be if all the vanity were eliminated. [8]

*

The man who can laugh when he isn't amused is always popular. [9]

*

One of the most pathetic sights in the world is a highbrow person trying to conceal his delight in the low comedy of a movie show. [10]

*

Often in our moralizing fits in these columns we have made reference to the futility of worrying. What indeed is there worth worrying about in this blessed country! If one is really desirous of worrying, is not happy unless worrying, anxious to worry, there are women built that way, let him go to a country where there is something worth worrying over. We have been in this country going on five years now and have yet to find the man, the condition, or the circumstance, no matter how untoward, that has succeeded in causing us a moment's worry. And yet we have been "up against it" all that time. The only man who could come anywhere near it is the chief of police. [11]

*

Most of us do things merely because other people do them. [12]

*

Forgive your enemies—but if you have no enemies, forgive a few of your friends. [13]

*

Applause has made a fool of more men than criticism. [14]

*

Don't meet trouble halfway. It is quite capable of making the entire journey. [15]

*

Other people's mistakes cause us a lot of trouble. Why will other people persist in making mistakes. Can nothing be done about it? [16]

*

Conscience is a watchdog that barks at sin. [17]

*

We never have much use for people who are smarter than we are. [18]

*

When you have no reason to smile, keep in practice anyway. Don't give way to the blues. Buck up! Be a man! Yellow ball in the corner pocket! [19]

*

Why does the bright idea we think of just before going to sleep depart, never to return? [20]

*

The world is full of queer people. Yes, you are one of them. [21]

*

When the average man has occasion to boast of his past he usually selects a part of it that others have forgotten. [22]

*

A man can always find time to do a thing if he has the inclination. [23]

*

A man who goes out to meet trouble will have a short walk. [24]

*

When a man begins to pay as much attention to a dime as he formerly did to a dollar, it's a sign he's getting rich. [25]

*

One's notions of happiness change with the years. When you're a young man you think happiness wears a skirt; when you're older you think it lives in a bank. [26]

*

Did you ever notice what a lot of friends you haven't got when you happen to need them? [27]

*

There never was a man as great as the average dog believes his master to be. [28]

*

A man always remembers his enemies, but he sometimes forgets his friends. [29]

*

A fussy man gets in his own way when he is in a hurry. [30]

*

The man who ought to listen and learn usually does most of the talking. [31]

*

There's a little wolf and a little sheep in every man. [32]

*

Great men sometimes make mistakes. If it wasn't for that, history would be mighty dull reading. [33]

*

Many a fellow who boasts that he is master of himself hasn't much of a boss. [34]

*

Character is what you are. Reputation is what you try to make people think you are. [35]

*

As a matter of cold fact, a lot of people have no use for you because they can't use you. [36]

*

Right here and now, pause and consider the fact that there are people in the world who never heard of you. So you're not such a hell of a fellow after all, are you? [37]

*

The tongue, like a race horse, generally runs faster the less weight it carries. [38]

*

Isn't it queer that only sensible people agree with you? [39]

*

One enemy will give a man more free advertising than a dozen friends. [40]

*

Few of us are half so good, half so bad, half so poor or half so rich as people imagine we are. [41]

*

Nothing pleases some of us more than being able to convey bad news to others. [42]

*

Money may be saved by avoiding sure things. [43]

*

Most people think they are virtuous merely because they are tame and inoffensive. [44]

*

Contentment may mean lack of desire. [45]

*

We admire a good talker who knows when to shut up. [46]

*

Never trust a man whose dog has gone back on him. [47]

*

Deciding where to go on one's vacation would be more difficult if one's bank account did not insist on casting the deciding vote. [48]

*

Your neighbors have a lot of nerve to imagine they are as good as you are. [49]

*

Some men are good because they find it cheaper than being wicked. [50]

*

Most of life's shadows result from standing in our own light. [51]

*

A little learning is a dangerous thing, but a lot of ignorance is just as bad. [52]

*

Play is merely work that you don't have to do. [53]

*

Ever notice how things that are none of your business will interest you? [54]

*

Don't worry about disagreeable people—it is only a matter of time when they get theirs. [55]

*

There is always a mystery about how the people next door live. [56]

*

Fat men are good-natured because good-natured men are usually fat. [57]

*

Old types gradually disappear, but the man who is always looking up things in the encyclopedia just to prove he is right is still with us. [58]

*

The man who never tried has no sympathy for the one who tried and failed. [59]

*

If every man was as fierce in action as he is in thought, all the jails would be full. [60]

*

Every man should master the art of concealing his bloody ignorance. [61]

*

A man's good deeds are limited, but there is no limit to the mischief he can accomplish. [62]

*

A fool and his money remind one of a bald man and his hair. [63]

*

A fellow never realizes how many friends he has until he doesn't need them. [64]

*

A man is never ridiculous for what he is, but assuming to be what he isn't. [65]

Sources

The best collections of original Calgary *Eye Openers* are in the Glenbow-Alberta Institute, Calgary, the University of Alberta Library, Edmonton, and the Legislature Library, Edmonton. In 1962 the Canadian Library Association microfilmed all copies it could find and sold reels to many Canadian and foreign libraries.

In addition, the Calgary chapter of the Historical Society of Alberta produced excellent reprints of the *Eye Openers* for March 9, 1912 and July 8, 1916. The Lethbridge Brewery also obtained some matrixes of five issues of the *Eye Opener* published 1916–17 and published these in the 1960s as sixteen-page giveaways at fairs and exhibitions.

The only book to date on Bob Edwards is the volume *Eye Opener Bob* by Grant MacEwan, published in 1957 by the Institute of Applied Art Ltd., Edmonton, and later reprinted by Modern Press, Saskatoon. A number of good articles on Edwards have appeared in the Calgary *Herald* and *Canadian Cattlemen*, as well as Max Foran's "Bob Edwards and Social Reform" in the Summer 1973 issue of the *Alberta Historical Review*.

The abbreviations used in the following footnotes require some explanation.

E.O. indicates *Eye Opener*, published variously in Calgary, High River, Port Arthur and Winnipeg. It carried such varying mastheads as *The Eye Opener*, *Eye Opener*, and *Calgary Eye Opener*.

Sum. Ann. means *Summer Annual*, followed by the year of publication and page number.

Wet. Free Lance means Wetaskiwin *Free Lance*. This is followed by the date in which a reprint of the article appeared in the Calgary *Daily Herald*. Only two or three original *Free Lances* are known to exist.

Wet. Breeze means Wetaskiwin *Breeze*, followed by the date the article was reprinted in the Calgary *Daily Herald*.

Alta. Sun means *Alberta Sun*, published variously in Leduc and Strathcona.

Introduction

1. Sum. Ann., 1924, 82.
2. Macleod *Gazette*, January 14, 1898.
3. Calgary *Daily Herald*, June 9, 1898.
4. Calgary *Daily Herald*, May 31, 1898.
5. Calgary *Daily Herald*, May 3, 1898.
6. E.O., October 9, 1909.
7. E.O., October 9, 1909.
8. E.O., June 8, 1912.
9. *Alberta Tribune*, Calgary, October 1, 1898.
10. Calgary *Daily Herald*, November 10, 1898.
11. Calgary *Daily Herald*, April 17, 1899.
12. E.O., October 9, 1909.
13. Macleod *Gazette*, September 21, 1900.
14. E.O., October 9, 1909.
15. E.O., October 9, 1909.
16. E.O., March 4, 1902.
17. Calgary *Daily Herald*, January 16, 1902.
18. E.O., October 9, 1909.
19. E.O., October 15, 1910.
20. E.O., January 16, 1903.
21. E.O., June 13, 1903.
22. E.O., June 13, 1903.
23. E.O., July 20, 1903.
24. E.O., February 21, 1919.
25. E.O., September 19, 1908.
26. Calgary *Daily News*, October 5, 1908.
27. E.O., April 9, 1910.
28. E.O., October 5, 1910.
29. E.O., August 3, 1912.
30. E.O., November 2, 1912.
31. E.O., November 25, 1906.
32. E.O., July 9, 1910.
33. E.O., August 12, 1911.
34. E.O., September 16, 1911.

35. E.O., March 31, 1911.
36. E.O., October 6, 1906.
37. Wet. Breeze, March 25, 1901.
38. E.O., August 25, 1906.
39. E.O., April 20, 1912.
40. E.O., April 18, 1908.
41. E.O., July 17, 1920.
42. E.O., November 2, 1912.
43. E.O., May 16, 1908.
44. Cited by Andrew Snaddon in a six-part series on the life of Bob Edwards, Calgary *Herald*, October 13, 1956.

1   The Fair Sex

1. E.O., February 21, 1919.
2. E.O., October 5, 1912.
3. Sum. Ann., 1920, 32.
4. E.O., August 14, 1920.
5. E.O., April 30, 1921.
6. E.O., December 6, 1913.
7. E.O., May 6, 1911.
8. E.O., December 4, 1909.
9. E.O., July 1, 1922.
10. E.O., February 19, 1910.
11. Sum. Ann., 1922, 77.
12. E.O., March 9, 1918.
13. Wet. Free Lance, May 21, 1898.
14. Sum. Ann., 1924, 61.
15. Sum. Ann., 1922, 51.
16. E.O., October 3, 1908.
17. E.O., July 8, 1916.
18. E.O., April 3, 1915.
19. Sum. Ann., 1920, 27.
20. Sum. Ann., 1920, 19.
21. E.O., October 5, 1912.
22. Sum. Ann., 1922, 7.
23. E.O., February 10, 1912.
24. E.O., December 18, 1909.
25. Sum. Ann., 1923, 56.
26. Sum. Ann., 1922, 7.
27. Sum. Ann., 1922, 13.
28. E.O., December 6, 1913.
29. Sum. Ann., 1924, 72.
30. Sum. Ann., 1922, 63.
31. E.O., August 14, 1920.
32. Sum. Ann., 1923, 19.
33. Sum. Ann., 1922, 84.
34. E.O., March 18, 1916.
35. E.O., April 30, 1921.

36. Sum. Ann., 1923, 60.
37. Sum. Ann., 1922, 17.
38. E.O., April 19, 1919.
39. Sum. Ann., 1920, 51.
40. Sum. Ann., 1923, 65.
41. E.O., September 11, 1920.
42. Sum. Ann., 1920, 24.
43. E.O., August 14, 1920.
44. E.O., August 28, 1920.
45. E.O., August 23, 1919.
46. E.O., July 29, 1911.
47. Sum. Ann., 1922, 28.
48. Sum. Ann., 1922, 28.
49. E.O., May 27, 1916.
50. E.O., March 18, 1916.
51. Sum. Ann., 1922, 58.

2 Politics

1. E.O., September 21, 1918.
2. E.O., October 25, 1911.
3. E.O., June 24, 1906.
4. E.O., June 15, 1907.
5. E.O., March 24, 1906.
6. E.O., November 19, 1904.
7. Sum. Ann., 1922, 24.
8. E.O., May 2, 1908.
9. E.O., April 3, 1915.
10. E.O., October 25, 1911.
11. E.O., January 29, 1922.
12. E.O., April 19, 1919.
13. E.O., September 5, 1908.
14. E.O., August 3, 1912.
15. E.O., March 6, 1920.
16. E.O., October 5, 1912.
17. E.O., July 3, 1915.
18. E.O., March 20, 1920.
19. E.O., October 6, 1906.
20. E.O., July 20, 1918.
21. Sum. Ann., 1922, 33.
22. E.O., April 21, 1906.
23. E.O., August 14, 1920.
24. Sum. Ann., 1922, 40.
25. E.O., March 23, 1907.
26. E.O., September 19, 1908.
27. E.O., September 19, 1908.
28. E.O., March 4, 1905.
29. E.O., September 5, 1908.
30. E.O., March 18, 1905.

31. E.O., August 12, 1911.
32. E.O., December 20, 1913.
33. E.O., May 15, 1920.
34. E.O., September 8, 1906.
35. Sum. Ann., 1920, 87.
36. E.O., March 20, 1920.
37. E.O., August 23, 1919.
38. E.O., October 25, 1911.
39. E.O., August 1, 1908.
40. E.O., August 3, 1912.
41. E.O., September 5, 1908.
42. E.O., November 22, 1919.
43. E.O., October 25, 1911.
44. E.O., March 9, 1912.
45. E.O., October 5, 1912.
46. E.O., June 3, 1911.
47. Wet. Breeze, June 20, 1901.
48. Sum. Ann., 1922, 51.
49. Sum. Ann., 1922, 40.
50. E.O., May 27, 1916.
51. E.O., September 24, 1921.
52. E.O., February 10, 1912.
53. Wet. Breeze, June 20, 1901.
54. E.O., August 20, 1921.

3 Religion

1. E.O., August 20, 1921.
2. Sum. Ann., 1920, 60.
3. Sum. Ann., 1920, 60.
4. Sum. Ann., 1920, 69.
   (Ponoka is the site of a provincial mental institution.)
5. Sum. Ann., 1922, 48.
6. Sum. Ann., 1924, 28.
7. Sum. Ann., 1923, 65.
8. E.O., December 6, 1913.
9. E.O., April 5, 1919.
10. E.O., October 24, 1906.
11. E.O., October 25, 1911.
12. E.O., September 3, 1919.
13. E.O., November 2, 1912.
14. E.O., March 23, 1912.
15. E.O., March 4, 1905.
16. Wet. Free Lance, May 25, 1898.
17. Wet. Free Lance, March 23, 1898.
18. E.O., April 11, 1902.
19. E.O., June 16, 1906.
20. Sum. Ann., 1920, 17.
21. E.O., September 27, 1910.

22. E.O., January 1, 1910.
23. E.O., July 17, 1920.
24. Sum. Ann., 1922, 63.
25. Sum. Ann., 1922, 33.
26. E.O., February 21, 1919.
27. Sum. Ann., 1924, 3.
28. Sum. Ann., 1922, 64.
29. E.O., June 29, 1906.
30. E.O., September 24, 1921.

4 Graft

1. Sum. Ann., 1920, 84.
2. E.O., June 16, 1906.
3. E.O., March 23, 1907.
4. E.O., December 2, 1906.
5. Sum. Ann., 1923, 10.
6. E.O., April 3, 1915.
7. E.O., April 20, 1912.
8. E.O., September 27, 1913.
9. E.O., February 9, 1907.
10. E.O., July 18, 1908.
11. E.O., March 9, 1912.
12. E.O., February 15, 1908.
13. E.O., June 16, 1906.
14. E.O., July 18, 1908.
15. E.O., August 3, 1912.
16. E.O., June 16, 1906.
17. E.O., January 27, 1912.
18. Sum. Ann., 1922, 20.
19. E.O., December 8, 1906.
20. E.O., January 2, 1903.
21. E.O., August 3, 1912.
22. E.O., November 2, 1912.
23. E.O., August 3, 1912.
24. E.O., January 13, 1912.
25. E.O., August 20, 1921.

5 Peter J. McGonigle

1. E.O., December 7, 1907.
2. E.O., February 15, 1908.
3. E.O., May 16, 1908.
4. E.O., May 2, 1908.
5. E.O., May 16, 1908.
6. E.O., September 19, 1908.
7. E.O., September 19, 1908.
8. E.O., October 6, 1906.
9. E.O., March 6, 1909.

10. E.O., January 1, 1910.
11. E.O., February 19, 1910.
12. E.O., May 16, 1908.
13. E.O., March 5, 1910.
14. E.O., April 9, 1910.
15. E.O., April 9, 1910.
16. E.O., June 4, 1910.
17. E.O., June 18, 1910.
18. E.O., September 27, 1910.
19. E.O., October 15, 1910.
20. E.O., May 6, 1911.
21. E.O., April 3, 1915.
22. E.O., July 17, 1920.
23. E.O., February 5, 1921.
24. E.O., May 20, 1911.

6   Booze

1. E.O., November 13, 1909.
2. Sum. Ann., 1920, 3.
3. E.O., April 18, 1908.
4. E.O., March 9, 1918.
5. E.O., December 12, 1908.
6. E.O., August 25, 1906.
7. E.O., July 3, 1915.
8. Sum. Ann., 1922, 59.
9. E.O., April 10, 1920.
10. E.O., reprinted in the Lethbridge *News*, June 11, 1903.
11. E.O., September 2, 1905.
12. Wet. Breeze, March 13, 1901.
13. Sum. Ann., 1920, 35.
14. Sum. Ann., 1922, 1.
15. E.O., January 4, 1908.
16. E.O., January 27, 1912.
17. E.O., August 12, 1911.
18. E.O., July 17, 1920.
19. E.O., November 1, 1919.
20. E.O., November 2, 1912.
21. Sum. Ann., 1920, 24.
22. E.O., July 3, 1915.
23. Sum. Ann., 1920, 11.
24. E.O., February 8, 1919.
25. E.O., June 27, 1914.
26. Sum. Ann., 1922, 15.
27. E.O., August 4, 1906.
28. E.O., June 4, 1910.
29. E.O., August 2, 1913.
30. E.O., December 6, 1919.
31. Wet. Breeze, June 18, 1901.

32. Sum. Ann., 1922, 58.
33. E.O., August 25, 1906.
34. E.O., February 10, 1912.
35. Wet. Free Lance, September 20, 1898.
36. Sum. Ann., 1923, 88.
37. E.O., May 22, 1915.
38. E.O., September 11, 1920.
39. Sum. Ann., 1922, 10.
40. E.O., May 8, 1915.
41. E.O., November 21, 1908.
42. Sum. Ann., 1923, 33.
43. E.O., March 23, 1912.

7 The Sexes

1. Sum. Ann., 1923, 56.
2. Sum. Ann., 1922, 77.
3. Sum. Ann., 1920, 36.
4. Sum. Ann., 1924, 35.
5. Sum. Ann., 1923, 78.
6. E.O., October 5, 1912.
7. Sum. Ann., 1920, 91.
8. E.O., April 3, 1915.
9. E.O., November 2, 1912.
10. E.O., August 3, 1912.
11. E.O., April 10, 1920.
12. E.O., September 3, 1919.
13. Sum. Ann., 1920, 9.
14. E.O., February 19, 1910.
15. E.O., August 4, 1906.
16. Sum. Ann., 1924, 70.
17. E.O., September 30, 1905.
18. Sum. Ann., 1920, 89.
19. Sum. Ann., 1923, 72.
20. Sum. Ann., 1920, 70.
21. Sum. Ann., 1922, 55.
22. E.O., April 9, 1910.
23. Sum. Ann., 1922, 30.
24. E.O., September 11, 1920.
25. Sum. Ann., 1924, 74.
26. Sum. Ann., 1922, 28.
27. E.O., August 14, 1920.
28. Sum. Ann., 1923, 56.
29. Sum. Ann., 1922, 79.
30. E.O., August 1, 1908.
31. E.O., April 3, 1915.
32. E.O., December 6, 1913.
33. E.O., February 10, 1912.
34. Sum. Ann., 1923, 55.

35. E.O., August 3, 1912.
36. Sum. Ann., 1923, 32.
37. E.O., November 1, 1919.
38. Sum. Ann., 1920, 45.
39. E.O., September 27, 1910.
40. E.O., January 27, 1912.
41. E.O., August 14, 1920.
42. Sum. Ann., 1922, 23.
43. Sum. Ann., 1923, 56.
44. E.O., July 29, 1911.
45. E.O., December 6, 1913.
46. E.O., October 5, 1912.
47. E.O., March 6, 1920.
48. Sum. Ann., 1920, 32.

8   The English

1. E.O., September 7, 1912.
2. Wet. Breeze, March 11, 1901.
3. Sum. Ann., 1920, 90.
4. E.O., August 28, 1920.
5. E.O., August 28, 1920.
6. Wet. Free Lance, December 27, 1898.
7. Sum. Ann., 1920, 71.
8. E.O., August 12, 1911.
9. E.O., December 2, 1906.
10. E.O., December 4, 1909.
11. Wet. Free Lance, April 5, 1899.
12. Sum. Ann., 1924, 9.
13. Sum. Ann., 1924, 8.
14. E.O., March 9, 1912.

9   Those Other People

1. E.O., August 28, 1920.
2. E.O., June 16, 1906.
3. Wet. Free Lance, January 20, 1899.
4. Sum. Ann., 1920, 7.
5. Wet. Free Lance, February 4, 1899.
6. Sum. Ann., 1922, 8.
7. E.O., April 10, 1920.
8. Wet. Free Lance, May 28, 1898.
9. Sum. Ann., 1920, 46.
10. E.O., February 23, 1907.
11. Wet. Free Lance, February 2, 1899.
12. Wet. Free Lance, December 27, 1898.
13. Wet. Free Lance, February 6, 1899.
14. Sum. Ann., 1920, 86.
15. E.O., March 4, 1905.

16. Wet. Free Lance, May 31, 1898.
17. E.O., August 20, 1921.
18. E.O., January 29, 1922.
19. Sum. Ann., 1920, 46.
20. Wet. Free Lance, December 27, 1898.
21. Sum. Ann., 1920, 3.
22. Wet. Breeze, June 18, 1901.
23. E.O., September 27, 1910.

10 Show Business

1. E.O., September 11, 1920.
2. Wet. Breeze, April 18, 1901.
3. E.O., July 29, 1911.
4. Sum. Ann., 1920, 91.
5. E.O., May 6, 1911.
6. E.O., November 2, 1912.
7. E.O., March 9, 1918.
8. Sum. Ann., 1924, 18.
9. E.O., April 20, 1912.
10. E.O., March 9, 1918.
11. E.O., August 20, 1921.
12. E.O., September 24, 1921.
13. E.O., February 5, 1921.
14. Wet. Free Lance, June 9, 1898.
15. E.O., October 5, 1912.
16. E.O., April 5, 1919.
17. E.O., July 1, 1922.
18. E.O., June 29, 1906.
19. E.O., July 29, 1911.
20. E.O., July 3, 1915.
21. E.O., July 8, 1916.

11 Morality

1. E.O., August 20, 1921.
2. E.O., December 2, 1916.
3. Sum. Ann., 1922, 77.
4. Sum. Ann., 1924, 86.
5. E.O., October 24, 1906.
6. Sum. Ann., 1923, 65.
7. E.O., May 16, 1908.
8. E.O., December 6, 1919.
9. E.O., January 25, 1919.
10. E.O., August 9, 1919.
11. E.O., July 3, 1915.
12. E.O., December 8, 1906.
13. E.O., September 24, 1921.
14. E.O., May 27, 1916.

15. E.O., September 18, 1909.
16. Sum. Ann., 1920, 80.
17. E.O., February 26, 1916.
18. E.O., March 23, 1912.
19. E.O., July 29, 1911.
20. Sum. Ann., 1922, 58.
21. E.O., July 1, 1922.
22. E.O., October 24, 1906.
23. E.O., December 2, 1906.
24. E.O., January 25, 1919.
25. E.O., October 9, 1909.
26. E.O., September 5, 1908.
27. E.O., July 29, 1911.
28. E.O., October 25, 1911.
29. E.O., December 7, 1918.
30. Sum. Ann., 1920, 10.
31. E.O., December 20, 1919.
32. Sum. Ann., 1923, 65.
33. E.O., June 27, 1914.
34. Sum. Ann., 1922, 29.
35. E.O., December 6, 1913.
36. E.O., January 29, 1922.
37. E.O., August 4, 1906.
38. E.O., November 20, 1915.
39. E.O., May 18, 1912.
40. Sum. Ann., 1920, 46.
41. Sum. Ann., 1923, 65.
42. E.O., February 10, 1912.
43. E.O., September 11, 1920.
44. E.O., December 4, 1909.
45. Sum. Ann., 1920, 14.
46. E.O., April 20, 1912.
47. E.O., August 1, 1908.

12 Life & Death

1. E.O., April 10, 1920.
2. E.O., May 17, 1913.
3. E.O., July 8, 1916.
4. E.O., July 29, 1911.
5. Wet. Free Lance, June 15, 1898.
6. Sum. Ann., 1922, 84.
7. Sum. Ann., 1922, 74.
8. E.O., January 27, 1912.
9. E.O., September 11, 1920.
10. E.O., March 23, 1912.
11. Sum. Ann., 1920, 23.
12. Sum. Ann., 1922, 65.
13. E.O., August 9, 1919.

14. Sum. Ann., 1920, 33.
15. Sum. Ann., 1922, 29.
16. Sum. Ann., 1920, 33.
17. E.O., April 3, 1915.
18. E.O., January 27, 1912.
19. E.O., September 27, 1913.
20. E.O., March 9, 1912.
21. Sum. Ann., 1922, 22.
22. Sum. Ann., 1923, 38.
23. E.O., April 3, 1915.
24. E.O., April 10, 1920.
25. E.O., December 20, 1913.
26. E.O., March 23, 1912.
27. E.O., May 17, 1913.
28. Wet. Free Lance, June 15, 1898.
29. Sum. Ann., 1923, 56.
30. E.O., August 3, 1912.
31. E.O., April 3, 1915.
32. E.O., May 4, 1919.
33. Sum. Ann., 1920, 24.
34. Sum. Ann., 1922, 74.
35. E.O., September 27, 1910.
36. E.O., December 6, 1913.
37. Sum. Ann., 1920, 74.
38. Wet. Free Lance, October 6, 1898.
39. Sum. Ann., 1922, 55.
40. E.O., May 17, 1913.
41. E.O., January 27, 1912.
42. E.O., March 23, 1907.
43. E.O., September 3, 1919.
44. E.O., December 20, 1919.
45. E.O., August 28, 1920.

13 Sports

1. Sum. Ann., 1922, 21.
2. E.O., August 25, 1906.
3. Sum. Ann., 1924, 73.
4. Sum. Ann., 1920, 39.
5. E.O., April 10, 1920.
6. Sum. Ann., 1922, 54.
7. Sum. Ann., 1922, 71.
8. E.O., April 10, 1920.
9. E.O., January 27, 1912.
10. E.O., September 27, 1913.
11. E.O., April 5, 1919.
12. Sum. Ann., 1922, 71.

14 Purely Personal

1. Sum. Ann., 1922, 9.
2. E.O., February 21, 1919.
3. Sum., Ann., 1922, 46.
4. E.O., December 4, 1909.
5. E.O., August 25, 1906.
6. E.O., March 11, 1905.
7. E.O., September 22, 1917.
8. E.O., May 16, 1908.
9. Sum. Ann., 1920, 36.
10. E.O., June 8, 1912.
11. E.O., January 27, 1912.
12. E.O., October 17, 1903.
13. E.O., January 16, 1903.
14. E.O., April 11, 1902.
15. E.O., September 21, 1918.
16. E.O., August 12, 1911.
17. E.O., August 1, 1908.
18. E.O., October 5, 1912.
19. E.O., April 4, 1902.
20. E.O., February 10, 1912.
21. Wet. Free Lance, October 8, 1898.
22. E.O., October 25, 1911.
23. Sum. Ann., 1920, 73.
24. E.O., May 30, 1902.
25. E.O., February 10, 1912.
26. E.O., September 27, 1913.
27. Sum. Ann., 1922, 30.

15 Personalities

1. E.O., June 29, 1907.
2. Sum. Ann., 1923, 31.
3. E.O., November 25, 1906.
4. E.O., July 13, 1907.
5. E.O., March 23, 1907.
6. E.O., August 8, 1903.
7. E.O., March 4, 1905.
8. E.O., March 11, 1905.
9. E.O., April 9, 1910.
10. E.O., November 11, 1916.
11. E.O., August 3, 1912.
12. E.O., November 10, 1906.
13. E.O., October 19, 1912.
14. E.O., July 29, 1911.
15. Sum. Ann., 1920, 45.
16. E.O., October 5, 1910.

17. Sum. Ann., 1922, 32.
18. Wet. Free Lance, March 22, 1899.
19. E.O., November 16, 1912.

16 Rural Life

1. Wet. Free Lance, May 23, 1898.
2. E.O., June 12, 1915.
3. E.O., December 6, 1913.
4. E.O., September 21, 1918.
5. Sum. Ann., 1923, 31.
6. E.O., October 25, 1911.
7. Sum. Ann., 1922, 8.
8. Sum. Ann., 1920, 11.
9. Wet. Breeze, June 20, 1901.
10. E.O., June 3, 1911.
11. E.O., June 29, 1906.
12. E.O., April 30, 1921.
13. Wet. Free Lance, November 10, 1898.
14. Sum. Ann., 1922, 59.

17 City Life

1. E.O., July 1, 1922.
2. E.O., May 20, 1911.
3. E.O., December 2, 1906.
4. E.O., November 24, 1903.
5. Sum. Ann., 1920, 24.
6. E.O., December 6, 1913.
7. Sum. Ann., 1924, 18.
8. E.O., July 14, 1906.
9. E.O., January 1, 1910.
10. E.O., May 20, 1911.
11. Wet. Free Lance, March 6, 1899.
12. E.O., February 4, 1905.
13. E.O., September 11, 1920.
14. Wet. Free Lance, February 20, 1899.
15. E.O., May 8, 1915.
16. E.O., March 20, 1920.
17. E.O., April 3, 1915.
18. E.O., August 3, 1912.
19. Sum. Ann., 1924, 89.
20. E.O., March 9, 1918.
21. E.O., March 23, 1907.
22. E.O., December 2, 1906.
23. E.O., October 5, 1912.
24. E.O., December 6, 1913.
25. E.O., February 23, 1907.
26. E.O., January 4, 1908.

27. E.O., November 19, 1904.
28. E.O., March 24, 1906.

18 Frenzied Finance

1. Sum. Ann., 1920, 85.
2. E.O., April 3, 1915.
3. Sum. Ann., 1922, 24.
4. E.O., February 23, 1907.
5. E.O., July 29, 1911.
6. E.O., September 16, 1911.
7. Sum. Ann., 1920, 65.
8. Wet. Breeze, January 25, 1900.
9. Sum. Ann., 1920, 65.
10. E.O., August 12, 1911.
11. Sum. Ann., 1920, 46.
12. E.O., February 19, 1910.
13. E.O., June 18, 1910.
14. E.O., June 15, 1920.
15. Sum. Ann., 1924, 12.
16. E.O., April 20, 1912.
17. E.O., June 27, 1914.
18. Sum. Ann., 1922, 29.
19. E.O., January 27, 1912.
20. Sum. Ann., 1920, 60.
21. E.O., September 13, 1919.
22. E.O., May 17, 1913.
23. E.O., October 25, 1911.
24. E.O., June 3, 1911.
25. E.O., October 25, 1911.
26. Sum. Ann., 1922, 25.
27. Sum. Ann., 1920, 58.
28. E.O., July 3, 1915.
29. Wet. Free Lance, February 20, 1899.
30. Sum. Ann., 1920, 69.
31. E.O., November 20, 1915.
32. E.O., July 1, 1922.
33. E.O., December 6, 1913.
34. E.O., September 27, 1913.
35. E.O., July 3, 1915.

19 Pure Philosophy

1. E.O., April 3, 1915.
2. E.O., November 2, 1912.
3. Sum. Ann., 1922, 10.
4. E.O., June 27, 1914.
5. Sum. Ann., 1920, 60.
6. E.O., September 3, 1919.

7. Sum. Ann., 1922, 10.
8. E.O., August 28, 1920.
9. E.O., June 4, 1910.
10. E.O., November 15, 1915.
11. Wet. Free Lance, December 1, 1898.
12. E.O., December 20, 1919.
13. Sum. Ann., 1924, 51.
14. E.O., August 14, 1920.
15. E.O., September 21, 1918.
16. Sum. Ann., 1922, 59.
17. Sum. Ann., 1924, 33.
18. Sum. Ann., 1922, 22.
19. Sum. Ann., 1922, 22.
20. Sum. Ann., 1922, 32.
21. Sum. Ann., 1922, 55.
22. Sum. Ann., 1920, 70.
23. Sum. Ann., 1920, 35.
24. Sum. Ann., 1920, 35.
25. Sum. Ann., 1922, 20.
26. Sum. Ann., 1924, 88.
27. Sum. Ann., 1922, 90.
28. Sum. Ann., 1923, 88.
29. Sum. Ann., 1922, 80.
30. E.O., August 28, 1920.
31. E.O., July 1, 1922.
32. E.O., January 27, 1912.
33. E.O., October 15, 1910.
34. E.O., October 15, 1910.
35. E.O., January 27, 1912.
36. E.O., January 27, 1912.
37. E.O., February 10, 1912.
38. E.O., February 10, 1912.
39. E.O., October 5, 1912.
40. E.O., September 27, 1913.
41. E.O., December 6, 1913.
42. E.O., December 20, 1913.
43. E.O., June 27, 1914.
44. E.O., April 3, 1915.
45. E.O., April 3, 1915.
46. E.O., April 3, 1915.
47. E.O., February 19, 1910.
48. E.O., July 8, 1916.
49. E.O., April 30, 1921.
50. E.O., May 22, 1915.
51. E.O., May 6, 1916.
52. E.O., August 20, 1921.
53. E.O., September 21, 1918.
54. E.O., April 5, 1919.
55. Sum. Ann., 1920, 50.

56. Sum. Ann., 1920, 24.
57. Sum. Ann., 1920, 85.
58. Sum. Ann., 1920, 86.
59. Sum. Ann., 1920, 27.
60. Sum. Ann., 1924, 18.
61. E.O., June 3, 1911.
62. E.O., January 24, 1919.
63. E.O., October 25, 1911.
64. E.O., August 14, 1920.
65. E.O., September 11, 1920.